HERE FOR A GOOD TIME

Albums by Trooper

Trooper
Two For the Show
Knock 'em Dead, Kid
Thick as Theives
Flying Colors
Hot Shots
Trooper
Money Talks
The Last of the Gypsies
Ten

HERE FOR A GOOD TIME

ON THE ROAD WITH TROOPER, CANADA'S LEGENDARY ROCK BAND

RA McGUIRE

INSOMNIAC PRESS

All interior photographs by Ra McGuire

Library and Archives Canada Cataloguing in Publication

McGuire, Ra
    Here for a good time : on the road with Trooper, Canada's legendary rock band / Ra McGuire.

ISBN 1-897178-10-7

    1. Trooper (Musical group). 2. Rock groups--Canada. 3. Rock musicians--Canada--Biography. I. Title.

ML421.T855M14 2006   782.42166'092'2   C2005-907627-5

The publisher gratefully acknowledges the support of the Canada Council, the Ontario Arts Council and the Department of Canadian Heritage through the Book Publishing Industry Development Program.

Printed and bound in Canada

Insomniac Press, 192 Spadina Avenue, Suite 403
Toronto, Ontario, Canada, M5T 2C2
www.insomniacpress.com

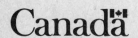

For
Debbie and Connor
and
Mom and Dad

TABLE OF CONTENTS

Introduction   **15**

Chapter One – May 30–July 3, 2002   **19**
Limbo in Toronto, She'll Do ANYTHING, Crack House Band Houses, Used Vacuums and Guitars, Dead Junkies, Raise A Little Hell Reggae, "Can I Have Your Shirt?", "What's That on Your Head?", Fish and Brewis with Scrunchions, Screech, Conception Bay, Boat in Garage, Subway Steve, My 52nd Birthday, Death at the Beach, Tear-Gassed at the G7, Trooper Karaoke, The Ontario Cookie Lady, Canceled Shows, Babe Cop Onstage, Pepper Spray Fun, Jimmy Rankin, Weezer, Mini-Plane to The Rock, Brian Greenway's Beer Sunday, Canada Day on George Street, More Screech, Great Big Fucking Trooper

Chapter Two – July 4–August 21, 2002   **55**
30,000 feet, Whatever Turns You On, Lance's Hometown, Turn 'Em On – Turn 'Em Off, Over 100 Trooper Shows, The Hard Rock in The Big Smoke

Chapter Three – September 15– October 22, 2002   **63**
The Island, The Authority at In Harmony, Victoria Hippies, Chip – Super Trooper Fan, eBay Weirdness, Frank Church, Botched Breasts at a Smelly Beach, DJ Violence, Gary MacLean – "Kick That Motherfucker's Ass," Harvest Time in Assiniboia, A Strange Night with Three Farmer's Daughters, Ten Days at Home, Anger and After, McGuire Artist Management, Mr. PG, Willie's Mudpuddle, Dancing Teens, Salty's in the Okanagan, Mullet Guy, Thanksgiving, The Truth About Squirming Woman, A Van Full of Flu, Rock and Country Collide, Something a Dildo Can't Do

Chapter Four – December 31, 2002–February 23, 2003   **81**
New Year's Reminiscing, Rock and Roll Dad, Take a Right at the Arctic Ocean, My Wonderful Wife, Out the Window, My Son's First Bra, It's a Living, Beachcombers, ATVs on the Tundra, "I Hated Fucking Spandex," Waiting for a Heartbeat, The Beatles and Buddy Clyde, The Epics, My First Gig, Hormonal Heroin, A New Drummer for Trooper, Three Auditions, Drummer X, A Trooper Armed Forces Tour, One-Sided

Interview, CBC Visit, Trooper's Graphic Artist, A Nervous Rash, Singing and Typing, Frankie Baker Rehearsals, Drugs, Drinking and Ego

Chapter Five – February 28–March 30, 2003   97
Frankie's First Night, Purgatory, Battle Conditions, Victory, Mic Stand Solo, Aunty Lena, 48 Below, Snowstorm, A Night Off, Creative Drift, Scott Richards, Road Mode, Venue Hijack, The Wee Hours of the Morning, Ferry Ride, 25 Shows – Four Weeks Later, Connor's Music, The Coming of Spring

Chapter Six – April 8–May 18, 2003   111
Hot Nights and Hearing Aids, Reason and Rhyme, Digital Recording Nightmares, "Cold Water" Is Born, Grandpa Smitty, Singing with the Doobie Brothers, Four-Letter Interview, Listen to the Music, Sabotage, Live or Memorex?, Rocky Mountain High, Dave, Making Music with My Son, The Trooper/Anger and After Show – a Major Moment, The 1965 Hit Parade, Sam the Sham and the Pharaohs, The Citations, Noon-Hour Concert, A+A Rules, Happy Together

Chapter Seven – May 26–August 15, 2003   125
Summertime and the Livin' Is Easy, On a Dark Ontario Highway, Steevo, Light Man Jeopardy, Fred Astaire and Ginger Baker, Rainstorm, Rock and Roll Haircut, Naked Woman Eviction, Mexican Movie Night Off, My 53rd Birthday with the Dwarves, Gary's Mr. T Haircut, Jammin', The OCL Again, Ontario vs. Nova Scotia, A Letter to Subway Steve, Naked Atlantic Ocean Action, War & Peace, Three Guys Walk into a Bar, My Cool Tools Review, The Fortress of Louisbourg, Airport Roulette, The Beatles' Hometown, White Point Beach Toga Party, Mr. Wolverine, A Cheap Trick All Round, "I Work for Trooper," Waking Up the Campers, Music vs. the Music Business, Takin' Care of Bullshit, Country Fest, Naked Pool Party, Church Jam, Gold Sandals, Sab, My Mouth Organ, Junk and Useless, Dangerous Driving, SARS Fest, 54•40 in St. John's, Sittin' In, "Barrett's Privateers," 20,000 Attend Newfoundland Trooper Party, Loverboy Geekfest, Screeching Frankie, Terrifying Security, Rockin' the Dock, Fred Penner Rocks Out, Extreme Bowling, Airport Chaos

Chapter Eight – August 30–December 22, 2003   163
A Songwriting Conversation, Canadian Music, The Irish Terrorist's Memorial Service, Uncle Jack, A Large Grey Blanket, A Changing Face,

Managing the Band Etc., My Wonderful Wife, Reviews of Five Favourite Movies, The Middle of Nothing In Particular, Technical Advice, On Songwriting, Cornering Phosphenes, David Gates on Songwriting, Our Van Blows Up, Highway Hero, Home Life, Fake Ra McGuire, Other Fake RMs, Crazy Talk, Our 32nd Wedding Anniversary, Connor's Fake Punch, Lord of the Rings, Merry Christmas!

Chapter Nine – January 2–March 15, 2004   185
Fifteen Songs!, The Blues Album, Dad's 84th Birthday, Mom and Her iMac, Alex's 75th Birthday, Con's New Song, "You Might Think It's Easy But It's Not," Dylan/Weezer/Wilco, Hal David and the Bridge, Our New Agent, "Where Do Songs Come From?", The Room With the Spring-Loaded Door, How to Start a Song, A Song's Progress, "I'm Not Prepared to Say That Something's Lost," Alchemy, Steve Allen Rocks, The "Instant Editor," Chasing the Moving Finish Line, All the Paraphernalia, Gear Slut Geek Spaz, The Hat on the Beat Before the Snare, A Reason to Celebrate, Song Number Two, Bad Day for Songwriting, Excuses?, A Poem, Shine Like You Do, Another Conversation, The Math, My Tools Are My Instrument, My First Guitar, When Right Is Wrong, The Winter's Green, Two Ex-Hippies Get Married, Applejack, Not "Rock" Enough?, Two for the Show – Randy and Me, Song vs. Arrangement, The Digital Player Piano, Composing AND Arranging, A Miracle of Modern Technology, Song #2 Technically Finished, An Artist Like My Dad, The Trooper Web Team, Out of the Closet

Chapter Ten – March 22–October 18, 2004   215
Fred Penner Sings with Trooper, Peter Jordan, The Singing MLA, Sardines in Saskatoon, Throat Trouble, Dazed and Confused in Ottawa, The National Gallery, Going Walkabout, The Wok Inn in Kingston, Shwartz's in Montreal, A+A's White Rock Show, Un-Sexy Women, The Southern Shore of Nova Scotia, With Our Scottish Brothers on The Rock, Eighty Pounds of Lobster, Annoyed and Aggravated, Grounded in Edmonton, The Writing Room, The F-Bomb, The Fredericton Fiasco, F-Word Update, 11 Hours Sleep in 4 Days, 110,000 People Since June, A Trooper Resurgence, Debbie and I and the Temptations, Dad Visits Hospital – Twice, Harry Clarke McGuire, A Turn for the Better, Love-Fests and Sell-Outs, Ra & Myles Sing the Blues, The Kuujjuaq Trip, All You Can Drink For Free, *Maclean's* Photo Shoot, Lederhosen, Mikey Leaves the Group, Plane Party, Truck Break-In

Chapter Eleven – October 19, 2004–July 4, 2005   **243**
Doug Bennett (cool with no regrets), Christmas 2004, Goodbye Dad,
Flickr Crack, The Wired Life, Singing Snowbird on the CBC, Spock Days,
Live in Calgary, Connor Graduates and Ra & Debbie Celebrate, The *Globe
and Mail* Writer Will Live with Us, 14,000 People Sing Happy Birthday to
Me, Atikokan, High Rise Threat in White Rock, The Tour – Written in
the Style of Mr. Cheney's Two-Page *Globe and Mail* Story, A Good Gig

Index   **261**

A Complete List of the Cities Where Trooper Performed During the Creation of This Book ...

2002
May – Iroquois Falls ON – **June** – New Liskeard ON, North Bay ON, Sault Ste. Marie ON, Sudbury ON, Tamiskamine PQ, Mount Forest ON, Bay Roberts ND, Glace Bay NS, Yarmouth NS, Dalhousie NB, Halifax NS, Whitby ON, Oakville ON, Strathroy ON, Port Colborne ON, Kingston ON, St. Stevens NB, Glace Bay NS, Saint John NB, Moncton NB – **July** – St. John's NL – **August** – Minnedosa MB, Vanderhoof BC, Terrace BC, Ottawa ON, Hamilton ON, Toronto ON – **September** – Victoria BC, Courtenay BC, Regina SK, Fort Francis ON, Winnipeg MB, Brandon MB, Assiniboia SK, Prince Albert SK, Saskatoon SK – **October** – Prince George BC, Williams Lake BC, Penticton BC, Kelowna BC, – Cranbrook BC, Vermillion AB, Grande Prairie AB, High Level AB, Lac La Biche AB – St. Paul AB, Medicine Hat AB, Moose Jaw SK, Black Diamond AB, Eston SK – **November** – Lac La Biche AB, Edmonton AB – **December** – Winnipeg MB

2003
February – Salmon Arm BC – **March** – Courtenay BC, Victoria BC, Nanaimo BC, Richmound SK, Slave Lake AB, Calgary AB, Rocky Mountain House AB, Drayton Valley AB, Brooks AB, Saskatoon SK, Black Diamond AB, Wetaskawin AB, Red Deer AB, Camrose AB, Edmonton AB, Lloydminster AB, Quesnel BC – **April** – Yorkton SK, Hudson Bay SK, Winnipeg MB, Regina SK, Lethbridge AB, Kamloops BC – **May** – St. Albert AB, Surrey BC, Maple Ridge BC, Banff AB, Trail BC, Penticton BC – **June** – Halifax NS, Liverpool NS, Liverpool NS, Yarmouth NS, D'Escousse NS, Port Hawkesbury NS, Glace Bay NS, Mount Forest ON, Kingston ON, Pointe Claire PQ, Barrie ON, Whitby ON, Oshawa ON, London ON, Sarnia ON, Thunder Bay ON, Marathon ON, Fort Francis ON, Thunder Bay ON – **July** – Toronto ON, Mattawa ON, Kapuskasing ON, Kirkland Lake ON, Merritt BC, Edmonton AB, Craven SK, Saskatoon SK, Camrose AB, Calgary AB, Ile-A-La-Crosse SK, Vermillion AB, Hamilton ON – **August** – Regina SK, Tobique NB, Sudbury ON, St. George's NF, Bridgewater NS, Sidney NS, Geraldton ON, Bay Roberts NF, Grand Falls NF – **September**

– Victoria BC, Pitt Meadows BC, Pitt Meadows BC, Powell River BC, Duncan BC, Cambridge ON, Russell ON, Oshawa ON – **October** – Barrhead AB, Black Diamond AB, Camrose AB, Brooks AB, Drayton Valley AB, High Level AB, High Level AB, Edmonton AB – **November** – Salt Spring Island BC, Flin Flon MB, Prince Albert SK, Regina SK, Winnipeg MB, Swift Current SK, Arcola SK – **December** – Edmonton AB

2004
January – Vancouver BC – **March** – Saskatoon SK, Winnipeg MB, Brandon MB, Regina SK, Lloydminster SK, Saskatoon SK, Edmonton AB, Calgary AB, Canmore AB – **April** – White Rock BC – **May** – Fredericton NB, Tracadie NB, St. Stephen NB, Kingston ON, Montreal PQ, Orillia ON, Ottawa ON, Cambridge ON, Cambridge ON, Cambridge ON – **June** – Vancouver BC, Sarnia ON, Toronto ON, Owen Sound ON, Saint Thomas ON, St Anthony NFLD, Triton NFLD, Stephenville NFLD, Clarenville NFLD, Mt. Pearl NFLD, Stellarton NS, Windsor NS, Bridgewater NS, Saint John NB – **July** – Wood Mountain SK, Red Deer AB, Nakusp BC, Cold Lake AB, Quesnel BC, Yellowknife NWT, Dauphin MB, Vernon BC, Port Moody BC – **August** – Darrington WA, Brantford ON, St Johns NFLD, Kuujjuaq PQ, Walkerton ON, Peterborough ON, Ottawa ON, Bathurst NB, Moncton NB, Liverpool NS, Antigonish NS, Halifax NS, Sydney NS, Saint John NB, Port Colborne ON – **September** – Hanna AB, Calgary AB, Regina SK, Mafeking MB – **October** – Campbell River BC, Duncan BC, Victoria BC, Vernon BC, Red Deer AB, Valleyview AB, Edmonton AB, Black Diamond AB, Penticton BC, Vancouver BC – **November** – Sun Peaks BC, Whistler BC – **December** – Saskatoon SK, Edmonton AB

2005
February – Vancouver BC, Chilliwack BC, **March** – Sun Peaks BC, Prince George BC, Prince Rupert BC, Terrace BC, Dawson Creek BC, Grande Prairie AB, Edmonton AB, Trochu AB, Banff AB, Airdrie AB, North Battleford SK, Lloydminster AB, Edmonton AB, Rimbey AB – **April** – Redcliff AB, Regina SK, Moose Jaw SK, Yorkton SK, Dauphin MB – **May** – Penticton BC, Black Diamond AB, Banff AB – **June** – Calgary AB, Vulcan AB, Thunder Bay ON,

Atikokan ON, Oshawa ON, Acton ON, Ottawa ON, Innisfil ON, Cambridge ON, Toronto ON, Trenton ON, Lucknow ON, Moncton NB, Glace Bay NS, Halifax NS – **July** – Grande Prairie AB, Gingolx BC

TROOPER

May 10, 2003 – Sunshine Village ski resort, Banff, Alberta

Brian (Smitty) Smith, Gogo, Ra McGuire, Scott Brown, Frankie Baker

All of the material in this book was originally presented online at http://www.ramcguire.com where the adventures of Ra McGuire and Trooper continue to be chronicled.

Ra McGuire's photographs were originally presented online at http://www.flickr.com/photos/ramcguire where new photos continue to be added regularly.

Trooper's official Web site is located at http://www.trooper.com

INTRODUCTION

December 31, 2005
In the air between Vancouver, BC, and Edmonton, Alberta

Jully Black closed her eyes and inched her lips toward the microphone. The first two words, the title of the song, seemed torn from a personal reverie... surrendered unwillingly—as though her thoughts and emotions had boiled over and out of her mouth by accident, or by mistake.

"Pretty Lady," she sang, and I let out an involuntary whoop.

"Here I am," she admitted, and other audience members gave it up. Spontaneous.

My nervousness turned to pride. Jully was singing the shit out of a song I wrote 40 years ago with my writing partner Brian Smith, and my wife and son and many of my peers in the music industry were there bearing witness. I grinned across the large round table, first at my family and then at Smitty. Debbie squeezed my leg.

After singing, Jully told the audience that her manager was a huge Trooper fan and had pulled strings to sit at our table...

"With God," she said.

She went on to describe our band as "honest-to-God Canadian legends." The crowd cheered as she called Smitty and me to the stage to accept our 2005 SOCAN Classic Awards.

Anne Loree, who wrote "Insensitive" for Jann Arden, was also sitting at our table and had shed a few tears when accepting her award, but Smitty and I were too buzzed for sentimentality. We could feel a palpable connection with the music-biz crowd arrayed before us, many of whom had become friends and compatriots over the years. The evening's awards ceremony played out like a personal celebration of a long and successful career that continues to offer up the elusive rewards of adventure, challenge, and straight-up fun.

I was proud to announce from the stage that night that my son, Connor, and I had just written our first song together. After the show, in Jully Black's dressing room, representatives of an independent record company approached Connor to talk about his music. He smiled and accepted their card appreciatively. Here he was, functioning comfortably in an environment that would have absolutely terrified me at 18.

I started singing in a band when I was 12 years old—six years younger than he is now. I recorded my first album 13 years later at the age of 25. I'm 55 years old now and have never had a real job. I've written hundreds of songs, performed thousands of shows, and have traveled tens of thousands of miles—most of those back and forth across Canada. Trooper is as viable today as it was in the 70s when songs like "We're Here For A Good Time" and "Raise A Little Hell" were knocking down doors and serving as our invitations to the best party in town. In many ways, our status has risen recently to a place just south of legendary where, for instance, total strangers embrace us as they would a favourite relative visiting from out of town. The party continues.

Trooper's first Web site went online in 1996. Little Timmy Hewitt and I hacked together the html for Rev. 1 long before Google, eBay, or Amazon.com had registered their now iconic domain names. I started my own personal site—they weren't called blogs then—not long after. I wrote about my life on the road and those things that someone unfamiliar with this kind of life might find interesting. I was surprised and encouraged by the enthusiastic response to that tentative and sporadically updated site, so, by the time Blogger launched their online interface, I had decided to maintain a semi-regular online account of a 53-year-old's rock and roll adventures.

This book represents the first three years of *ramcguire.com*. It was written in real time as journal entries. It has no beginning and no ending, but it surprised me by telling more than a few seemingly complete stories.

It was written in airports and rented vans, on ferries and planes, in billet rooms in remote high north villages and luxury hotel suites in the heart of the Big Smoke. Some of it was dashed off quickly at four in the morning. Some of it might be more carefully considered than it needs to be. Often it reveals much more than I'd intended at the time. And sometimes, the story is fleshed out by that which wasn't written down at all. Each entry came as a complete surprise to me—as did, of course, the unfolding events I was chronicling.

The SOCAN Awards were held in Toronto at the end of November. I'm writing this on a plane on the way to Edmonton, Alberta, on the last day of 2005. Our New Year's Eve show tonight will be at Reds, a very large club in the West Edmonton Mall. It's going to be a total sold-out zoo!

CHAPTER ONE

May 30–July 3, 2002

Limbo in Toronto, She'll Do ANYTHING,
Crack House Band Houses, Used Vacuums and Guitars,
Dead Junkies, Raise A Little Hell Reggae, "Can I Have Your
Shirt?", "What's That on Your Head?", Fish and Brewis with
Scrunchions, Screech, Conception Bay, Boat in Garage, Subway
Steve, My 52nd Birthday, Death at the Beach, Tear-Gassed at the
G7, Trooper Karaoke, The Ontario Cookie Lady, Canceled Shows,
Babe Cop Onstage, Pepper Spray Fun, Jimmy Rankin, Weezer,
Mini-Plane to The Rock, Brian Greenway's Beer Sunday,
Canada Day on George Street, More Screech,
Great Big Fucking Trooper

May 30, 2002
Toronto, Ontario

Today was a limbo day, neither here nor there: not home, but not really on the road yet. Right now, here in my airport hotel room just outside of Toronto, I feel disconnected, lonely, and not part of any useful reality. This will change.

On the flight here, Isaac Grimnebulin began an intensive investigation of the mechanics of flight so as to be able to create some kind of artificial wings for Yagharek, whose real wings were sawed off as punishment for an as yet undisclosed breach of Garuda ethical law. Meanwhile, Isaac's lover Lin, a red skinned Kheprin with a head described as a "huge iridescent scarab," is having second thoughts about her acceptance of a commission to create a Kheprin spit-sculpture of New Crobuzon crime boss Mr. Motley.

Perdido Street Station (by China Miéville) has 710 pages. As we landed in Toronto I folded the corner of page 140 and packed it away in my backpack.

I should probably stay up 'til at least three a.m. to get a start on resetting my bio clock. That's three or four more hours. Tomorrow, I will become more of my road-self. Tonight, though, I'm just a guy in an anonymous Toronto hotel room who misses his wife and son and his home in White Rock.

It's always like this.

View from my airport hotel room – Toronto, Ontario

View from my airport hotel room – Toronto, Ontario

Friday, May 31, 2002
Iroquois Falls, Ontario

It was touch and go with dinner tonight. The very French-Canadian front desk guy/probable owner of the Glendale Motor Hotel here in Iroquois Falls, Ontario, seemed convinced that there was no Chinese food available for delivery this evening. In a situation like this, the restaurant sections of the inch-thick, multi-town phone books are essentially useless to me. Timmins, for instance, has several Chinese restaurants listed and is, apparently, a nearby town, but *how* nearby is a relative question. For some small towns, thirty kilometers is a short drive. For others, it's an unthinkable hardship. I called and asked about the Motor Hotel's restaurant.

"Closed," he said perfunctorily.

I asked him if he had any ideas about what I could eat for dinner. He thought for a moment and then said, "You will heard from me in three minutes," and hung up.

He called back in two minutes and said, "Call this number." Which I did.

The call was answered by a very nice, obviously Chinese, lady. The man who delivered my Chinese food was not Chinese, maybe 70 years old, had only two or three teeth left, and a painful looking stoop that gave the impression that he was about to fall through the open door and into my room.

After I paid him he said, "If you need a taxi, I can give you a number."

I did manage to stay up till three a.m. last night. In fact, I had difficulty sleeping once I'd turned out the light. I filled the several extra hours trying, unsuccessfully, to pour my first on-the-road blog entry into the customized Web page/blogpage template that I had made (and that had worked fine for the only other entry). Finally, around 2:30, I gave up and went for the dramatically less attractive, but fully functional (and free), BlogSpot option.

Today we drove 680 kilometers from Toronto to Iroquois Falls in a brand new Budget 15-passenger van. Happily, the Ontario Budget vans still have cassette decks—allowing me to plug a cassette adapter into my PowerBook, wherein I have almost four days' worth of music and the ability to play both CDs and DVDs. Today we listened to the first CD by some good friends of ours who had asked for a no-holds-barred critique of their work. The result was a two-page saga—the upshot of an hour-long discussion about what makes an excellent album excellent. The playlist thereafter careened from Rufus Wainwright to Ryan Adams to Cozy Bones (from White Rock) to Ray Charles and on... until I remembered the copy of the *Best of Trooper* karaoke disk that I had brought for Smitty (by way of *karaokemaker.com*). We filled the last hour of the drive listening to extremely well-rendered versions of Trooper hits without... uh... me.

In two hours, Trooper will take the stage in the Jus Jordan Arena in Iroquois Falls, Ontario. True to form, we will not have seen the stage before we walk onto it.

Let the party begin.

Saturday, June 1, 2002
New Liskeard, Ontario

I've come to believe that towns have a personality—a communal civic character. It's not as evident or definable in a bar or nightclub because those venues often have a culture of their own that attracts (or repels) a particular clientele—but, when I'm on stage at an arena show, like the one we did last night in Iroquois Falls, I feel as though I'm jacked straight in to the temporarily exposed heart of the community.

Iroquois Falls was a great town for the first gig of the tour. The Jus Jordan Arena was packed with a spirited collection of good-hearted, fun-loving souls. I also sensed a high level of passion in the audience—they seemed to feel the music very deeply. This may or may not have had something to do with the fact that the population was 60 percent French-speaking. The great vibe combined with our surfeit of first-night energy made for a very successful and fun show.

Following up on yesterday's post: Smitty also called the front desk last night, asking about Chinese food. He was also told there was none available, but, unlike me, was not eventually given the mysterious Chinese food phone number. Scott told us in the dressing room that he had ended up buying food at a grocery store.

A thunder and lightning storm, accompanied by high winds and torrential rain, that raged outside my window yesterday afternoon for about ten minutes was responsible for some serious damage in the town last night. Roofs were removed and trees fell. Today's weather, though, was warm and sunny.

We're in New Liskeard, Ontario, tonight—a short 170-kilometer drive away from last night's show. We played a speedboat festival here two or three years ago. I remember that night very well. At one point in the show, as I was kneeling at the front of the stage, I found myself being slowly pulled off the large outdoor stage and out into the sea of people. During my unintentional crowd surf I continued singing, and when the song ended, I was very carefully surfed back and hoisted up onto the stage. Tonight's show is in the arena—and it's time for my shower.

Sunday, June 2, 2002
North Bay, Ontario

New Liskeard was a great show. Another arena—packed right out with a loud and extremely appreciative crowd. Our gigantic upstairs dressing room came complete with a bar and two attractive bartenders. When I asked why we had been so honoured, I was told that it was against liquor regulations to do otherwise. I did not tell them that this was only the second time in our 27-year career that our dressing room had come so equipped.

I saved a note that was passed up to me on stage last night. Here it is verbatim:

"Trooper. Ra. My name is Sherrie. I'm a big fan. There's a song that I beg you to sing, but I would do ANYTHING (underlined three times), ANYTHING (also underlined three times) to sing it with you. Please. I beg you. I'll do ANYTHING (underlined twice), ANYTHING. Song is: Thin White Line."

I read the note out to the crowd and then said, "Sure."

After I helped her onto the stage I reminded her that I hadn't yet decided what "ANYTHING" was going to be. Smitty leaned in and whispered the punch line to an old joke into my ear. I turned to Sherrie and said:

"So you'll do ANYTHING I ask?"

She smiled coyly and said, "Yes."

I looked deep into her eyes and said:

"Paint... my... house."

After which, Sherrie sang "Thin White Line."

Monday, June 3, 2002
Sault Ste. Marie, Ontario

It occurred to me last night that no one other than a working musician would know about Band Houses. I was reminded of this because our dressing room was a multi-room Band House setup, upstairs in the old building that houses the club we played in North Bay, Ontario.

I removed a sign from the wall of the "living room" area that really tells the whole story... in a creepily ironic way. Once again, I quote verbatim:

"FREE" (This is centered at the top of the page in large bold letters—there is also, in the middle of the page, a clip art illustration of a pile of cartoon dollar bills.)

FREE DOES NOT (Underlined) MEAN THAT YOU CAN TAKE WHAT YOU WANT WHEN YOU LEAVE.

FREE DOES NOT (Underlined) MEAN THAT YOU CAN WRITE ON EVERYTHING THAT YOU CAN REACH.

FREE DOES NOT (Underlined) MEAN THAT YOU CAN PUT HOLES IN THE WALLS.

FREE MEANS THAT WE HAVE TO PAY TO REPLACE THINGS THAT DISAPPEAR.

FREE MEANS THAT WE FLIP THE BILL FOR REPAIRS, CLEANING SUPPLIES, AND STAFF.

FREE MEANS THAT WE ARE PAYING FOR YOU (In Italics) TO STAY HERE.

PLEASE TREAT THE BAND HOUSE WITH RESPECT AND BE GRATEFUL FOR WHAT IS GIVEN TO YOU FOR "FREE"

Everyone in Trooper has stayed in Band Houses at some point in their career.

Far from being "free," band accommodations are actually part of the contract—an important part of what a band receives as compensation for playing—often for weeks at a time—in a nightclub or bar. More often than not, these Band Houses have all the charm and comfort of a skid row crack house. It should be noted here that none of us have stayed in a Band House for a *very* long time.

We swapped stories—comparing the North Bay Band House to others that we were forced, in our dues-paying days, to stay in. This one had the traditional junkie-grade Salvation Army furniture, the mandatory "bedrooms" that housed four single beds and nothing else, and the early 70s console TV with the power knob that comes off in your hand.

The carpet in the combined living room/kitchen area, which was our official dressing room (and the room where the "BE GRATE-FUL FOR WHAT IS GIVEN TO YOU FOR FREE" sign was posted) had almost completed its transition from beige to a speck-led shit-brown—a metamorphosis made possible over time by an accumulation of dirt, grime, splattered food, spilt beer, hash burns, black circles of chewing gum, and, probably, bodily fluids. It was worn thin enough to no longer really qualify as a carpet and, as a result, it bunched up into darker clumps here and there underfoot.

Instead of art, the walls were adorned with computer-generated signs like the "BE GRATEFUL FOR WHAT IS GIVEN TO YOU

FOR FREE" one. There was: "USE YOUR HEAD—DON'T SMOKE IN BED," "PLEASE LEAVE THIS KITCHEN AS YOU FOUND IT," "NO SMOKING BETWEEN THE HOURS OF 8:00 a.m. AND 6:00 p.m." (Does this mean you can chain-smoke from 7:00 a.m. to 8:00 a.m. without fear of violating the Band House regulations?), and finally, my favourite, the mind-boggling: "PLEASE DO NOT BRING IN ANY FOOD FROM THE OTHER SIDE OF THE STREET."

(Okay, I nicked that sign too—I *needed* it for my collection. I'll put it on my garage wall with "ABSOLUTELY NO SUNFLOWER SEEDS ALLOWED. (Signed: The Management.)"

The club's stage sounded, with the exception of the nearly non-existent vocal monitors, absolutely awesome and inspired one of the best musical nights in a long time. The North Bay crowd was witness to some amazing playing and improvisation that will never be heard again.

This audience stayed in their seats for two-thirds of the night—preferring to experience the show as a concert rather than the go-for-it free-for-all that we're more used to. Despite the fact that they remained seated, they were extremely attentive and noisily responsive... encouraging us to push the limits a bit. This was one of those shows where the band might have had more fun than the audience.

Today's 430-kilometer drive to Sault Ste. Marie was fun as well.

Before we left town we stopped at Omer's. The big sign on the front of the store read: "USED VACUUMS AND GUITARS." How could we pass that up?

Omer's – North Bay, Ontario

Later, on the highway, I fired up *iTunes* on my PowerBook and, as the result of a random conversation, began playing only songs by... well... uh... dead junkies. We imagined a radio station whose motto was "All Dead Junkies—All of the Time." I managed to find, and play, songs by: Nirvana (too obvious, really), Little Feat (the wonderful Lowell George), Grateful Dead (although we couldn't come to consensus about whether Jerry Garcia was, in fact, a junkie), Billie Holiday (duh), The Average White Band (whose drummer, Hamish something-or-other, OD'ed), Sublime (singer Bradley Nowell), Miles

Davis (another junkie-status question here), John Lennon, and, the one I was most proud of having in my collection... Judy Garland (although, to be fair, I have never heard conclusively that Junk was one of her drugs of choice).

Good fun.

ADJR—All Dead Junkie Radio.

Tuesday, June 4, 2002
Sault Ste. Marie, Ontario

We had a night off last night. I watched two DVDs on my trusty PowerBook: *Dude, Where's My Car?* and *Jerry Maguire*. It was a fun night on my own. Went for a long walk today. I took a few pictures. It was a low-volt day, overall.

Wednesday, June 5, 2002
On the way to Sudbury, Ontario

I'm sitting in the passenger seat of the van watching as the northern Ontario rural landscape slips by. It's a grey day. Cold again. The "In Search of Summer" Tour continues.

There's not much I can say about The Sault. I downloaded the pictures that I took on my walk yesterday and wasn't surprised to see that they all worked better in black and white. I walked the entire downtown for almost two hours and saw only five or six people on the street. All of them seemed disoriented and distracted—as though they had arrived there by accident. The downtown seemed to be retreating into itself—the old buildings wrestling the clock back, with the sheer weight of concrete and stone memory, to a time where they could once again be relevant. When we talked, in the dressing room before the show, 'lonely' is the word we all agreed upon.

Downtown, Sault Ste. Marie, Ontario

The gig last night at the Canadian Hotel in Sault Ste. Marie was another fun one for us—although the talk-to-music ratio might have been a bit off its usual balance. I like to think I would have stopped talking so much if the audience wasn't so clearly getting it, but I can't be sure of that.

I tried on a reggae version of "Raise A Little Hell" in the middle of the set. It says on our Web site that we have been "tinkering with" the idea. Actually I'm the only one that has been tinkering—Smitty heard about it for the first time onstage last night. I tried to sing him his parts, but I couldn't seem to make the all-important musical connection: Lance, on the drums, was immediately grooving like Robbie Shakespeare; Gogo rasta-fied impressively on the keys while Scott stood with his bass hanging free—wisely chose to play nothing... but my flustered partner, Smitty, just stared like the proverbial deer-in-the-headlights. He played the reggae groove with the same chord, changing occasionally (and randomly) to chords that clearly did not support the melody of the song. I like the idea of doing things spontaneously onstage—it makes the show more interesting (for us and, hopefully, the audience) and it usually works. Last night's improv, though, more accurately resembled spontaneous combustion.

"It's only two chords," I yelled at Smitty in mock frustration, "... and you wrote them!"

Despite the lack of correct chord changes, the audience seemed to like our not-quite-arranged-yet effort. They cheered and yelled encouragement and gave it an appreciative hand... once it had finally collapsed under its own weight.

If you ever plan to drive from Sault Ste. Marie, Ontario, to Sudbury, Ontario, first download the song "Essence" by Lucinda Williams so that you can play it over and over. It's the perfect one-song soundtrack for this run.

Thursday, June 6, 2002
(On the way to) Temiskaming, Quebec

It's Connor's 15th birthday today! I'm very sorry that I can't be in White Rock to celebrate it with him. He is the joy of my life and everything I had hoped he would become. Happy B'day, Con!

This is one of those days where I'm torn between two realities. Here's what I wrote in the van on the way to the beautiful town of Temiskaming:

In the past year, I have had at least 20 girls/women ask me to give them the shirt I am wearing.

They just walk up and say: "Can I have your shirt?"

I find this phenomenon alternately amusing, baffling, annoying, disturbing, and, when I think about it later... endlessly fascinating. The fact that the girls/women in question are nearly always attractive makes it even more intriguing.

Lately, instead of making polite excuses, ("sorry, no, it's... uh... my favourite shirt") I've started asking these women/girls if they honestly expect me to strip my shirt off and give it to a complete stranger. They all seem as taken aback by my question as I am by theirs. They're all dead serious. To compound the strangeness, most of them seem downright insulted, and then pissed-off, when I refuse their request.

Does this happen to non-singers? Do men actually give the shirts off their backs to attractive women just because they ask them to? Last night in Sudbury a woman/girl walked right up to the stage and interrupted one of my introductions...

"Can I have your shirt?"

Because I have given this behaviour so much thought, I was prepared with an answer.

I blurted out: "Can you have my shirt??... What the fuck?!"

There is some weird-ass, gender-related, sexual-socio-political shit going on with this shirt thing—and I would really like to understand it better.

Sudbury was a great show—packed-out—with a good vibe all round.

Friday, June 7, 2002
Varley, Ontario (There were no rooms for us in Mount Forest)

Whoa...

This will be an interesting weekend.

We play tonight in Mount Forest, Ontario, and tomorrow night in... Bay Roberts, Newfoundland! In order to pull off that trick, we have to leave here at around four a.m. Luckily, tonight's (sold-out) show is at eight p.m., so we might actually get a few hours in.

Temiskaming, Quebec, was a very peaceful town... until Trooper showed up! The fans were sardined into the "Topspot" cabaret... it was another fun one. Today's five-and-a-half-hour drive was quiet. No music, just the clicking of laptop keys. I have an hour and a half 'til our lobby call. Not enough time to sleep—it takes my throat at least an hour to start working properly again after a nap.

It's a theatre show tonight. We love those.

Tuesday, June 11, 2002
Halifax, Nova Scotia

My real-time weblog has fallen a bit behind real time. I'll use today's drive through the beautiful Cape Breton Island to try and reconstruct the past few days.

Mount Forest, Ontario, was a sold-out, extremely successful show in a beautifully renovated movie theatre. During the drum solo I left the stage and climbed the dark backstage stairs to our dressing room, wiping the sweat from my head and forehead on the way up. The room was empty, so I came back down the stairs and pushed through a door at the stage level and looked in. The light was on and Smitty was there.

"What's that on your head?" he said.

I made my way to the mirror and saw the black, greasy mess on everything above my eyes. My hands were still covered in the remainder of the grease that must have come from the backstage handrail. With only a minute or so left in the drum solo, I scrambled for paper towels, thankful that I had avoided a painfully embarrassing return to the stage.

We slept for a couple of hours after the show before leaving, at four a.m., for Toronto International Airport. We arrived in St. John's, Newfoundland, eight and a half hours later and were driven to our hotel in the bayside town of Harbour Grace, Newfoundland.

Harbour Grace, Newfoundland

Our driver, Steve Bradbury, was the perfect host, a priceless well of Newfoundland lore and culture, and a great guy. He called ahead to Harbour Grace to arrange for some traditional Newfoundland cooking for us and stopped at a store along the way to pick us up some Purity Hard Bread (also known as Hard Tack) and some Purity "Kisses"(rum & butter candies). Purity is a St. John's-based company that makes a wide variety of locally loved products. I still have some of the small, rock-hard Hard Bread loaves in my suitcase. Hard Bread, soaked overnight, is the "Brewis" in "Fish and Brewis," the traditional Newfoundland meal that I was served when I arrived at our small, waterfront hotel. The softened hard bread is mixed with potatoes and salt fish and "manged together." Scrunchions, fried onions, and fat come in a bowl on the side. Scrunchions are fried, rendered pork fat chopped into small, salty, quarter-inch squares. The fat was... well... fat. The meal was delicious, but too rich to finish.

Harbour Grace, Newfoundland

The sold-out show at the Bay Roberts Arena will probably be the best of the tour. Newfoundland is, without question, our favourite place to play, and Newfoundlanders clearly our favourite people. The show was less a concert than a noisy, sing-along, love-in. After the show, we returned to Harbour Grace, where we attended a small but spirited hallway party with some fun-loving Wendy's employees from Mount Pearl.

Scott Brown on Bay Roberts, Conception Bay, Newfoundland

The following day we cruised the waters of Conception Bay with Bob and his son Robert. (We later met Bob's dad, Bob—no wonder they call it Bay Roberts). Trooper is blessed with a charmed social status that is similar to (but in some ways better than) that of a family member. People all over Canada know us well, and like us, before we've even met. This makes for amazing adventures, seeing and doing things that no tourist's money could buy. We are quickly and warmly welcomed into the lives and communities of the people we meet. This may be the best thing about being in the band. Our afternoon on the bay was one of those great, magical experiences.

Bay Roberts, Conception Bay, Newfoundland

After our boat trip we visited Bob's dad, a 63-year-old retired fisherman who is building a 28-foot cabin cruiser, by hand, by himself, from scratch, in his garage. Bob logged all the wood for the boat from local forests and has a steamer in the back of the garage that helps him to bend the milled boards into shape. Removing the finished boat will require the removal of the garage's front wall.

Boatbuilding in Bob's garage – Bay Roberts, Newfoundland

On our way to the St. John's Airport, Steve drove us through Brigus, a charming, cliff-wandering village that looks much as it must have looked one hundred years ago.

We arrived in Halifax in time for a late dinner. We've stayed at the Best Western so often that the front desk ladies offered, once again, to do our laundry for us! This alone is a good enough reason to stay at that hotel.

The following day, (yesterday actually) we drove for six hours up the convoluted and extremely bumpy road to Glace Bay for an early show at the Savoy Theatre. The eight o'clock start left us no time to eat or sleep. It was a cold and rainy Monday night and it was a welcome buzz to hit the stage and see that beautifully restored old theatre packed to the gunnels with cheering fans.

One of those fans, the one-man cheerleading squad that we've come to know as "Subway Steve," was there once again in the front row. Steve's enthusiasm is inspiring. I've traditionally feigned annoyance at his chants and shout-outs, and pretended that I don't like him—it's made for some funny moments—but I think by now that charade has worn thin and the people of Glace Bay know how much I like him. Last night I asked him if he wanted to sing.

Subway Steve's version of "We're Here For A Good Time" brought the house down and was the high point of the set. After the show, Steve told me that he's been reading this blog, so... Hi Steve!

We are nearing Halifax, where we'll have the night off. I'm going to watch DVDs on my PowerBook.

After I post this.

Thursday, June 13, 2002
Dalhousie, New Brunswick

It's my birthday today. I'm 52 years old. I'm a very lucky guy—thankful for my wonderful family, my excellent job, and a life that gets more and more like the one I've always dreamed of.

I'm in my hotel room in Dalhousie, New Brunswick, about ten hours away from Yarmouth, Nova Scotia, where we played last night. The Yarmouth crowd has always been politely appreciative, until the very end when they go nuts. Last night was no exception.

We watched *Sling Blade* (one of my favourite movies) on today's long drive.

I'm tired. We call this a "two-week moment," which is twice as bad as a "weak moment." Two more shows and we're off to Wasaga Beach for our annual three-day band holiday. We've been watching the weather reports with our fingers crossed.

Thursday, June 20, 2002
Wasaga Beach, Ontario

Since my last post, I've traveled several thousand miles, sung karaoke for the first time, basked in the 27-degree heat of Wasaga Beach, sold-out three more shows, was tear-gassed by a riot squad in Halifax, and, finally, a few minutes ago... watched a man die.

Smitty hosted a band barbeque tonight... he went to town and picked up all the fixin's and flipped burgers for us out in front of the resort. It was a happy time for us all. Coincidental to our party was a gathering of golfers who also barbequed and then gathered, about

20 yards away from us, for a casual, outdoor awards ceremony. At some point in the ceremony, their laughing came to an abrupt stop. One of the golfers was on the ground. We watched in stunned disbelief as three or four others kneeled over him—beginning CPR. Their efforts at reviving him, and the subsequent efforts of the paramedics who arrived soon after, were unsuccessful. We quietly packed up our picnic and returned to our rooms. I may still be in shock.

I'm back in my room at the Dyconia Resort in Wasaga Beach, Ontario. This is the last day of our now-traditional band holiday in one of our favourite places. Today, we went to the beach—like we did yesterday. Once again, our gamble paid off. Monday was a cold, windy, and distinctly un-beachworthy day, and weather reports had not been optimistic. I walked for two straight hours on the longest freshwater beach in the world, and after dinner, Scott, Patrick, and I drove to Midland to see *Spider-Man*. When we returned home, I watched my newly purchased DVD of *Grey Gardens*—one of the most fascinating movies I've ever seen. Tuesday was 25 degrees, and today 27. Perfect beach weather.

Gogo at Wasaga Beach, Ontario

There have been several jarring cultural changes since my last posting. The Dalhousie, New Brunswick, gig was another sold-out, mega-enthusiastic arena show in yet another predominantly French-speaking town. The Halifax shows, while fun and successful in every way, were overshadowed by the bizarre events taking place in the heart of that otherwise beautiful and charming city.

On Saturday morning, I left the Citadel Hotel to go to the Lower Deck Pub for sauerkraut and sausages, one of my favourite tour meals. My usual route through the city was blocked by a 15-man team of mean-looking RCMP, outfitted with helmets, billy clubs, shields, and canisters of tear gas clipped to their belts. The G7 conference had turned parts of downtown Halifax into an armed camp.

Riot police in downtown Halifax, Nova Scotia

After my usual walkabout, I returned with my camera. Feeling like a war correspondent, I made my way to the heart of the action where a crowd of protesters faced off against a phalanx of helmet—and gas mask—wearing robocops. Almost as soon as I had positioned myself for a good shot, a cry went up and the crowd of protesters (of which I was now one) turned as one and ran in a panic. Instinctually, I joined them, not know what I was running from. This was a very strange feeling.

A block or so away, the crowd slowed and began doubling back. It was then I realized that many of them wore goggles and scarves pulled up over their mouths and noses. Some of the protesters were collapsed on the curb, rubbing or pouring water on red, swollen eyes. The sting in my eyes, nose, and throat began slowly and built up as I made my way back to the hotel. A shower and a contact lens replacement took most of the pain away and I was fine for that night's show. You can see that kind of action on TV all the time these days, but actually being there to see it in person was a chilling experience.

Less interesting, but kind of funny, is the story of my first karaoke experience. Someone in the band told the owner of the Dyconia Resort that there was a Trooper karaoke disk in Smitty's suitcase. To make a long story short, I found myself, the only member of the band in attendance, in the small Dyconia bar at two a.m., singing Trooper songs for, and with, four or five very drunk, golf-shirt-wearing men.

Tomorrow we're back at it, in a place called Whitby, Ontario, where I'll post this. I've been offline for the past four days because there are no telephones in the rooms here.

The Beach – Wasaga Beach, Ontario

Friday, June 21, 2002
Oakville, Ontario

There's a smog alert today. The stuff's so thick you can't see the CN Tower. Here in Oakville, Ontario, the sun appears to be shining, although the forecast for tonight is for rain. Outdoor shows are always considerably less fun when it rains. Sometimes, depending on the quantity of rain and the quality of precautions taken in preparation for rain, we are unable to play at all. That would truly suck. The next three shows are outdoor festivals... I have my fingers crossed.

Whitby, Ontario—last night—was a hoot. The venue was small and packed-out. It was hot and sweaty, the crowd was into it, and the band was amazing. When we were about to leave, the owner loaded us up with two giant bags of wings covered in five or six of their special sauces. This led to an extremely unhealthy but tons-o'-fun two a.m. grease-fest that eventually pissed off my next-door neighbour enough to get him out of bed and hammering on our mutual wall. As Paul Simon would say: "One Man's Ceiling Is Another Man's Floor."

Whitby was also the scene of another visit from the "Ontario Cookie Lady." She brought us two big Tupperware boxes full of cookies and five individual metal lunch kits full of fudge. Each of the lunch kits was emblazoned with the Trooper logo and the band member's name. All of the other boxes and bags had big Trooper logos professionally printed on them. This extremely generous lady has a tattoo on her hand that reads: "Ontario Cookie Lady." Underneath is a picture of three little cookies. If you read Gogo's road stories (which you really should!) you will already know that there are currently three lovely ladies who bring us cookies when we're in their parts of Canada. There were, at one point, *two* Ontario Cookie Ladies— which was a problem that Gogo settled by renaming one of them "The Ultimate Queen of Baked Goods"—or something similar. On our last time through, we learned that the current OCL also makes cookies for April Wine. As you might guess, she took some good-natured ribbing about her loyalty to our band, but she was forgiven when she made it clear that no other bands are the recipients of her excellent handiwork. We play with April Wine tonight, so we're going to snoop around their bus and see how many cookies *they* got.

The last couple of days have seen some scrambling around on the business side of this touring machine we call Trooper. The Richibucto

Festival, where we were scheduled to play on the 29th and 30th has gone belly up. This sucks because this festival was the "anchor date" for the second Maritime leg of this tour. That means that it was the highest-paying gig of the tour. Also, the club in Mississauga canceled our show on the 27th. Our agent had warned us that the venue's mandatory deposit was very late arriving and that he suspected they didn't have enough money to pay out our full fee. We then received an e-mail from SDTF (Super Duper Trooper Fan) Ian Winsor, warning us that Honeymoon Suite had canceled their show there a week or two ago. More than likely theirs was a situation similar to ours; often, the venue will blame the artist for a no-show.

Thanks to the quick thinking and hard work of George Elmes, our east coast agent, we have recovered somewhat from these cancelations by adding a show in Moncton, New Brunswick, and a 75th Anniversary show (theirs—not ours!) back at the Savoy Theatre in Cape Breton. You hear that, Subway Steve? You'd better start rehearsing another Trooper song.

Saturday, June 22, 2002
Strathroy, Ontario

Two hours before our 6:10 lobby-call yesterday thunder cracked like a cannon and the skies lit up. The rain came down in sheets ... bouncing eight inches above the pavement outside my hotel room's sliding glass door. Mikey called an hour later, with the storm still raging, to tell us that the Oakville Waterfront Festival show was going on as scheduled.

When we arrived at the site, I could see no one at all in front of the stage. The rain continued to fall heavily. By the time we went on, half an hour later, an impressively large crowd had assembled— umbrellas and rain suits deployed—to welcome us, cheering, to the stage. There is no better audience than the one that has suffered in order to see you! We loved those people immediately and they returned that love disproportionately.

Oakville was my favourite show of the tour so far. My connection to the crowd was palpable and I ranged far and wide with the confidence that they would venture out there with me. I have many favourite moments from this show.

I was thrown several hats in the first half of the set—all of which I wore for a song or two. Waiting backstage, during the drum solo, I asked an OPP officer if I could wear his hat on stage. He said no; he would get in trouble. I turned to his partner, an attractive, blonde female officer and asked her. "Sure," she said. We worked out some stage business. I went back out with her hat on.

The OPP hat got the expected response from the crowd, but as I stood there waiting to return to the verse of "Boy With A Beat"... this great-looking cop walked out onto the stage, pulled the hat from my head, and smacked me on the ass with it... and walked off. The smack on the ass was her improvisation. I love show biz.

There was other funny stuff: the pit photographer that I accused of being Jerry Mercer from April Wine; the guy I threw the mic (a long way) to so he could finish the vocal improv at the end of "$100,000.00"; and the moshing teenagers with the homemade Trooper shirts. Unbelievably, the sun came out during the encore and we returned to the stage with the short version of "We're Here For A Good Time," including the line: "and the sun is shining, in this rainy city." I want to thank everyone who came to the Oakville show for making it so damn fun for me!

Thanks also to our buddy George Elmes for coming out and hanging with us backstage after the show. He's been working particularly hard for us this week.

One other thing I have to pass on to you: one of the cops backstage told me that a fun cop trick is to pepper-spray another cop's butt when they're not looking. Apparently, it takes a little while for the effects of the spray to kick in...

We're on our way to Strathroy, Ontario, right now—eating Ontario Cookie Lady cookies and drinking Tim Hortons' coffees. The weather is, once again, questionable. I love my job.

Monday, June 24, 2002
Port Colborne, Ontario

Last night's gig in Strathroy, Ontario, was a dream. It was a hot and very humid night on a big pro stage in front of a noisy and incredibly appreciative audience of several thousand. After our one-hour set in Oakville, it was a real pleasure to settle back into the full show. Once again we could do no wrong. The roar at the end of "Raise A Little Hell" was the longest and loudest I can remember on this tour.

Jimmy Rankin (formerly of the Rankin Family) and his band opened up for us. I met Jimmy for the first time at a SOCAN Awards banquet in Toronto two years ago. Last night, in the backstage tent, he told me about going to see Trooper at the Misty Moon in Halifax.

We're on our way to Port Colborne, Ontario, where we play at 2:30 in the afternoon. That's *way* too early to be doing what we do! I've been doing extra vocal exercises already so that I'll be warmed up. Although, as Jimmy was saying last night, this humidity is the perfect environment for a singer's voice.

Thursday, June 27, 2002
Kingston, Ontario

This room could be larger, and have a window that opened—and real pillows instead of these bags of chipped foam—but it has a great view of the Kingston harbour and I can easily walk from here to all my favourite places in the city.

Out my hotel window – Kingston, Ontario

I have added another restaurant to my small list of favourites. The Cambodian Village has the same Cambodian/Thai menu as my old fave, the Wok Inn. I've eaten there three times—and at the Wok Inn once.

Classic Video, a few blocks from here, has a wonderfully eclectic collection of DVDs and has rented me nine movies over the last three days. I have watched: *The Dream Life of Angels* (very cool); *Crumb* (a fascinating but disturbing documentary about artist/cartoonist R. Crumb); *My Life in Pink* (also fascinating but disturbing in an altogether different way); *Lumumba* (powerful but sad); Roger Vadim's *And God Created Woman* (too old now to really have an impact); *The Princess and the Warrior* (excellent—my fave of the film-fest—directed by the guy who did *Run Lola Run*); and Atom Egoyan's *Exotica* (well-made and thought-provoking). Beside my PowerBook on this small desk are *Powder* and *Boys Don't Cry* which I may or may not have time for between now and the 10:45 show at AJ's Hangar.

Our usual work schedule is six nights on/one night off, a different city every night. Most of our so-called days off are consumed by a long Sunday drive and usually only amount to an evening without a show. Monday was like that. We drove for six hours from Port Colborne. Yesterday, though, we had the pleasure of having the whole day to ourselves in a great city. I walked for several hours. Kingston is a beautiful, intelligent, and cultural town—my favourite city in Ontario.

We have another night off tomorrow, which was supposed to be the canceled Mississauga show. Unfortunately we can't stay here in Kingston because we have to wake up near the Toronto airport for our flight back out to the Maritimes.

Friday, June 28, 2002
St. Stephen, New Brunswick

I have a particularly strong memory of my Wednesday morning checkout from the Howard Johnson Hotel in Kingston. The 20-something customer service representative printed my telephone bill and said:

"Awesome show last night!" Two other front desk guys appeared behind him.

"Awesome!" they echoed. "That was more than just a show, it was..." they struggled for words but failed to finish the sentence.

"Thanks," I said. "It was a lot of fun." It's true, the Kingston show was extremely fun. It was also the best response I can remember at that venue.

"Everything about your show was so..." again, the sentence remained unfinished.

"It was a great night for us," I said truthfully, "we were playing really well."

"Oh my god... your band is *so good*..."

"Loved your Weezer cover."

"Weezer's my favourite band," I laughed.

"I know. I heard about an interview with you when you were in Alberta last year and the band started playing 'Hash Pipe' to surprise you on your birthday."

"Right..." I said, knowing right away that I would remember this conversation.

Forgive me for reveling for a moment in our odd version of celebrity, but I just love the nature of our current position in the Canadian music scene. I am proud to be part of a band that is the "guilty pleasure" of college students who are supposed to be fans of Remy Shand, Sum 41, or, for that matter, Slim Shady or Alicia Keys. In a small, Canadian way, it's like Weezer's career—they're a band that was never considered cool but continue to exist happily because of their loyal fan base. I am still surprised and delighted by nights like Kingston where the audience we can see, the ones pressed 20 deep against the stage unabashedly waving their arms in the air, are between the ages of 18 and 25. I am also very proud of our over-40 fans who brave the potential indignity of a modern-day rock show to come out and support us, after all these years. This would be a good time to thank you all—whatever your age—for showing up and making these shows such joyous events.

Last night in our hotel near the Toronto airport, I ordered in Japanese food and watched an excellent Japanese anime movie called *Princess Mononoke*. Early this morning we swapped out our Budget 15-passenger van for eight Executive Class seats on an Air Canada flight to Halifax, Nova Scotia.

At this moment, we're in a different 15-passenger van, about an hour into the six-hour drive to St. Stephen, New Brunswick. We play tonight at the Border Arena, so named, I think, because St. Stephen sits on the border between New Brunswick and Maine. It was odd to do my pre-show radio interview with a DJ with such a strong American accent.

We are trying to prepare ourselves mentally for the next four days. Tomorrow we drive ten hours to the 75th Anniversary show at the Savoy in Glace Bay. We leave right after that show and drive through the night to St. John, New Brunswick, where we play at two o'clock the following afternoon. After that show we drive straight to Moncton, New Brunswick, where we play, again, that night. (That was two shows in one day, for those of you not paying attention.) The following morning we drive to Halifax and—get this—jump on the premier of Newfoundland's charter jet to fly to St. John's for what promises to be our best Canada Day show ever! The next day, we will spend fifteen hours, either in the air or in airports, making our way back to our homes in British Columbia.

Then we will sleep.

Saturday, June 29, 2002
Sydney, Nova Scotia

We're four hours into a nine-hour drive on our way from St. Stephen, New Brunswick, to Glace Bay, Nova Scotia. I slept for three of those hours with my feet up on the dashboard and an inflatable airplane pillow around my neck. I've been thinking about what we're going to play tonight at the Savoy Theatre. We did a great Savoy show only two and a half weeks ago—how do we improve on that?

In all the years that we've traveled all over the Maritimes, we've never been down to the St. Andrew/St. Stephen part of the province. It's very beautiful down there, more like the south shore of Nova Scotia than the rest of New Brunswick. The gig was another sold-out, extremely loud, and enthusiastic arena show. It was very hot and humid on stage and it felt like most of the oxygen in the arena had already been consumed before our show began. This made the early part of the set difficult—it took a while to acclimatize my lungs to the humidity and the apparent lack of oxygen. I've had lots of experience with this phenomena and the trick is, of course, to deal with it without appearing to be gasping for air, which, at several points, I was wishing I could do.

My room at the Winsome Inn was so clean and well-maintained that I felt I had to make my bed and fold up my used towels before I left. I particularly liked the pen and pencil set with a protractor, ruler, and eraser. Mostly, though, I loved the motel's name.

The conversation continued here in the van about when we should leave for St. John. We may sleep for four or five hours after the show before we leave instead of going right after the show. This makes things a little tighter at the other end, especially considering the unknown factor of how far away the festival is from downtown St. John.

Monday, July 1, 2002
St. John's, Newfoundland

I'm sitting behind the pilot in a tiny, ancient Piper Navajo prop plane, looking out at the lake-studded greenery of Nova Scotia below. The pilot's name is Dianne, and the co-pilot's name is Kathy. Dianne told me that she was a flight attendant until the day she said to herself: "I can do that." These are the first female pilots we've ever flown with.

We had to leave a major part of our gear behind; the plane is that small. No "Thin White Line" in the set tonight: the guitar wouldn't fit. Scott and I are shoulder to shoulder—it took two or three minutes to crawl into our seats from the door at the back. There's a guitar case filling up the tiny aisle. The engines are roaring so loudly that there's no point trying to talk. I am having difficulty believing that this is the premier of Newfoundland's plane. A beautiful new Lear Jet was sitting outside the window of the waiting room when we arrived. We thought it was ours 'til they pointed out this little plane that had been skulking in behind the Lear.

We fly to Sydney, land and refuel, and then fly on to St. John's, Newfoundland, where we play at 9:30 tonight. This should be the best show of the tour.

Yesterday started with a five a.m. departure from Sydney, Nova Scotia, and a six-hour drive to St. John, New Brunswick. A grinning Brian Greenway, the lead guitar player for April Wine, greeted us, at the backstage gate of the Mispec Beach Canada Day Festival. Brian was celebrating "Beer Sunday," a weekly tour ritual that he appears to have invented. He continued celebrating with us and, in fact, joined us on stage for several hilarious guest appearances—including the traditional band bow at the end. The show was a ton of fun for us, and for the audience. It was a loose-boned hoot of a performance that made up for the fact that we had to be the first band on in order to make it to Moncton for our second show of the day. As we left the site, April Wine's road manager, Kenny, was surprised to see Brian in our van with us. "Tell Myles I quit—I'm joining Trooper," he shouted out the window. It was also good to see the boys from Honeymoon Suite, who have now, according to a local newspaper story, graduated to "classic rock" status. In response to my traditional, pre-show, "break a leg" salutation, Johnny told me about being hit by a car at the airport and having his leg broken.

Five-and-a-half hours later we were onstage at the Voodoo Lounge in Moncton, New Brunswick. We dug into our full-length set with a vengeance and soon had the whole room shouting with their arms in the air. It was another predominantly 18-to-25-year-old crowd up front with us—shouting up a hot and sweaty vibe for us to work off. Afterwards, we sat for a while at a quiet picnic table out behind the club and caught our breath.

As we pulled out onto the street to head back to the hotel, a car full of young fans swung in beside us honking the horn. Gogo honked back. The other car replied with a rhythmic honk, which Gogo answered. Soon van and car were making their way through Moncton with horns blaring in intricate rhythmic patterns. Gogo grinned at one point and said, "This guy's good!" This lasted for the entire ten-minute run back to the hotel and was incredibly funny at the time.

We just landed at Sydney Airport to gas up again so that we can get across the water to Newfoundland. We picked up some sandwiches at Muddah's in the small airport lobby. Sitting in the first seat behind the pilot, I got to climb out of the plane through the pilot's window. We just broke out the fruit plate and the bag of Werther's and we're out over the vast stretch of water between the mainland and The Rock.

Our pilots – on the way to St. John's, Newfoundland

Tuesday, July 2, 2002
On the way to Halifax

We've just taken off from Sydney, on our way back to Halifax. Cathy says the weather (and visibility) is bad in Halifax. She didn't seem too pleased about that. Could be some more adventure soon.

The Canada Day gig on George Street in St. John's, Newfoundland, was as wild and fun as we had all expected. Thousands of people were jammed into the street in front of the stage. Instead of our usual introduction, I walked out alone, waited for the cheering crowd to settle, and then sang "O Canada," hockey game style. I knew that the whole audience would sing it with me, which they did, loudly. We went straight from that into "Good Time" and the crowd went nuts, singing the first half of the song louder than the band. We had nothing but fun after that.

The only thing that wasn't ideal about the George Street setup was the large space between the audience and the stage. I told the crowd that the reason there were big security guys in the space between us was so that they could ferry us on their shoulders out to meet them. Then, after warning the security guy in front of me twice, I climbed on his shoulders and he carried me out to shake hands with the crowd. The other two guards came in on either side and the three of them moved me right along the front of the barricade.

What an incredible way to end a great tour: Canada Day in our favourite city in Canada. After the show, and a long stay at the T-shirt booth, we all dispersed into the George Street crowds. There is no way to accurately describe the interaction that takes place out on that street. At one point, Scott said to me that he wished that the whole rest of the world could be like that. I have to agree. You can't stand in one spot for more than two minutes without a conversation starting, without a funny story being told, without meeting yet another kind-hearted, good-spirited person.

Patrick, our talented and charming merchandise manager, got screeched in at Trapper John's (a favourite George Street Bar) in a very funny ceremony that was cheered on by the whole club. I sang a song or two with the guy who was playing there. He plays a right-strung guitar upside down, which is the way I've played for years. (I play left-strung onstage). I was so surprised to see him playing upside down that I wanted to show him how I did it. Next thing you know, I was playing, and singing, "Darlin' Be Home Soon," an old favourite Lovin' Spoonful song that The Barra MacNeils covered a few years ago. I also sang "Hash Pipe" with him.

Scott and I were heading back to the hotel... until we heard some excellent traditional music that we followed into another bar. Just as we entered, someone was calling out to the band for Stan Rogers, so I started singing "Barrett's Privateers" loudly. Moments later, the singer in the band belted out: "Oh the year was seventeen seventy-eight" and the whole crowd, including me, shouted back: "How I wish I was in Sherbrooke now." By the end of the song, Scott was confidently singing the choruses with everyone else in the room. After that, chants of "Trooper, Trooper" got me up to sing a song with the band. We did "Norwegian Wood" by the Beatles. I sang an octave to the Stan Rogers-like lead of the singer and it sounded great. Even our walk back to the hotel was fun. We were joined by two semi-punk guys who called out: "Hey... great big fucking troop-er!" When we played in Bay Roberts last summer, we were on the bill with Great Big Sea and Big Sugar... so, remarking on that, I introduced the band to the audience as... "Great Big Fucking Trooper." It has amazed me how many times I've heard about that since. "Bif Naked had a pretty good show last night," they told us, "but it was totally mild compared to you guys."

Pub – St. John's, Newfoundland

Yesterday's flight in this little plane was four hours long. Today's will be the same. There is virtually no air conditioning and it is very hot up here. Crammed in like sardines, most of us are attempting sleep in these small, low-backed chairs. At this altitude, the weather is beautiful, and we hope things have cleared up over Halifax.

Later:

Fifteen hours of flying today. Thankfully, Debbie and Connor wait for me at the end of this cross-continent journey, making the whole trip beyond worthwhile. The separation from my family is a subtext to this job that I try not to dwell on, for fear of not being able to deal with it as well as I sometimes manage to do. I will be a very happy man when I turn on my cellphone at Vancouver International and call my wife, who will be circling the arrivals level.

CHAPTER TWO

July 4–August 21, 2002

30,000 feet, Whatever Turns You On, Lance's Hometown,
Turn 'Em On – Turn 'Em Off, Over 100 Trooper Shows,
The Hard Rock in The Big Smoke

Thursday, July 4, 2002
White Rock, BC

I'm home. The tour has ended. I now, happily, begin a month off with Debbie and Connor. Whoohoo.

The pier – White Rock, BC

Saturday, August 17, 2002
In the Air

I'm currently at 30,000 feet, pecking away on my PowerBook, headed for Ottawa, Ontario, where we're playing the Ottawa Exhibition tonight. Actually, we're playing it about an hour after we get off the plane. It's going to be a tight one.

Speaking of tight, I swear that my economy seating area (the seat and proximate personal real estate) shrinks every year. I vaguely recall reading about airlines pulling out seating and reconfiguring in order to create an extra row (and—it seems—an extra seat per row). That particular renovation would account for the proportionate change in comfort that I'm experiencing (so I tend to believe), urban legend or not.

Five days, three shows. Ottawa tonight, followed by a day off in Hamilton, then Flamboro Downs—a race track/casino in Hamilton on Monday, and on to Toronto and the Hard Rock Cafe on Tuesday. Wednesday, we fly home.

For our day off I've brought along a few DVDs: the first nine episodes of *Oz*; the British TV version of *Gormenghast* (the bizarre Mervyn Peake epic, of which I've read the entire, brain-warping trilogy); a documentary on Louis Armstrong (one of my favourite singers); and six episodes of *Fawlty Towers*. There is also a video store a few blocks from our Hamilton hotel. I refuse to be bored.

I wonder sometimes about my need for entertainment. In my heart of hearts, I would prefer writing a book to reading one. I procrastinate on the Great Canadian Novel concept only because writing a book takes a *lot* more time and effort than reading one. Watching a movie requires even less.

Sunday, August 18, 2002
Near Ottawa, Ontario

I'm sitting in the shotgun seat of the Pontiac Montana that we picked up at the Ottawa airport a few hours ago. We've just left Lance's Mom and Dad's house in Ottawa, where we had an excellent lunch, a fun visit with Lance's very cool parents, and a short walk down Lance's memory lane. Before we left we watched a video that was brought to our dressing room last night by a guy named Jim Clark. In the late 70s, Jim worked on a TV show called either *You Can't Do That on Television* or *Whatever Turns You On*. The former is the name I remember from 1979 when we did it; the latter is the name written on the VHS cassette that Jim brought for us. I remember flying to Ottawa, from Toronto, the day after the Juno awards in 1979, to do this show. Anyone who remembers Ruth Buzzi from *Laugh-In* will understand why my favourite moment of the show was when Ruth (who was the other guest on the show) hit me repeatedly over the head with her famous black purse. Inexplicably, the purse scene cuts off prematurely on the tape. The entire rest of the show is intact, and just the purse whipping is missing! I hope Heather, our Web meister, still has Jim's e-mail address! By the way, thanks Jim.

Ottawa is Lance's hometown, and the Civic Centre, where we played last night, is a pivotal landmark in his rock and roll memory core. Last night was the first time he'd performed in the building where he has witnessed countless shows by a long list of his rock heroes. His whole family was in attendance to commemorate the event, along with a boisterous and appreciative collection of Ottawa locals.

When we were making our way to the dressing room, we had passed a guy sitting near the big back doors, at a table upon which was a small black box with a few switches. He was wearing headphones. During the drum solo, when I left the stage, I went to the back of the building and asked him what his job was.

"House lights," he replied. He was playing solitaire.

Turn 'em off, turn 'em on... that's it. That's all he did all night. Turned 'em off when we went on... turned 'em on again at the end of the show. It's hard to believe that "house light guy" is a complete job description (or, for that matter, a complete job!).

Our old pal (and ex-soundman/road manager) Paul Cloutier also showed up at the dressing room.

"You guys are on the wrong stage," he shouted. "This stage is the Britney Tribute."

Paul lives in Coquitlam, BC, and works with Lance (with whom he has been friends since their early teens in Ottawa), so it was a big surprise to see him there. Although I missed the after-show party, I understand that most of the fun was generated by Paul and the two non-English-speaking Italian tourists who he insisted join them all for drinks.

Traffic here on the 401 is grinding to a halt. We've just pushed our ETA ahead another hour.

Wednesday, August 21, 2002
Near Ottawa, Ontario

K' well, it's all done. We're on our way back down the highway to Ottawa to catch our plane home. I have a couple of spare hours.

We arrived in Hamilton in the early evening for our night off. I moved the desk in my room over to the couch, set up my speakers and PowerBook, and settled back to watch the first few episodes of

Oz, an explicit, hard-edged drama that takes place in a maximum-security prison. The series paints an unrelenting, darkly unflattering picture of the human condition and, because it's a serialized story, allows no conflict to be resolved in any significant way. What I saw left me unsatisfied and disturbed. I watched 'til four a.m. By the end of the first three episodes, I had learned only that, in prison anyway, you can trust no one and there is no depth of evil to which a man will not sink. Probably because of *Oz*, I slept badly that night.

On Monday, I slept late, and the Hamilton show was early. We played at eight in a tent outside of the Flamboro Downs Slots. It was a chilly and drizzly evening. The show, though, was anything but chilly. There are quite a few people who have seen the band more than 100 times. At the Hamilton show, there were five of these serious Trooper fans in attendance! By now we know all of them by name, and they were invited, along with the casino's VIPs, back to the trailer after the show.

We left Hamilton early so that we could be in Toronto on time for my noon interview with Ripkin on the Mojo Radio Network. During the interview, Ripkin sang "Two for the Show" on the air, accompanying himself on an acoustic guitar. I sang a bit of back up. It was a funny show. Afterwards, the band met up at The Hard Rock Cafe and headed down to Queen and Spadina, where we split up and dispersed into the Queen Street action. My trek took me to the Bamboo for Kah Kai soup and to The Silver Snail—one of the best comic book shops in Canada—for a big bag full of graphic-novel fun.

Club 279 at the Hard Rock is very cool. They've obviously poured millions into that Hard Rock corner of Yonge Street. I was expecting a crowd like the one we had at the Horseshoe, the last time we were in Toronto. That collection was very urban and pretty eccentric. The crowd waiting for us at the Hard Rock last night turned out to be totally Trooper-centric: intensely fan-heavy and a joy to perform for. We totally revved out for our "last show of the tour."

Conversation here in the van has turned to Ra and Brian's rock and roll past. Interesting.

Our next shows are on September 13 and 14 in Victoria and Courtenay, BC. The following week we go to Regina, and there is talk of a midwest week bumped up against that. A western tour is shaping up to start almost immediately after that. See ya then.

Queen Street artist – Toronto, Ontario

CHAPTER THREE

September 15–October 22, 2002

The Island, The Authority at In Harmony, Victoria Hippies, My
Son's First Bra, Chip – Super Trooper Fan, eBay Weirdness, Frank
Church, Botched Breasts at a Smelly Beach, DJ Violence,
Gary MacLean – "Kick That Motherfucker's Ass,"
Harvest Time in Assiniboia,
A Strange Night with Three Farmer's Daughters,
Ten Days at Home, Anger and After, McGuire Artist Management,
Mr. PG, Willie's Mudpuddle, Dancing Teens,
Salty's in the Okanagan, Mullet Guy, Thanksgiving,
The Truth About Squirming Woman, A Van Full of Flu,
Rock and Country Collide, Something a Dildo Can't Do

Sunday, September 15, 2002
Vancouver Island, BC

I'm sitting in the Duke Point Ferry terminal building, just outside of Nanaimo, BC, waiting for the 12:45 p.m. ferry to take me home to White Rock. It's 11:45 now, so I have an hour to write. The ferries are often backed up for what they call a "two-ferry wait," so, being savvy west coast residents, Smitty and I left Courtenay at 10:15 so we'd be sure to get on the boat. It's a perfect west coast morning—the sun is shining and sailboats and other pleasure craft are tooling around in the bay beyond the terminal windows.

Smitty is wandering the perimeter of the parking lot, admiring the boats and no doubt regretting the fact that, because he was building his new place in Desolation Sound this summer, he had no time to get his boat out on the water. I know this piece of information because I've been riding with him in his Beemer since Friday morning. This is one of those very rare occasions where we didn't rent a van to transport the five band members from show to show. Since the two shows (Victoria and Courtenay) were both on the Island (Vancouver Island—we west coast people just call it "the Island" although there are hundreds of islands off our coast), both Scott and Gogo, who live in Nanaimo (on "the Island"), bring their own cars so that they're free to travel on their own schedule. Lance and Vesna shortened their honeymoon in order to do these shows, so they came over from Whistler (Mountain—an extraordinary ski resort a few hours north of Vancouver) in Lance's truck.

I left White Rock reluctantly. Connor's band, The Authority, was playing at The In Harmony Music Festival on Friday night. Con and I have attended this festival for the past three or four years. It's where we first saw White Rock's Cozy Bones, who have since become one of our very favourite bands. This was a very Big-Deal show for the band and I was really sorry to have to miss it.

I was dying to see how their set worked out. The local music critic had already picked The Authority and Rio Bent (Connor's good pal Allie's band) as the two acts to watch at the three-day festival. Pictures of both bands illustrated the Entertainment Section pre-show story in the *Peace Arch News*. Two weeks of rehearsals had tightened them up amazingly and I fully expected them to burn the stage down at 8:15 that night—I would have liked to have been there for the stage burning!

I'm on the ferry now—sitting in the very front row of seats at the "bow" of the ship. (Smitty was waxing nautical as we came aboard.)

The Friday crossing was as perfect as today's. I took a ton o' digital pics of scenery that I've grown so accustomed to over the years that I've nearly come to take it for granted. I live in an amazingly beautiful part of the world. A pod of killer whales paced the ferry for a few minutes during the trip and I tried in vain to will my digital camera to take a picture at the same moment that I pressed the shutter. I was rewarded with an unimpressive collection of bubbly water photos.

Victoria is one of the five or six great Canadian cities. Like all great cities, its greatness begins with the people who live there. The place is an interesting blend of conservative Victorian (get it?) small-town and wide-open-minded hippy commune. Vancouver Island has always been a magnet for the original 60s hippies, and the most recent generation of flower children (the third, I'm guessing) wanders the streets of Victoria—flashing me back to my days of long hair, striped orange bell-bottoms, and a firm belief that a better world was on its way. I spent my afternoon wandering the streets, enjoying the great shops, the well-maintained architecture, and the unusual abundance of beautiful hippy chicks.

I would like to add the Lotus Pond Vegetarian Restaurant on Johnson Street to my very short list of favourite Canadian eateries. I would never have thought that I could enjoy tofu more than chicken, beef, pork, or seafood. It's a small place and the window is nearly full of photocopied great reviews. I had the tofu, vegetables, and cashews dish, which I recommend, although everything I've eaten there has been incredibly good.

My Victoria walkabout also took me to A&B Sound (a place I should really try to stay clear of) where I bought some headphones for Connor and a three-disc DVD collection of the movie *Brazil*. *Brazil* is not a movie I recommend to everyone. It's dark, sad, and, I guess for some, ultimately depressing. I also think, though, that it's brilliantly conceived and executed, occasionally hilarious, and, when approached from the right direction, uplifting and exhilarating. It's a movie about, among many other things, the human spirit and its sometimes hopeless battle with an increasingly restrictive "reality." When director Terry Gilliam presented the finished movie to the

American studio that was financing it (Universal), they refused to release it until it was shortened by more than an hour and... get this... re-shot to include a "happy ending"! One of the three discs (disc two) documents the "Battle of *Brazil*" as the Director and Giant Corporation fought tooth and nail for the right to the "Final Cut." Both sides ultimately won. A shortened but uncompromised version of the movie was released (disc one), *and* a second 90-minute version with a re-shot happy ending was edited together by a Universal executive and a team of editors unrelated to the film for television release (disc three). I find this kind of thing endlessly fascinating. Others, I'm sure, see it as anal beyond all imagining.

Passing ferries – Strait of Juan de Fuca, BC

I watched disc two: "The Battle of *Brazil*," killing time 'til 9:30 when I figured it was safe to call Connor on his cellphone. Rio Bent was roaring in the background when he answered. I asked him how it went. "It was fucking amazing!" he shouted over the din. "We have never played better."

"Hey Dad... I got my first bra thrown at me!" I was grinning so hard I could hardly respond.

"K', I gotta go mosh to Allie's band... hope *your* gig goes good..."

he shouted. I am so proud. I am *so* proud.

The Fleet Club gig was fresh and fun. It was one of those rare shows where the audience was primarily comprised of "grown-ups." Thankfully, they were grown-ups who loved to party (and loved our band!). After the show, at T-shirts, we met Chip Ryle, a Super Trooper Fan from somewhere in Idaho. Chip had driven up from the US for the show—his first in a planned series that included Courtenay last night and a trip to the prairies for at least the two Regina shows and possibly more! He presented us with a complete collection of Trooper albums to autograph. He had found two of the albums on eBay where he had bid big bucks ($70.00 US for one) for them. In one of those very strange coincidences that seem to haunt us, Chip met a Victoria native at the show against whom he had been eBay bidding for one of those albums!

Chip was sitting front-row on a hay bale when we walked onstage in Courtenay last night. The Harvest Festival show was a magical outdoor concert on one of the most beautiful evenings so far this month. People aged from five to fifty cheered, sang, and danced in the fresh evening air. My good friends Bruce, Maggie, and Morgan Rutherford were there for the show, as was my equally good pal (and well-known west coast singer and performer) Judy Norbury. Bruce had visited with me at the hotel in the afternoon. Although he's my age, he had just returned from a week-long mountain biking adventure in Nelson, BC. This was his first serious ride since he broke his collarbone in June. After the show, I returned a copy of the book *Geek Love* to "Santa Morgie," Bruce's daughter, who has also become a great friend. Morgan is an Emily Carr Institute graduate and a brilliant fine artist. We are proud to have one of her paintings hanging in our home.

I can see the mainland in the distance. I should wrap up. I'll pick this up again on September 20, when we play for two nights at Casino Regina and then head out for six more shows, concluding with a double bill in Saskatoon with our new friends Farmer's Daughter (who, I have just learned, have changed their name to "The Daughters"). Our first meeting with "the daughters," last year in Rankin Inlet, Nunavut, was a hoot and a half, so Saskatoon should be fun.

Out my hotel room window – Victoria, BC

Saturday, October 12, 2002
Penticton, BC

First of all—because I need to write it somewhere...

Frank Church was a great man, and the world is a lesser place now that he's gone.

Frank's son, Larry Church, played bass with Trooper for years. We used to meet at Frank and Vi's house, drink some coffee, shoot the shit... and then Frank would drive us to the airport to begin the tour. My Dad, who is almost ten years older than Frank, would have called him "a good egg" if he had known him—which is high praise from my Dad—and, without question, "a helluva guy." Frank Church was a helluva guy. I will seriously miss him. Larry and Sue's Christmas singalong party (a much-loved yearly tradition) is going to be very difficult this year.

All right...

Well, I don't know where to begin.

Seriously, as more stuff happens, it becomes more difficult to make a start.

I figure I'll just leave things out. Hell, I totally left out the gig in Ontario where we played on a beach that smelled like shit and was populated by some of the scariest people I've ever seen (including the extremely unattractive topless woman with the badly botched boob job). I'll just leave things out.

Right now I'm driving from Williams Lake, BC, to Penticton, BC. It's a crisp, sunny Cariboo day.

I'll try to summarize. In my last post, we were on our way back to Winnipeg. The Winnipeg gig was SRO again and tons of fun. An interesting moment came when I slugged the radio station DJ (I didn't know who he was at the time.) He had decided, without asking anyone, that he was going to say something before we started. He hit me on the shoulder when I wasn't looking (and certainly wasn't expecting anyone to be up there, as the intro march was blaring and we were just walking on). I didn't hit him hard, but even after I smacked him back, it still took a few minutes for him to assimilate the idea that we weren't going to stop playing and that he should get the fuck off the stage. Patrick told us later that the DJ was planning to give away some tickets to the upcoming Cher concert. He gave the tickets to Patrick. Patrick threw them away.

After the amazingly love-charged set, Gary MacLean's widow, Monica, brought us a homemade booklet full of pictures of the Tribute/Benefit Concert that was held in his honour, along with newspaper clippings and family shots of his last few weeks alive. Gary was, of course, one half of MacLean and MacLean, Canada's funniest and most foul-mouthed comedy duo. He had been diagnosed with throat cancer. The concert was, in many ways, a "wake" that Gary could attend, and enjoy, with his many friends. The first page of the booklet she gave us was a copy of the message we sent to Gary because we couldn't make the show. It read: "Gary, kick that Motherfucker's ass. Love, your pals in Trooper." The booklet was hard going. I didn't make it to the last page.

The next night in Brandon, Manitoba, was excellent. That's all I remember about it.

Somewhere in Saskatchewan

Assiniboia is a very small Saskatchewan town. The gig is in the old Hotel on the main street. We stayed in the little one-level motel next door. We all attended the Hotel's weekly "Steak Night" again. (This was our second visit to Assiniboia.) There, the owner of the hotel apologized to us, saying that he hadn't sold this show out a week in advance like the last one. Because of the terrible weather this year (floods followed by drought), the timing of the harvest was critical. Most of our potential audience was frantically trying to finish before the imminent first frost. As it turned out, he needn't have worried; the place filled up and we were happy to give the locals a much-needed night of stress relief. It was a classic good-vibe-small-town night.

Prairie frost – somewhere in Saskatchewan

By contrast, the Prince Albert, Saskatchewan, venue was an upscale room with a large, high stage, great lighting, and perfect sightlines. It was a total sold-out rock concert kinda deal. The tons-o'-fun we had that night was completely different from the kind of fun we had the night before...

Chamberlain, Saskatchewan

Saskatoon, Saskatchewan, is one of my favourite Canadian cities. On the Saturday night, we played at the Convention Centre with Farmer's Daughter. Our first gig with them was one of the great adventures of my career. The hook-up was instant; the two groups got on like a house on fire. Shawna-Rae has since left the group, and they've changed their name to The Daughters, but it was great to see Angela and Jake again. This was a woefully under-attended gig. Every now and then there's a show like this one where something has gone terribly wrong. This was a bill that should have seriously sold out—even the promoter was baffled. Despite the large, dark emptiness of the room (in fairness, there were hundreds of people there, but thousands would have been better) both bands put on amazing shows. The Daughters sang a couple of songs with us, and I sang one with them. An excellent way to end the mini-tour.

I returned home in time to attend a photo shoot for the poster advertising a show that Connor's band (now called Anger and After) will be doing at the White Rock Playhouse in November. Connor is growing into a great songwriter, guitar player, singer, and performer and as his "career" progresses, I see, more and more, that I will be unhappy leaving the overseeing of his affairs to a management company. I have a strong feeling that this is something I need to think about. I know I could do a better job for him than all but the very best outfits in Canada. McGuire Artist Management. Hmmm... He's only 15... there'll be time.

My ten days at home was short but very happy. As I get older it becomes harder and harder for me to leave my family and my home behind. I give thanks to my phone company and their nine-cents-a-minute Calling Card.

The first show of this run was Prince George, BC. Five hundred miles north of Vancouver, I've played this town hundreds of times. It's never been one of my favourite gigs. It's always seemed like a hard place—the downtown populated by a sad collection of drunk, forlorn, and mostly native street people. The gigs have traditionally been hard-drinking affairs—sometimes a little scary. For years, a large log man called "Mr. PG" marked the entrance to the city. The story goes that a metal replica eventually replaced the log sculpture because locals kept burning the log ones down.

Mr. PG – Prince George, BC

We returned to a venue we haven't played since the early 90s. It has a new name now, but it used to be called the Rock Pit. Every musician I know called it the Snake Pit and stories of the former (now deceased) owner and his scuzzy "Band House" are legendary. Strangely, the sold-out gig was like a reunion with old friends. It was awesome—easily the best Prince George gig I can remember. The hard edge has softened, and the vibe improved. Everyone in the band sensed it and commented about it later in the dressing room. It was a nice surprise.

Last night was Williams Lake (my parents, who spent a good part of their youth in the vicinity, always called it "Willie's Mudpuddle"). This is the town where my Mom and Dad first met. My Mom was waiting for a train. My Dad was in uniform. Mom sent me an e-mail the day before the show, asking if I could take a picture of the Lakeview Hotel where they had dined that fateful day. The Hotel was still there but, to my great dismay, suffering in its old age from several devastating renovations, which have left it completely devoid of any character or interest. I took a few pictures, then went in to the Lakeview Restaurant and ordered some Beef and Broccoli to go. The food, at least, was great.

Lance had risen early in Prince George and bragged, on the way down, about picking up the *Reservoir Dogs* DVD for ten bucks at one of the many Prince George pawns. On my way to my Williams Lake photo assignment I stopped in at Cariboo Pawn and bought four DVDs (*Full Metal Jacket*, *Strictly Ballroom*, *Romeo & Juliet*, and an early Adrien Brody movie called *Tenbenny*) for $35.00. I watched half of *FMJ* after the gig. Vincent D'Onofrio is fast becoming one of my favourite actors.

The gig was sold-out, fun, and full of very nice people, all of whom, it seemed, stopped by the T-shirt booth to say hi before they left. The last time we did this gig, two teenage girls danced, for the whole set, outside a large window that was right beside the stage where the audience couldn't see them. At the end of the night, we called them in—I embarrassed the security guys into letting them dance the last couple of songs in the (much warmer) club. The fact that they did not return to entertain us again was the only thing wrong with the Williams Lake show.

We're heading down into the usually sunny Okanagan for three days: Penticton, Kelowna, and a day off in Kelowna. (Shit, there's an

A&B Sound there... must be very careful). Tonight we will dine at Salty's Beach House, one of my favourite Canadian restaurants. It may be the first place I ever had Kha Kai soup and, for that matter, Thai green curry. I just now tried to phone in our reservation but, of course, there's "no service" in this particular neck of the woods.

Tuesday, October 15, 2002
Cranbrook, BC

Penticton T-shirt booth moment:
Ra: That's the longest Mullet I've ever seen!
Mullet Guy (proudly): Thanks. I had this hairstyle way before it was popular.

Penticton was another sold-out funfest, as was Kelowna. The beautiful Okanagan Valley has always brought us a high-spirited crowd of happy people. Saturday's and Sunday's shows maintained this tradition.

We stayed, for the show day and our day off, at the Grand Hotel on the Kelowna lakefront, in rooms that would normally cost almost four hundred dollars each. Thanks to our friend Billy at Flashbacks, we paid less than that. The rooms contributed greatly to an idyllic day off on Monday. I won't bore you with my DVD watching schedule (*Simply Ballroom* and, for the fourth time, *Sling Blade*) but I did manage to get my laundry done; buy soap, shaving cream, toothpaste, and a card for Flo Church; pick up the new Gregory Maguire book, *Lost*, at Chapters; and have a happy hike around Kelowna on a warm summer-like afternoon. I passed on the $23.00 Thanksgiving turkey dinner buffet and ordered pizza to eat while movie watching.

Speaking of Thanksgiving, I am thankful and grateful for the life I currently lead. My family, my home, my work... are all as I have always hoped they could be. I give thanks for them and, in the case of my family, to them.

Gogo and I have been discussing the fact that we could never give an accurate picture, in the road stories we post, of what it's really like out here. There are just too many stories that can't be told.

The stars of these stories would be mortified to read detailed descriptions of their entertaining/fascinating behaviour, and blameless citizens could be hurt by perceived (or real) slights to their hometown.

Since the Trooper Web site address is displayed over the T-shirt booth, I assume that some people surf over after seeing the band play. Imagine a small-town Ontario resident linking up to my blog and reading, last week, that their beach smelled like shit. Worse, imagine the witless 40-year-old woman from said beach stumbling on to my description of the misplaced gel-sacs in her proudly displayed naked breasts.

Stories told after the fact about what happened in an unnamed city at some undefined time would lack the details that make a good story come alive. Often the context of the odd behaviour is what makes that behaviour odd. Take, for example, the woman who climbed onstage after a show and... uh... "squirmed around on the floor" on the spot where I had been standing. This uninhibited act of misdirected sexual energy wouldn't have raised an eyebrow in the bar at Port Hardy, BC (another story entirely), but this particular squirming took place on the stage of the multi-million dollar dinner theatre at Casino Regina, in front of a well-dressed, sold-out, Saturday night crowd.

This story, reported the following day, could suggest that Regina women, in general, lack a sense of decorum. As funny and/or fascinating as her behaviour might be, my commenting on it could be perceived as mocking not just the hapless squirmer but also her entire community. This is not the kind of thing a performer, who lives or dies by public perception, should do.

So that's my dilemma. How do I share these stories without inferring a deeper or broader criticism of a person or place? The squirming lady may have been deeply ill, uncontrollably drunk, or in the process of winning a hundred-dollar bet. I cast no judgment. I generally love every audience equally. Unusual people and their baffling behavior is what distinguishes one gig from another and keeps my life on the road interesting.

Sunday, October 20, 2002
Somewhere between High Level Alberta and Edmonton Alberta

We're driving to Edmonton, Alberta, for our day off. We left High Level, Alberta, at ten this morning. I slept sitting up for the first three hours: I have an inflatable airplane neck support that helps with that.

Yesterday, I slept in, went for a walk around the town, and returned to my room, where I stayed until show time. These days, it's unusual for us to do two shows in one place, and it was strange not to pack up my gear and hump it into the van for another drive. This has been a hard tour with six- to ten-hour drives every day and the weather slowly but resolutely turning colder each day. The five of us have been sharing a change-of-season cold—a low-grade congestion accompanied by stinging eyes that seems to come and go—moving from me to Scott, back to me, over to Smitty, on to Gogo, to Lance in the back of the van, and then around again. Since we last spoke, we have driven another 2500 kilometers. Although we drive all day again today, tonight's night off in Edmonton will be a welcome one. I have been sleepwalking through the past few days.

Cranbrook, BC, was a great show: a lively crowd pushed right to the front of the stage with arms in the air all night. My favourite musical moment of the tour so far came in "Happy Together" (which we moved into the encore) when, for about a minute at the end of the song, the singing crowd and the grinning band blurred into one sweaty, euphoric being.

Somewhere on the road

Vermillion, Alberta, was sold-out and successful, but a little mysterious. After the show, the people were extremely nice to us and I enjoyed meeting all of them, but, while we were playing, they all seemed tense and self-conscious and... well... busy with something more important.

Grande Prairie, Alberta, was a good gig, but the crowded dance floor was a long way from the stage, so I felt disconnected from the audience. Without real feedback from the people I'm performing for, it's difficult to keep my mojo on. Truthfully, I get bored. The show kicked in at the end, with more people crowding into the space in front of the stage—and the four-song encore brought the kind of audience action we thrive on.

Roadside — Somewhere in Alberta

We played two sold-out nights in High Level, Alberta, with The Poverty Plainsmen, a popular Canadian country band that was just nominated for Group of the Year at the CMA Awards. The posters read: "Rock and Country COLLIDE!!" There was no collision in High Level. The Plainsmen were a great band, a great bunch of guys, and we really enjoyed hooking up with them. At the end of the show last night, after singing a few songs together, the two bands linked arms right across the full length of the High Level stage and took their bows together. This was a very successful weekend and, after the show, there was some serious talk of future Rock and Country collisions!

Tuesday, October 22, 2002
St. Paul, Alberta

I spotted a pawn shop across the street from the Chinese food place and went in for a quick look around. A 60-something man stood behind the glass counter.

Pawn Shop Guy: "Hi."

Me: "Hi. Looks like it's starting to be winter."

Pawn Shop Guy: "Startin' to be..."

Pause in conversation while I peruse the small, scantily stocked store.

Pawn Shop Guy (once I had circled back to the counter): "So I said to my sister-in-law yesterday: 'why do you keep my brother around?' and she says: 'because a dildo can't mow the lawn'."

Me: "..."

Chapter Four

December 31, 2002–February 23, 2003

New Year's Reminiscing, Rock and Roll Dad,
Take a Right at the Arctic Ocean, My Wonderful Wife,
Out the Window, It's a Living, Beachcombers, ATVs on the
Tundra, "I Hated Fucking Spandex,"
Waiting for a Heartbeat, The Beatles and Buddy Clyde,
The Epics, My First Gig, Hormonal Heroin,
A New Drummer for Trooper, Three Auditions,
Drummer X, A Trooper Armed Forces Tour, One-Sided Interview,
CBC Visit, Trooper's Graphic Artist, A Nervous Rash,
Singing and Typing, Frankie Baker Rehearsals, Drugs,
Drinking and Ego

Tuesday, December 31, 2002
New Year's Eve 2002/2003

A passionate roar erupts as the house lights go down. The MC steps out in front of the red velvet curtain and, through the mounting screams, shouts an introduction. The curtains part and slowly draw open. The noise of the crowd drowns out the music. Two guitar players stand, in dark silhouette against the red stage lights with their backs to the crowd. As the song kicks in, they turn. The tall one with the black Les Paul steps up to the mic. The crowd screams. He grins slightly, then sets his jaw. I cheer loudly as my eyes dampen. He's my son.

Connor McGuire – September 1, 2002

I think this is my strongest, proudest, and happiest memory of 2002—a year full of proud and happy moments for all three of us. It was a year where Connor came into his own as a performer, singer, songwriter, and musician. Unbelievably, to anyone that knows her, Debbie turned 50 this year—and realized that she has become the girl she always wanted to be. I arranged to spend more time with my family in 2002, which made me very happy. In addition to a very successful 17 weeks of touring (with what still seems to be one of Canada's favourite bands), I also found time to re-visit two of my old passions, photography and writing, with very rewarding results.

Here are a few more vivid memories from the year:

Marty's SUV turns from the main drag—the one that boasts the most northerly traffic light in North America—and heads down toward the wide, frozen MacKenzie River. The road ends where the ice begins and we make a right out onto the ice road. We pass a large ship, frozen upright 'til the spring. We drive up the MacKenzie for two hours. We see only two other vehicles. Then we make a right onto the Arctic Ocean.

Ice road on the Arctic Ocean – Near Tuktoyaktuk, NWT

I am singing with my favourite singer. We have been singing along, rollers in hand, to the songs from a playlist called "Paint House." We've been working from eight in the morning 'til eleven at night for several days and we are extremely happy.

The tiny, ancient Piper Navajo touches down on the tarmac 50 yards from the small Sydney Airport building. The pilot opens the window and gracefully pulls herself out onto the wing. There is so much gear in the plane that it's taking some time to get the rear door open. I swing out and around the pilot's seat, careful not to bump anything, and follow her out the window.

There are five thousand roaring Trooper fans in front of me, shaking the building to the tempo of "Raise A Little Hell." To my right is a cameraman hoisting a large camera, to my left is Peter Jordan (the host of a Canadian TV show) and a guy I've come to really like over the course of an intensely compressed day. I am supposed to be singing, but I'm laughing too hard to get anything out. Peter is swinging wildly with a drumstick at a lone cymbal on a stand. He's loving it. The crowd's loving it. And I'm loving it.

My family settles in to watch the new *Beachcombers* movie on TV. As the first scene opens, I experience a warm rush of prideful recognition as the camera pans over the BC Ferry on its way to Gibsons Landing. As the camera moves closer to the ferry, "Here For A Good Time" begins to play.

I wish you all a year full of adventure and inner peace. We truly are here for a good time, not a long time.

Sunday, January 5, 2003
Strong Memory—Wrong Year

On New Year's Eve, as I thought back over the events of the previous year, I wrote this little flash of memory before I realized that it came from the end of 2001:

I have fallen behind to the point that I cannot see the other four riders. My thumb is aching from the cold and the strain of pushing the throttle as far as it can go. There are two possible routes in front of me, two Vs cut out of the high, rough tundra. I veer to the right, only because it is the easiest turn to negotiate at speed. I hit the crest of the hill faster than I had intended and, flying almost out of control into the Arctic air, I see four ATVs racing erratically in the broad sandpit under me. As the five of us race back to Rankin, I realize, in a moment of great joy, that my thumb is no longer hurting.

Monday, January 13, 2003
White Rock, BC
Thank God I Turned Down the Photo Shoot

The picture is huge—12 by 9 on the front page of the Saturday entertainment section. Al Harlow from Prism, Doug Bennett from Doug and the Slugs, and Tom Lavin from Powder Blues are posed like the Three Stooges—grinning broadly, arms extended—just like Al Jolson when he sang: "Mammy, how I love ya, how I need ya."

Thank God I turned down the photo shoot.

The three-page *Vancouver Sun* mega-article is called: "Rockin' Away the Years." The smaller headline reads: "The hair's a little thinner and the bodies a little thicker, but many of BC's 'classic' acts still barrel down the rock 'n' roll highway."

"Oh, sweet Jesus," I whispered, in an unintended moment of intimacy with the counter guy at J&H Market. Between the dignity-challenged photo and the glib ageism of the headline, I was terrified to read the story—for which I had done an hour-long interview with its author, Kerry Gold.

It's so easy, in a long interview (which a good writer will turn into more of a "conversation"), to say something that will look ridiculous when quoted out of context. I've learned, over the years, to watch out for the questions that elicit casually conceived, but subsequently often brutally inappropriate, answers. I'm happy to say that (after a jaw-clenching read-through) I came off OK in the article. I know all these guys well and like them, so I was nervous for them, too. Doug was his usual witty self and Bill Henderson was perfect as always. Others, though, were not so lucky.

Al Harlow felt the need to discuss "the old fart concert series that goes across Canada in the summertime...". Tom Lavin pointed out that he's been "running some really big companies, so I have to curtail myself to being a weekend warrior." Harlow gets the Spinal Tap Prize, though, for "I think we're bigger in England and Germany now than we are here."

Although I came out of the story relatively unscathed, I still feel embarrassed and uncomfortable about the whole thing. I dislike being roped in with wildly different bands simply because we had hit records in the same decade.

...and I cringe at the media's constant, snickering references to spandex. I never wore spandex. I hated fucking spandex.

Tuesday, January 14, 2003
White Rock, BC
Waiting for a Heartbeat

I am in professional and personal purgatory. So much of what I am and what I do is currently dependent on someone I have not met yet. I yearn for closure but am powerless to hasten its arrival, so I wait for the audition tapes with my fingers crossed.

The beat and the voice. That's all my mother-in-law hears. That's all many people hear.

Every drummer has a different groove. We've had great drummers who were just unable to play... say... "Ready" with enough authority to keep it in the set. The slightest millisecond difference in emphasis in the groove can change everything—sometimes in every song. My phrasing bumps and wobbles. My old moves don't work. Onstage every night, there is an invisible set of horizontal puppet-strings running from the drum kit directly to my body. Changing the puppeteer can be unnerving.

Usually, the change is invigorating. As good as—better sometimes—than a rest. A new guy injected into our close-knit brotherhood kicks new life into everything. The van chatter improves dramatically. We experience a renewed pride in the musicality of the set and the tightness and professionalism of our touring routine. And... our last set of auditions brought us the best drummer we've ever had.

We have made some mistakes, though. One drummer in particular lasted for only one excruciating tour. His audition was impressive. He was young, energetic, and ambitious. Once the tour began, we learned quickly that he was also undisciplined, arrogant, headstrong, and, most significantly, not a very nice guy. It didn't work, at any level, and he was the only one who didn't know that. It was a very long tour.

So I wait for the audition tapes with my fingers crossed.

Sunday, January 19, 2003
White Rock, BC
The Beatles Changed EVERYTHING

The first Beatles song I ever heard was not performed by the Beatles.

In 1962, at the age of 12, I enrolled in a "DJ course," a questionable educational opportunity offered by Buddy Clyde, a popular Vancouver disc jockey. My parents sponsored me for the course because at home, on Muirfield Drive in South Vancouver, I had built a small radio station that could broadcast from my bedroom to the family living room on the opposite side of my bedroom wall. My mother and father and my two brothers were my entire listening audience.

Although Buddy's TV show, *Dance Party*, was a must-watch teenage staple, his DJ course attracted only five or six students—of which I was the youngest, by five years. I graduated top of the class from the course, which was undertaken in a tiny, rustic guest house in the backyard of a North Vancouver millionaire's estate. There was a party, probably celebrating the end of the course, that, for reasons I cannot imagine, my parents allowed me to attend.

I recall a dark room—not the cabin—lit by Christmas lights and full of many more people than just my classmates. I remember that the Vancouver singer Del Erickson was there and lip-synched his latest 45. My new friend and fellow classmate, Wayne Eichendorf—a courageous kid who wore one of eight identical red corduroy shirts every day—was also there. Midway through the party, Buddy stopped the music and dramatically announced a new 45, which he placed onto the small vinyl-covered record player. The song began and the room came alive. I loved it immediately and was thrilled when the party guests demanded that it be played again. By the time my parents picked me up, the Beatles' "From Me to You," as performed by Del Shannon, had been playing, over and over again, for an hour.

It was my DJ training that landed me my first gig in a band.

Although I had been invited to the band's lunch-hour auditorium rehearsal solely for the purpose of standing with my foot firmly planted in front of the bass drum to prevent it from sliding forward, I soon convinced them that my recent training with Buddy qualified me to introduce the band at their next show. This announcing gig ultimately expanded to include individual song intros:

"And now, the Epics will play 'Walk Don't Run'."

Since the Epics' repertoire consisted entirely of "instrumentals," it took very little time to convince them to let me add singing to my duties with the group. At my first paying gig, at Bonsor Hall in Burnaby, I was paid four dollars for singing four songs. "What'd I Say" by Ray Charles was one of them. The other three were most likely Motown and R&B favorites, adapted for drums, two electric guitars, and, occasionally, Gerry's Hammond organ. Soon, I was singing James Brown, The Temps, Sam Cooke, and—my favourite— a blissfully extended version of Ben E. King's "Stand by Me."

Singing brought me unimaginable happiness. I had been convinced that a job as a radio DJ was the closest I could ever get to the music. After Bonsor Hall, I gave no further thought to a DJ career.

Other than my rapidly waning interest in UFOs, music was my entire world. My red transistor radio—tuned to CFUN, Vancouver's first teen-oriented radio station—was constantly at my ear. I was walking down 44th Avenue, near Nanaimo Drive, with a group of friends when I first heard them. The radio was at my ear, as always, when "I Want to Hold Your Hand" came on.

There is nothing in recent musical history to compare to it. I cannot express how completely revolutionary their music was. It was immediately so much more than music: it was teenage hormonal heroin. I had never heard anything like it. There had never been anything like it. I shouted at my friends to listen; the Beatles poured into us and surged through us.

From that moment on, the Beatles changed *everything*.

Sunday, January 26, 2003
White Rock, BC
There are three drummers auditioning with Trooper next week

I was successfully taking the weekend off from drummer madness, until a piece in Dave Chesney's column, "Canada Calling," reminded me: "Trooper is looking for a new drummer."

My immediate thought process was to do the math: drummer reads newspaper Saturday; goes to Trooper site for instructions; finds video recording of himself playing; makes dub by Sunday; mails copy to Calgary address on Monday; tape arrives in Calgary Wednesday; tape is overnight couriered to me Thursday; I watch the tape Friday; I like the drummer and overnight courier him the live versions of the songs Friday afternoon; CDs arrive at drummer's home on the "next business day" (Monday)... at about the time we start our auditions at the Wired 4 Sound Rehearsal and Pro-Demo Studio in Surrey.

There will be three drummers auditioning. The first guy had his video in within three days of the original "Trooper needs a new drummer" post. A respected musician friend recommended the second guy. The complication was (and is) that he currently plays for a very popular Canadian rock band. Several hasty and carefully worded phone calls and e-mails ensued, after which Drummer X couriered his tape to my home address. The third guy heard about the gig through Bob Dog. His video rocketed out of Vancouver and had bounced back from our Calgary mailing address by early last week.

Viewing their videotapes was an interesting responsibility. The first guy sent a recording of a Friday night in a Whitehorse bar. He played the smallest kit I've seen in a long time, but nailed a couple of sets of rock standards with authority and grace. Drummer X's video showed him laying it down solidly behind songs (and players) I know so well that it was difficult to be objective. He fit perfectly into the arena-rock format. The remaining drummer's video (and audio CD) featured him perfectly duplicating all of John Bonham's licks in an impressive Zeppelin cover band!

There were at least 20 drummers who contacted us. Some wrote that they were "very interested" and planned to submit a video. A couple of them asked for "more information" and were reminded by our Web meister that *all* the necessary info was on the site. One promised a tape of himself "playing the entire *Hot Shots* album" that he was sure we would be impressed with. Others sent e-mails describing their history in the music business. Some, after responding to the post that warned that the auditions were scheduled for the first week of February, sent us a second e-mail, last week, reiterating their interest in the gig. So far, we haven't seen tapes from any of them.

I tied up the auditions on Wednesday. I confirmed the booking of the rehearsal studio for four days, sent out the CDs of the live show, and sent a group e-mail to the band and the three drummers, with a map, a list of songs, and the times for each audition. The first day will be auditions; the next three days will be rehearsals.

The next day, more e-mails came in. And our west coast agent, Bruce Bromley, alerted me to two more possible candidates.

I'm not going to call them. I like the three guys that are coming to audition. They want to be in the band enough to be professional about their first interaction with us. They got on the job right away and took positive action. I really like that.

It's a good start.

Friday, January 31, 2003
White Rock, BC
Since we last spoke...

There's been a last-minute flurry of new-drummer-related activity this week, including a passionately intense e-mail from an old friend who played (without credit—but that's a whole other story) on the *Money Talks* album with us. Jason-from-Digby's video, consisting of him playing along with the *Hot Shots* album, has arrived in Calgary, as has another from a drummer who plays in an Ontario Iron Maiden tribute band. Smitty e-mailed me, asking me to fill him in on my progress, and several people have been calling regarding friends that they are "sponsoring" for the gig. I do not know yet what to tell any of these people. The auditions, scheduled about a month ago, are in three days.

Bruce Bromley has called me three or four times a day for the past week regarding the overwhelming abundance of Trooper booking requests coming in for shows that are scheduled to take place all over Canada between now and... next Hallowe'en! Three of today's six calls were regarding a four-day tour with the Doobie Brothers in April. The show will move from Kamloops to Lethbridge, and on to Regina and Winnipeg. My guess is that the Doobies won't be driving that one. We have to decide whether or not we are. The imminent March tour, on the other hand, hangs in the air like a house of cards—tentative weekend dates on hold 'til we know if there's enough weekday shows to justify a full six days on the road. The tour is a month away, so the weekend offers want a bottom line... meanwhile, the early-week people are skittish. My opinion on this situation has been repeatedly sought.

A very nice lady named Brenda sent an e-mail regarding Trooper taking part in Armed Forces tours: shows that fly in to Canadian Armed Forces bases in Israel, Beirut, and other exotic, often war-torn, and occasionally godforsaken locales. Think Bob Hope. No, really... think Bob Hope. Turns out, after a couple of in-depth conversations, that Brenda needs to find exactly 13 people (as mandated by the "tender" posted by the military): an MC, a band, a comedian, at least one female, and a dancer or dancers, the sum total of whom must be able to offer 20 percent of the "show" in the French language. There are eight of us that travel with Trooper. I remember trying to keep a straight face while suggesting that all she needed to do was search out a garrulous and funny French songstress who could accompany herself whilst singing—and dancing—in the manner of Natalie McMaster. Not long after that suggestion, Brenda casually mentioned, "These shows don't usually pay that well." I prepared a summary of what I had learned and e-mailed it to my partner, Brian, our west coast agent, Bruce, and our Web meister, Heather.

That same day, I also recorded my side of a conversation with a Halifax radio DJ. The DJ in question, who was unavailable at the time, added his side to that conversation at a later date. Having finished that oddly unfulfilling task, I called collect to a newspaper office in Salmon Arm, BC, and did a forty-minute interview with a writer there, while simultaneously mocking up the first version of the new T-shirt design and putting the finishing touches on an "employer" letter to a loans officer in Nanaimo, BC, where Gogo is currently assembling the down payment on a Protection Island building lot.

Monday morning we visited with Mom and Dad. I brought *The Bay of Love and Sorrows*, *The Informant*, and *Neverwhere* for them to read. On Monday after school, Connor and I visited the giant CBC building in downtown Vancouver, where Producer Rob Kirby was editing the *It's a Living* episode that will feature host Peter Jordan onstage with Trooper. I did a short interview and a "voice-over"— altering slightly something I had shouted into the mic... hopefully helping to tie up the segment more gracefully. It was a great opportunity to hang with Connor for four hours and to show him how big-time Canadian television works. Rob was the perfect host, and a true professional: he's someone who can have fun while doing great work.

Mikey called three days ago to remind me that we need to do a T-shirt order soon, and did I want to do a new shirt for this tour? Once, long ago, I was shown a new Trooper T-shirt, designed by a T-shirt designer, depicting a large white '57 Chevy (*not* a sports car by a long shot) with a Gibson Flying V guitar in the back seat, flying serenely over a sparkly gold map of Canada. It was then that I decided to take a shot at the position of graphic artist for the group. I've designed all the shirts since then. The newest is the "Trooper— Fukeneh" shirt (one of my favourites so far), and it's over a year old. So, yes, Mikey... I should do a new one. I've been working on it for a solid three days now. I have a telephone headset that allows me to Photoshop and talk on the phone at the same time—a trick of multi-tasking that I've been performing almost constantly since Monday. My original shirt idea involved a male pattern baldness skull and crossbones, but several attempts to make it work failed miserably. My subsequent, and more focused, efforts have since produced what may be my new favourite shirt, but it's not done yet.

I broke out in a rash a little over a week ago. My doctor says it's viral; I think it's nerves.

A CNN story a few days ago featured my favourite quote of the week. The story was about a recent appeal of the judgment settling the lawsuits between Mattel (the maker of Barbie dolls) and MCA (the record company that released "Barbie Girl" by Aqua). The appeals court judge, Alex Kozinski, concluded:

"The parties are advised to chill."

I can't tell you how much I like that.

Tuesday, February 4, 2003
Surrey, BC
Watch this: typing and singing AT THE SAME TIME!

In another amazing display of multi-tasking, I'm reporting live from the Wired 4 Sound Rehearsal and Pro-Demo Studio where we are now, as I write, happily rehearsing with the amazing Frankie Baker on drums.

Particularly, we are examining the "down section" in "$100,000.00" where the introductions are. I have just discovered that the CD player in my big, customized, $70.00, Japanese-girl ghetto blaster *can*, in fact, fast-forward and rewind. I have my PowerBook on a stool in front of me and a mic on a boom stand swung in front of my face.

In a sec I'm going to sing. There. Now I'm back to typing. Cool, huh?

There's a lot of stopping and starting at this kind of rehearsal—going over parts 'til they're perfect. There's not a lot for a singer to do. I do play an organizational role relative to arrangements, tempo, etc., and, of course—I'm operating the big, customized, $70.00, Japanese-girl ghetto blaster.

The auditions were a close call: all three drummers were excellent. Frankie Baker, though, was the one with the buzz. Frank was the one that elicited whoops and "ya!"s from the rest of the band while we were playing. Frank was the one where a vibe set in. Everyone, including Frank, was grinning broadly. The consensus was that he's going to be a lot of fun in the van.

I am very relieved.

"Cold Water" now. Working up a different kick drum feel.

"Ba-dum-pa-dum."

The March tour will be a continuing audition in many ways. I found myself using the same phrase with all the potential drummers:

"If there are any drugs, alcohol, or ego problems, that will be his..." I always said "his," suggesting that the problematic drummer I was referring to was not the one I was speaking to, "...last trip with Trooper."

Drugs are always bad. Drinking isn't always. There have been some hard-drinking Trooper members whose onstage performance (and their day-to-day interaction with the world) was unaffected by their alcohol intake. Others were not so fortunate.

Ego is a tricky one. A healthy ego is important in this business. It becomes a problem only when it grates on the other players or the people we work with from day to day.

"Pretty Lady" now. (I'm singing and typing at the same time!) Fuck, he plays this well.

I'm getting the strong feeling that we're not going to have any problems with Frank. He's feeling very comfortable, and the songs are *really* coming together.

Sunday, February 23, 2003
White Rock, BC
On Writing:

"Writing is no trouble: you just jot down ideas as they occur to you. The jotting is simplicity itself — it is the occurring which is difficult." —Stephen Leacock

CHAPTER FIVE

February 28–March 30, 2003

Frankie's First Night, Purgatory, Battle Conditions, Victory,
Mic Stand Solo, Aunty Lena, 48 Below, Snowstorm, A Night Off,
Creative Drift, Scott Richards, Road Mode, Venue Hijack,
The Wee Hours of the Morning, Ferry Ride,
25 Shows – Four Weeks Later, Connor's Music,
The Coming of Spring

Friday, February 28, 2003
Salmon Arm, BC—The First Night of the Tour

I have an hour before lobby call. Tonight is the first show in two months and our first show ever with Frankie Baker on drums. We had arranged to go straight to the arena as soon as we arrived in Salmon Arm so that we could go over anything that Frankie was unsure of. When I brought it up in the van today, he said he'd rather just go up there and go for it. It's been a while since I was this excited about a gig.

My room tonight is the "Victorian Suite" here in the Prestige Harbourfront Resort and Convention Centre. The large whirlpool tub in the middle of the room is the only thing not carved from dark-red wood. There is an elaborate red velvet construction above the ornately carved bed and the lamps all glow a gaslight yellow. I've had my shower and shave and am now in that vague purgatory between being ready and being on.

I am in another purgatory as well—that place between being home and being away. I'm never ready for the Spring tour. After nearly four months of virtually uninterrupted time at home with my family, my heart was vehemently unwilling to pull up stakes. Soon, "Road Mode" will click in—until then I have to deal, once again, with this ghost-like state that is neither home-Ra nor road-Ra.

Sunday, March 2, 2003
Quesnel, BC

Last night, deep under the usual pre-show bravado, pump, and adrenalin, I harboured a small but well-concealed concern that Frankie would not pull through for us on his first onstage Trooper performance. He played amazingly well in rehearsal, but there are many players who just can't cut it under what Frank Ludwig used to call "Battle Conditions."

The obvious fear is that a new player will choke. A live performance requires a high level of confidence, delicately balanced against a dependable supply of sheer nerve. There are many who simply cannot muster the necessary combination. Other players can't interact successfully with the intensity of a pumped-up live audience. They attack their instrument with the unnecessarily high amount of energy that they are unwittingly channeling from the crowd. The resulting vibe hemorrhage results in playing that is, at best, musically un-subtle and, at worst, completely out of control. In the case of drummers, there is also the chance that what sounded like an ass-kicking pounding in the rehearsal hall will become wussy-assed tapping on stage.

Halfway through the first song, I began grinning so broadly it was difficult to sing. I could tell already that Frankie totally had it...

The Salmon Arm Sunwave Centre Arena and the Trooper dressing room were packed with very happy people last night. The band clicked perfectly into gear after the two-month rest. The crowd jumped to their feet in "Good Time" and stayed up and rocking for the duration. In the dressing room after the show, Frankie collected handshakes and hugs from the band and crew. If he was *that* good on the first night, Scott said, think about how good it's going to get.

Monday, March 3, 2003
On the Road, BC
The Drive Back Home

We went from a large concert stage in the Salmon Arm arena on Friday to no stage at all in the Cariboo Hotel last night in Quesnel, BC. This kind of booking plan really keeps us on our toes. My most intense memory of last night's show was the look of absolute joy on nearly every audience member's face. Everyone seemed to be having an extremely good time. Our second night with Frankie Baker on drums was better than the first. The band was huddled together in a tight space, so we could all work very closely musically. Frankie just oozes talent and showmanship. During his drum solo last night he left his kit, came to the front of the stage with his sticks, and began playing a solo on two mic stands. Since the stands had live mikes at the ends of them, the resulting performance was amplified through the PA system. I complimented him on the mic stand solo after the show and he said: "Did you like that? It's the first time I've ever done it." I really admire this guy.

I had only a couple of hours between arriving in Quesnel and getting ready for the show during which I could visit with my Aunt Lena and her growing family. I dropped my bags at the hotel and drove out of town to her trailer, where most of the family had assembled. Lena had made dinner and we all enjoyed a short but fun visit, catching up on family news. Lena, my Mom's older sister, and Ray, my Dad's younger brother, are my two favourite relatives.

The van has just passed through Hope, BC, as we make our way back to the coast. It's raining, but the weather has been mild—better than expected. We have a few days off at home and then we're off for a three-week western Canada tour.

Saturday, March 8, 2003
Edmonton, Alberta
And so it begins...

Even the locals, who usually pretend not to notice, are talking about the weather here in Alberta. Yesterday the temperatures reached a record low in Edmonton: -38 C and -48 C with the wind chill. This is the kind of cold I remember from the Northwest Territories, dry and painful on exposed skin. It's a perfect day for the West Edmonton Mall.

The Lloydminster show was another love-fest. The Kooler, a big new club, was packed out with very sweet people. It was a great way to start the tour. We're out, now, for three weeks in western Canada—mostly six nights on and one night off, a different city every night.

Ours was one of the last vehicles to struggle through the Coquihalla Highway before they shut it down on Thursday. Visibility was limited because of a raging snowstorm. The snowplows were fighting a losing battle. We crawled along behind one for a while. Once we were through the mountains, I plugged a three-way splitter into my PowerBook and Frankie, Gogo, and I watched the movie *Minority Report*.

Snowstorm – Coquihalla Highway, BC

Monday, March 10, 2003
Edmonton, Alberta

His body is splayed across the plaid hotel room couch, propped up by pillows at one end, his legs supported by the couch's arm at the other. The legs of his sweatpants are rolled up past his knees. His feet are bare. His socks were removed one at a time: the first during a tense scene in Vidocq, *the second in the opening minutes of* Road to Perdition. *The round table pulled up close in front of him is crowded with wires, two black speakers, a cellphone in its charging cradle, a pile of CDs, four DVDs in their cases, the television remote, a rooming list displaying the names of eight traveling companions, a white telephone, two room keys, and a wide-screen G4 PowerBook. He is unshaven and wearing headphones. The computer screen lights the otherwise dark room. A small red light glows from the left side of the headphones. Beside the couch, on the floor in the dark, are two trays: one containing the remnants of lunch—a grease-laden creation referred to on the room service menu as "Portobello Bruschetta"—the other containing just about all of the so-called "Vegetable Thai Red Curry" that was supposed to have been dinner.*

During Road to Perdition *his mind multi-tasks, a habit he often wishes he could avoid. His admiration for the great craft he recognizes in the movie leads him to thoughts of writing, painting, and creating that elusive something that he's never quite been able to put his finger on. His mind skips like a stone over the promising but mysterious surface of his creative impulse, tantalizingly connecting with vague images for milliseconds and then moving on. The resulting circles move out hopefully from their points of contact but ultimately fail to connect with one another.*

He'd like to write a novel, but he is unclear about the point he'd like to make should he begin to do so. He is toying with the idea of a collection of very simple songs, but he has assembled only a page or two of less than half-finished lyrics. He would love to do a series of paintings with a vaguely religious flavour, but he cannot imagine, yet, what their subject matter should be. He often has glimpses of a project that resembles a comic book but is somehow multi-dimensional... and someday he would love to be the editor of the kind of magazine that he would passionately read and support.

These thoughts are concluded by a blast of machine gun fire. He glances at the glowing red numbers on the bedside clock. He would normally be walking onto the stage at this time. He grins and returns his full attention to Tom Hanks.

Tuesday, March 11, 2003
Camrose, Alberta
Scott Richards

Trooper's six-times-Platinum Greatest Hits album, *Hot Shots*, was Scott Richards' idea.

Scott was the man in charge of MCA Records Canada in 1975 when Trooper's first album was released on that label. He became our champion at MCA, our guide through the music business jungle, and, by virtue of his kind and good heart, our lifelong friend.

Scott Richards died on Saturday. He had a heart attack while shoveling snow.

Scottie was a wonderful human—fun, intelligent, and deeply spiritual.

I picture him now with a cigar waving in his hand, his eyes wide, mid-thought, exploring a cosmic riff—half Steven Wright, half Groucho Marx—with a silly grin forming because he knows the thought may be going nowhere and he doesn't give a shit.

Thankfully, we had a chance to hang out with Scott and his son Eric at an outdoor show in Ontario recently. I think he left there knowing how much we loved him. I truly hope so.

Saturday, March 15, 2003
Saskatoon, Saskatchewan
Road Mode

I'm 52 years old. I've been on the road since I was 15.

Over those 37 years, I've had responsible grown-up friends ask me seriously about coming on tour with the band as part of the crew. They imagine that the experience would be fun, exciting, and free of the constraints of the straight world. In fact, it is all of those things. A few of those friends have tried coming along for a few days. All of them, at the end of their two or three days of vicarious rock and roll, ask the same question:

"How do you do it? How do you keep it up?"

Trooper has always been a hard-working band. When we tour it's usually in three to four week blocks. We work six nights on—each night in a different city—and one night off, with that day usually being a travel day. Every day we drive a minimum of three hours and often as long as six or seven.

"It's like any other job," I say glibly, "you learn how to do it over time."

That's an easier answer than an attempt at explaining Road Mode.

Road Mode is that state of consciousness that lies somewhere on the neural highway between Vacation Mode and what behaviourist Mihaly Csikszentmihalyi refers to as "Flow," that state of focused alpha brainwave activity wherein you and what you're doing merge into one seamless reality.

Road Mode is partly innate survival instinct, partly learned behaviour, and partly the inevitable effects of this rock and roll life on our minds and bodies. A sleep system that acknowledges seven hours of sleep regardless of when those seven hours were slept or in what increments they were accumulated, is an instinctual necessity. The ability to sleep some of those seven hours sitting up in the passenger seat of a 15-passenger van is a learned ability. The even-keeled, calmly focused, drug-like state, which is the most obvious manifestation of Road Mode, is borne of high-intensity late nights, long hypnotic drive days, and the overall surreal nature of what it is we do for a living.

Today, driving across the snow-covered prairies, and after seven consecutive sold-out shows, I am definitely in Road Mode.

Friday, March 21, 2003
Slave Lake, Alberta
After an Unscheduled Day Off

There are only two shows left on this tour. Every show (12 since Salmon Arm) has been sold out—SRO—standing-room-only. The gigs have all been awesome. So uniformly awesome, in fact, that I can't distinguish one from the other in my mind right now. This does not mean I'm bored, just a bit confused about what happened on what night.

Last night is still clear in my memory. I ate Thai food in my hotel room while watching an excellent movie, called *Quitting*, on my PowerBook. We were unable to perform our show in Calgary because the venue was hijacked, not by Bif Naked and I Mother Earth (the bands who played there), but by some combination of promoter, agent, and club management who needed a venue at the last minute and for some reason chose ours. Although Trooper had a binding contract for a show there, local radio had already announced that the Bif/IME show was being moved to the venue— before we had even arrived in town.

The apologetic promoter and club manager have promised us a buy-out of sorts. The agent involved is, unfortunately, employed by the same agency we have worked with for our entire career. We are not happy about this at all.

I spent the afternoon and early evening on the phone. My early hopes of hanging on to the gig were completely undermined by someone who, not surprisingly, represents the artists who needed a room to play. His insider status was the key to expediting a solution to his problem. Unfortunately, that meant keeping us out of the early loop. I have written a letter to the founder of the agency in question. Although it is unlikely that heads will roll as a result, it is my deep and fervent hope that one particular head will be smacked around in a sincere and meaningful way.

I'd like to thank Bif for the sincere apology, to Trooper and Trooper's fans, that she made at the start of her performance last night.

We are once again rolling down an Alberta highway. Today we're on our way to Slave Lake. Tomorrow, another long drive to Richmound, Saskatchewan, to play their arena again, and then we go home for a few days before a three-show trip to Vancouver Island.

Harris, Saskatchewan

Monday, March 24, 2003
Richmound, Saskatchewan

A few minutes ago—at 2:30 in the morning, Saskatchewan time—I was sitting on the floor in the office of the Richmound Hotel with my PowerBook balanced on a brown plastic garbage can in front of me. My 'book was jacked into the only phone line in this small hotel that could get me online. I checked my mail, the Trooper message board, CNN, and one of the five blogs I frequent daily.

Sitting there on the floor of that silent room in this small Saskatchewan community, I experienced an extreme reality warp. I have no particular revelation to offer here, because I have yet to parse the experience, but the overall effect was calming and reassuring. I felt, for a moment, that all was well with my multicultural, multi-reality, multi-tasking world.

The most sleep I can expect between now and our lobby call is three and a half hours. The very sweet lady who owns the hotel was waiting in the lobby/restaurant/pub/big-screen TV room when we came in. She has promised to serve toast and coffee at seven a.m. God bless her... and all the people in this kind-hearted, clean-living town.

Steins Grocery, Richmound, Saskatchewan

Sunday, March 30, 2003
The Strait of Juan de Fuca, BC
End-of-Tour Thoughts

It's a rainy west coast afternoon. There is no particular view beyond the grey windows of this large, full BC Ferry. I'm sitting at a table just beyond the restaurant, surrounded by hundreds of fellow passengers on their way back to the mainland from Vancouver Island, where the last three shows of the tour—Nanaimo, Victoria, and Courtenay—took place. In about three hours I'll be home in White Rock where I will stay, happily, for three weeks before heading out again.

I have been thinking back to January when I was overwhelmed with uncertainty about the musical future of the band. Lance's departure was a serious setback, and one I was not sure we would be able to recover from successfully. I was dogged daily by an unpleasant combination of fear and loathing that propelled me into a state of manic activity. The nationwide search for a new drummer became all-consuming.

Today, at the end of almost four weeks of touring with Frankie Baker, I'm happy to report that the band has improved dramatically. The buzz that Frankie has brought has inspired us all. The show pops and sizzles with a newfound positive energy that is the result of much more than just the infusion of a new bandmate. Frankie *loves* to play. You can see from looking at him that every moment on stage brings him joy. All of us are playing, singing, and performing better. The set has mutated. The fans can tell.

The 25 sold-out shows we've played are a bit of a blur to me. I do remember the music though: the arrangement changes and refinements, the new stage bits, the parts we've changed. The set has a new momentum that it had lost. It barrels along like a freight train now, careening wildly from song to song in a seamless journey through the hills and valleys of tension and release. Throughout the tour, I recall the many onstage smiles, winks, and shout-outs between the band members—acknowledging just how fucking excellent the band is. I remember the post-show dressing room hugs and high-fives, and the pride we shared over a job well done. I love the fact that we are surprising audiences again—and in the process, surprising ourselves occasionally.

I return to White Rock happy and content. This is a great band. This has been a great tour.

Connor's band has a couple of important gigs coming up. They start recording again on April 6; they're playing at the South Surrey Youth Centre on the 8th; and they're opening for Trooper on May 15—in the gym of their high school. There's tension and excitement in the air at rehearsals. They're getting stronger and stronger, heavier and heavier. The new songs thunder with "drop D" tuning and a new and focused appreciation of groove and texture. Connor has begun to sing harder—often screaming the lyrics in a way that makes me fear for his throat. The rehearsals are intense; the new songs are borderline brilliant. I'll be going into the studio with them next Sunday to help them try and capture some of that brilliance.

The coming of Spring demands a return to yardwork and home improvement. The rest of my time off will be filled happily with home chores and the non-routine of our unpredictable home life.

"Your attention, please. We are now approaching the Tsawwassen terminal... would all vehicle passengers please proceed to the car deck..."

CHAPTER SIX

April 8–May 18, 2003

Hot Nights and Hearing Aids,
Reason and Rhyme, Digital Recording Nightmares,
"Cold Water" Is Born, Grandpa Smitty,
Singing with the Doobie Brothers, Four-Letter Interview,
Listen to the Music, Sabotage, Live or Memorex?,
Rocky Mountain High, Dave, Making Music with My Son,
The Trooper/Anger and After Show – a Major Moment,
The 1965 Hit Parade, Sam the Sham and the Pharaohs,
The Citations, Noon-Hour Concert, A+A Rules, Happy Together

Tuesday, April 8, 2003
White Rock, BC
The Sound and the Fury

A lady in her "early forties" from Edmonton, Alberta, has written an e-mail to the Trooper site to complain. She complained about the fact that we didn't go on 'til 11:00 and that she had arrived at 7:00; she pointed out that my microphone didn't work for the first verse of the first song—she even mentioned that it was 40 below in Edmonton that night. Mostly though, she wanted to complain about the volume.

That night in Edmonton, 1500 people packed themselves tightly up against the stage. It looked to me as though every single cheering member of that crowd was having an excellent time. No one at any time gave us the universal signal for "it's too loud" (also the universal sign for "hear no evil"). Often the crowd's roar completely drowned out the band. How could I have guessed that, somewhere in that mass of seemingly ecstatic humanity, there was at least one person already composing a letter of complaint.

Our incredible Web meister, Heather Uhl (who happened to be at that Edmonton show), wrote a thoughtful reply that detailed the difficulty of mixing sound in a long, low room like "Nashville's" and diplomatically suggested that the members of the sold-out crowd behind the mixing board were probably complaining that it wasn't loud enough. She also explained that a phone call to the club could have determined the 11:00 show time, and that my microphone had been inadvertently unplugged by a member of the backup band—a problem that our crew remedied as soon as they could make their way through the packed nightclub and onto the stage. (One of the guys in the band also wrote a reply that was sent only to other band members. His hilarious e-mail contained my favourite response to the criticisms—one that involved "bon-bons" and a "snug hospital bed".)

Smitty wears stereo hearing aids. I should probably get some soon. I hear about two-thirds of what's being said in all but the quietest rooms. There is no doubt that 37 years of exposure to jet-take-off volume levels has badly damaged my hearing. Nonetheless, I still believe that real rock music needs to be played very loud.

Last night I roadied for Anger and After at a local gig. The PA system onsite was small and inadequate. The soundman, who had mic'd the guitar amp, asked me to turn the amp down so he had "more control" over it. I told him that the Marshall amp was the best sounding thing in the room and I wasn't going to turn it down so he could bring the intensity (and volume) of the band down to the lowest common denominator of their two tiny Peavey speaker boxes. Surprisingly, he agreed with me. As it turned out, A&A rocked. The Marshall rattled and thumped as only a Marshall can do, and the band retained that all-important sense of something about to career very badly out of control. I cannot wait for Anger and After to experience the power and the glory of rock music played through a real PA system.

Because… that's a large part of what a live show is all about—the power and the glory. The joyful rattle and hum. The feeling of being physically involved in the performance—and the music. I love the scene in *Children of a Lesser God* where Marlee Matlin, a genuinely deaf actress, dances erotically to the sheer physical volume she feels from the music in the disco. Onstage, I love to be pushed around by that thump and roar. It's what I love about attending a live show—being overwhelmed by the power of it, being inhabited by the groove, lost in the noise. More about body than ears.

So…

I am unapologetic. Live rock shows aren't for everyone. I'm not fond of opera.

Tuesday, April 22, 2003
Kamloops, BC

I have set a challenge for myself. By the end of this week-long tour, I hope to have developed a working knowledge of the amazing music production program *Reason*. Mastery of this software is part one of a larger plan: by the time I return to White Rock, *Digital Performer 4.0*, a digital audio recording program, should have been released. Once I wrestle down the learning curves and synch these two programs together, I will have, literally at my fingertips, a whole new way of making music and writing songs.

In 1996, I spent thousands of dollars on similar gear. After almost a year of trying unsuccessfully to get it to work, I learned that the software was not ready for primetime and unable to perform as advertised. I staggered away from the experience with a very bad feeling about digital recording.

Time spent with a faulty program is the opposite of a learning experience. When your best efforts fail to have the desired effect, the implication is that you have done something wrong. Repeated failures suggest that you are doing something very wrong. In my case, eight months of believing that I wasn't "getting it" had me pretty shook up. My digital insecurity was compounded by countless calls to tech support who insisted that I was, in fact, the woefully ignorant cause of the many problems I was experiencing. As it turns out, I was not the cause of the problems—but that knowledge could not return the time I had wasted.

My second attempt at digital audio involved a system that cost well over twice what the first did. This set-up was brutally slow— mind-bogglingly convoluted and... surprise... didn't always work properly. Just to turn the system on took more than ten minutes, after which something inevitably went wrong.

Over the next few years, dogged determination was rewarded with five or six useful recordings. The song "Cold Water," for instance, was written and arranged with that cumbersome pile of beige boxes. Eventually, though, any reasonable excuse was enough to keep me away from the room that contained the digital recording experience.

For years, my very wise wife would tell me that she didn't want a computer because they weren't yet able to perform well enough to be genuinely and dependably useful. With the release of the 500MHz G4 PowerBook, she determined (correctly, I believe) that computers were finally ready for her. I think that digital audio might now be ready for me.

I have a three-hour *Reason* video tutorial in my backpack, a mini-keyboard in my suitcase, and a copy of *Reason 2.0* installed in my PowerBook. I have five or six very long drives coming up this week and just enough space, here in the passenger seat of this 2003 15-passenger GMC van, to fire them all up. How cool is that?

Wednesday, April 23, 2003
Lethbridge, Alberta

My long-time musical collaborator and compadre, Brian Smith, got a phone call as we were driving to Lethbridge this morning. The reception was bad so all he heard was:

"You have a grand..."

Later, when the phone worked, he learned that Madeleine Aaron Bedard had officially entered this crazy world—making Brian William Smith, my partner since I was 15... a Grandfather.

In other news:

I sang with The Doobie Brothers last night. Their road manager approached us at the side of the stage.

"Patrick wants you guys to come up and sing."

"Cool. When?"

"Four more songs. Right after 'China Grove'... in 'Listen to the Music'—you know that one?"

Everybody, including the road manager grins broadly.

After "China Grove," Patrick announced:

"We're going to bring Trooper on to sing." The crowd roared...

Friday, April 25, 2003
Regina, Saskatchewan
Doobie Brothers Tour

Lethbridge was fun from the git-go.

When we arrived in the dressing room, I found myself almost immediately engaged in an interview with the local Global TV station. The camera guy sat across the table, the producer beside him, and the host settled in beside me with his microphone. I liked the guy. He was a pro. He asked good questions and had great, very natural pacing. I was having a lot of fun working with him. Near the end he threw me this:

"What do you say to those people—and I'm not one of them—who say 'your last record was ten years ago and you're not relevant any more'...?"

I looked into the camera, smiled, and said...

"I just tell those people to go fuck themselves."

After the interview, there was intense discussion, among the Global crew, about the use of "bleeps." If you live in Lethbridge and saw the interview, I'd love to know if that bit made it in.

Our Lethbridge show was *so* much more fun than the one in Kamloops. The stage sound was way better and we played brilliantly. I, of course, teased Grampy Smitty mercilessly on the eve of his entry into grandfatherhood. Once again, we stayed on in the arena 'til the end of the Doobies show. As they launched into "Listen to the Music," Skylark, the bass player (yes, that's his real name), yelled and waved at us from the stage to join them again.

An uncomfortable moment came as I leaned into the mic with Patrick Simmons. In front of us, a girl frantically waved a *Hot Shots* CD and a pen. I pretended not to notice.

I am so impressed by Patrick Simmons. He appears to be a true, clear spirit. He seems, even for just those few minutes we sing together, to be sincere, genuine, and truly "in the moment."

Tonight, here in Regina, was Gogo's birthday party. There were probably many interesting occurrences, events, and epiphanies that will, because I am rapidly becoming uncontrollably sleepy, have to wait 'til tomorrow's post for recounting. Goodnight everyone.

Saturday, April 26, 2003
Hudson Bay, Saskatchewan

Every night, after the Doobie Brothers finish their show, they gather in a large backstage room for a catered meal. Last night, just before leaving the Winnipeg Arena, we stopped in to say goodbye. As we leaned into room, all nine of the Doobies began clapping their hands and cheering.

Over the years, Trooper has opened for hundreds of very successful bands—none have been as easygoing, fun, and generous of spirit as the Doobies.

Last night, Patrick Simmons gave Gogo his address and phone number on Maui and invited him to come by for a visit sometime. Just down the wide backstage hall, I passed Tom Johnston's 15-year-old son hanging out with our crew—listening raptly to their totally inappropriate party stories. Further down the hall, Matt Russo, the incredible sax player for the band, high-fived me. Before the show,

I'd heard him warming up with some ultra-intense licks and challenged him to play some of that stuff onstage. He later surprised his bandmates with some new solos.

"Ya, I played some shit..." he said, grinning broadly.

During the "Listen to the Music" encore, where we again joined the Doobies onstage, Patrick leaned way back from his mic, encouraging me to scat out some high stuff. The higher I sang, the bigger his smile. After the show, many high-fives and hugs were exchanged. Early in our drive today, we shared our Doobies stories. We all agreed that we are going to really miss playing with them.

Spirits are very high in the band. Our sets have been intense and passionately played; the responses from the arena audiences have been roaringly loud and overwhelmingly appreciative. As we drive down the road to Hudson Bay, Saskatchewan, it's a good day in Trooper-Land.

Somewhere in Saskatchewan

Monday, May 5, 2003
White Rock, BC
Neither Here nor There

I'm enjoying a very short break from the action, here in White Rock, before heading out for Penticton, BC, on Thursday. I hope to resume blogging then.

Monday, May 12, 2003
White Rock, BC

Since this mini-tour began, I have written several blog entries that I subsequently decided not to post. The first was a long rant about how crewmembers of headline bands sometimes blatantly handicap our crew's efforts to make us sound and look good. I decided that post was too whiney and lacking in class.

The next day, I wrote an in-depth exposé that involved digital recorders (in playback mode) hidden backstage and operational during some headliners' sets. I documented investigations and conclusions, revealing that a large part of many concert performances are pre-recorded and played back via an auxiliary board at front of house. As I wrote this, I thought that non-musicians might find it interesting. When I read it back, it also came off like a classless example of sour grapes.

Yesterday, I took a stab at describing the dreamlike environment at the top of the mountain in Sunshine Village where we have played for the last two days. I wrote: "These shows are like no other. It really is like visiting another world. Our set, rather than being the focal rock concert that we're used to, is more like our contribution to a mountain party at which we are special guests." I then attempted to describe the surreal quality of the vibe up there—and experienced a complete failure of my descriptive abilities.

Mount Rundle, Banff, Alberta

Last night after the show, back in my Banff hotel room, I watched the movie *Waking Life*—a unique piece of work that's brilliantly effective on many levels and that altered my consciousness like no drug could. During the movie, for reasons I don't yet understand, I became convinced that it was imperative that I tell an important story. By the time the movie ended, I was too tired to sit up typing, and went to sleep. So yesterday, even though some of the previous night's fervour had been burned away, I felt obligated to attempt to honour that conviction.

Driving home, I wrote a long and heartfelt post about a friend who is battling mental illness. I posted it when I returned home. I got a call the next morning from another friend who took offense at what I had written because some of the critical information in the post came from him. He demanded that I remove the post.

So I did. If it weren't for bad luck, writing-wise, I would've had none at all this week.

Wednesday, May 14, 2003
White Rock, BC
The Anger and After show

I wish so much for Connor tomorrow.

He'll be playing on a big, professional stage with big, professional lights... backing up his dad's big, professional band—all for the first time. His friends, his family, and his community will be there to see him play—it's a rock and roll bar mitzvah. I want him, and Simon and Nik, to play well, to interact well with the audience, and to blow Trooper off the stage. I try to give them tips. I remind them that they should react to the crowd's applause after the first song, otherwise the crowd will be less inclined to react thereafter. I fret about a two-beat-per-minute speed difference in one of their songs; I cheer at their rehearsals like the rabid fan I have become. I roadie for them.

I don't want to accelerate their music career. There's plenty of time for that; Connor's only 15. I don't want to teach them the things that are so much fun to learn on your own. I especially have no interest in any reflected glory from their success. I simply want them to experience the joy that comes from making the music and from pulling off a successful performance.

So, if it's all for fun, why am I so nervous about it?

Friday, May 16, 2003
White Rock, BC
So Much to Say...

The show was amazing. It was everything we could have hoped for.

And exhausting.

I'm not answering the phone today. We've been sitting on the deck in the sun looking out at the bay and being extremely thankful for so many things.

Last night, Debbie and Connor and I sat up around the table 'til 2:30 in the morning, laughing and telling stories about our night—piecing the picture together, drinking Sprites, and eating taco chips left over from the afternoon Trooper/Anger and After sandwich party. This morning we picked up where we left off. Soon I will have the complete story of what happened last night—a major moment in the life of my family—and will try to share it with you.

And now, back to the deck...

Sunday, May 18, 2003
White Rock, BC
The Earl Marriott Trooper/Anger and After Show

I was 15 years old in 1965. At the time, I could sing the verse and chorus of virtually every song on the top 50; I probably still can. "Yes It Is" and "Ticket To Ride" by the Beatles was the double-sided number one song in Canada for the week of May 10, 1965—exactly 38 years ago today. "Silhouettes" and "Mrs. Brown You've Got a Lovely Daughter" by Herman's Hermits were numbers two and three respectively, and "Shakin' All Over," the first hit for a Canadian group called The Guess Who, was number seven. "Go Now" at number 15, by another new group called The Moody Blues, is still one of my all-time favourite songs. "King of The Road" by Roger Miller, "Stop! in the Name of Love" by the Supremes, "It's Not Unusual" by Tom Jones, "Help Me, Rhonda" by The Beach Boys, and "Wooly Bully" by Sam the Sham and the Pharaohs were all on the chart that week.

In a box downstairs there is a fragile reel-to-reel recording of a noon-hour concert that my band, The Citations, played in the Killarney High School auditorium that year. We opened with a version of "On Broadway" by The Drifters. On the tape, you can hear the squeak of the thick velvet curtains drawing back during the opening chords. Halfway through the first song we segued suddenly into "I'm Down," an over-the-top Beatles song in the style of Little Richard. Even without the recording, I could never forget that show. It was a turning point in my life.

On Thursday night, my son, Connor, whose birthday is seven days before mine and who is 15 now, took the stage in the gym of his high school, Earl Marriott Senior Secondary, backing up his dad's band for the first time. Rangy and skinny at six-foot-one, with his hair dyed bright blue and armed with a black Gibson Les Paul slung casually over his shoulder, he stepped to the mic, looked out at the crowded gym full of his friends, neighbours, and family members and said: "Hey...".

Debbie watched proudly from the VIP section in the middle of the gym floor where she sat with a group that included my beaming Mom and Dad on a very rare night out, her Mom and sister, and the Mayor of White Rock. Most of the friends we have made in our 14 years in White Rock were there. Friends from the past were there with their teenaged children. A large crowd of Connor's school-mates and other adrenaline-pumped adolescents jostled happily in front of the stage. I watched from a small opening in the movable wall of the upstairs weight room—our dressing room for the night—careful not to be a distraction for Connor.

Connor, Simon, and Nikhil played a tight, powerful, and pas-sionate set. Their grasp of music and performance is twice that of my high-school band. The songs Connor has written are awesome, his playing is more and more impressive, and his singing voice con-tinues to mature. Simon's stage moves are at once kinetic and grace-ful while his playing locks in the groove, and Nik's drumming is stronger and more precise with every show. The mosh pit swarmed and boiled, and a scream-heavy roar followed every song. There is no way to describe the pride I felt while watching them. Weeks of anx-iety, much of which I had been oddly unaware of, fell away as I wit-nessed their total command of the stage and the intensity of the crowd's reaction. Anger and After completely rocked the house.

We live in a small community and, in many cases, this was the first time that friends and neighbours would see me in my rock and roll mode. As always, I damned the torpedoes and held my breath as the Trooper intro began to play. The love remained in the room. The joy multiplied. Trooper also rocked the house.

Bringing Anger and After out for the encore was the highlight of the night. We had rehearsed an amalgamated band version of the song "Happy Together" at the afternoon sound check. Both Smitty and Connor played their Les Pauls, Simon played bass while Scott sang, Gogo played keys, Nik played tambourine and sang, and Frankie played drums. The resulting performance was larger than life and joyous. Singing the verses with Connor—my arm around his neck—is something I will never forget. Tears pressed at my eyes while my jaw hurt from smiling. The two bands took a long, happy bow together at the end of the show.

This was a milestone moment for our little family. Love, pride, and happiness whirled around the three of us as we later pieced together the many events and conversations of the evening. It was a coming-of-age moment for Connor in more ways than musical. It was a galvanizing moment for the three of us in our community and with our families. We talked about how thankful we are for what we have. It was a long, satisfying exhale.

Friday and Saturday were peaceful beyond belief. It was as though we would never have anything important or stressful to undertake again. Ever. We ignored the phone. We ate pizza. We went to see *The Matrix Reloaded*.

CHAPTER SEVEN

May 26–August 15, 2003

Summertime and the Livin' Is Easy, On a Dark Ontario Highway,
Steevo, Light Man Jeopardy, Fred Astaire and Ginger Baker,
Rainstorm, Rock and Roll Haircut, Naked Woman Eviction,
Mexican Movie Night Off, My 53rd Birthday with the Dwarves,
Gary's Mr. T Haircut, Jammin', The OCL Again,
Ontario vs. Nova Scotia, A Letter to Subway Steve,
Naked Atlantic Ocean Action, War & Peace,
Three Guys Walk into a Bar, My Cool Tools Review,
The Fortress of Louisbourg, Airport Roulette,
The Beatles' Hometown, White Point Beach Toga Party,
Mr. Wolverine, A Cheap Trick All Round, "I Work for Trooper,"
Waking Up the Campers, Music vs. the Music Business,
Takin' Care of Bullshit, Country Fest, Naked Pool Party,
Church Jam, Gold Sandals, Sab, My Mouth Organ,
Junk and Useless, Dangerous Driving, SARS Fest,
54•40 in St. John's, Sittin' In, "Barrett's Privateers,"
20,000 Attend Newfoundland Trooper Party, Loverboy Geekfest,
Screeching Frankie, Terrifying Security, Rockin' the Dock,
Fred Penner Rocks Out, Extreme Bowling, Airport Chaos

Monday, May 26, 2003
White Rock, BC
...and the Livin' is Easy

I feel the summer beginning, and I feel the joyous abandon of audiences that feel it too. The heat, the quickened pulse, the reborn passion after a winter of greys. The sweat, the warm evening breeze, bare arms in the air. The tribal jump of a crowd united by a power they welcome, but that is beyond their capacity to fully grasp. The sticky oneness, the thunderous shared pulse, the one-throated roar.

Everything is easier in the summer. My throat, after months of tightening dryness and cold, relaxes, open and rejoicing. The travel is faster, less dangerous, more beautiful, less trouble. No more snow-plowing my suitcase across a frozen hotel parking lot. No more warm coats in cold dressing rooms. I can take long, aimless walks again, and wear sandals in the van.

I am still full of the spirit conjured this weekend in Peace River and St. Albert. As we make our way down through the mountains, I am warm from the energy I absorbed from those two crowds. Summer is definitely beginning. Bring it on.

Saturday, June 7, 2003
Marathon, Ontario
Very Late at Night on a Dark Ontario Highway

Last night we were forced to leave Fort Frances after the show as a result of some very mysterious confusion regarding our rooms for the night. According to the parties involved, neither the hotel manager nor the club manager (whose responsibility it was to provide the rooms) had done anything wrong—it was, apparently, simply a case of the wrong outcome resulting from no actual wrongdoing.

Because all the hotels and motels in Fort Frances were sold-out last night, we arranged for rooms in the small town of Atikokan, an hour and a half away. Once we had done our duty at the T-shirt booth, we packed up and headed out on the virtually deserted northern Ontario highway.

In the passenger seat, I strapped on my noise-canceling headphones and ran myself a playlist of night music: Joe Henry, Harold

Melvin and the Bluenotes, Lucinda Williams, and, oddly, Frank Sinatra, among others. Lost in a dark, three a.m., soulful reverie, I was returned to reality when Smitty hit the brakes hard.

The van came to a stop on the highway. In front of us—oblivious to both our bright headlights and the threat of our looming 15-passenger van—a young fox stood concentrating its full attention on a spot four or five feet in front of us. Suddenly the fox leapt to the right, repositioning its focus on a new point on the highway. A small, pavement-coloured frog was leading the fascinated fox in rough, jumping circles in the yellow spill of our headlights. The fox pounced from spot to spot, passing by obvious opportunities to end the chase, prolonging the play. His long tail twitched happily as their nocturnal dance played out exactly as it would have, had we not been there.

We looked on in amazement, laughing at the real-life *Looney Tunes* episode unfolding before us. It went on for minutes, but I was so enthralled that I left my camera untouched beside me in my bag. Finally, either bored with the game or overcome by hunger, the fox grabbed the frog in its teeth and ran into the forest at the side of the highway.

I put my headphones back on as the van accelerated down the highway.

Sunday, June 8, 2003
Thunder Bay, Ontario

I'm not sure how it began...

One minute I'm talking to a guy at the T-shirt booth, the next minute, I'm standing in the middle of my room and he's kneeling in front of me, and I'm shaving his head.

Our stage yesterday was two flat-decks parked adjacent to the highway in front of the McKenzie Inn, about 20 minutes outside of Thunder Bay, Ontario. The crowd of about a thousand people spilled from the licensed veranda of the inn out into the parking lot in front of us. The sun was shining hard. People brought their own chairs. There were young people, old people, little babies... and "Steevo," a 30-something ex-banger in tight jeans and wraparound shades who danced seductively, by himself, in the wide empty space in front of the stage... for the whole show.

The set was fun, and funny from the git-go. Steevo helped a lot with both. I was on his case for the whole show, at one time kneeling down at the front of the stage asking him questions like: "where did you receive your dance training?" and "do you expect to get lucky tonight?" It would be charitable to say that he was a good sport. In fact, he was too blown-out to grasp much of anything beyond the fundamental groove, to which he ground his hips menacingly.

The show was full of surprises. Early in the set, during Frankie's now famous mic-stand solo, Gogo took the stage, carrying an aluminum sink found on the site a few hours earlier. Frank played it. Gary then walked out with a *double* sink. Frank played that too.

When we play outdoor shows in the daytime, I usually ask the crowd whether or not we should pay our lighting director. On the mountain in Banff, for instance, I asked Gary to come to the front of the stage and said: "Should we pay him today... or ... should we all just throw snowballs at him?" after which our hapless lighting director was pummeled by hundreds of simultaneously thrown snowballs. Yesterday, it was decided (well, I decided, actually) that Gary should dance... with Steevo... to earn his afternoon's wage. Laughter defeated singing during the first verse of "Cold Water" as we watched Gary mirror Steevo's sexy hip moves. He continued dancing, expanding into an arm-waving hippy-dance—tripping blithely over the gravel. Steevo didn't miss a beat. The first half of their performance was hilarious beyond description but, as the song progressed, it became a thing of surreal beauty. It is so rare to see that kind of unselfconscious and, in Gary's case at least, courageous abandonment, in public. Trying to say something completely different, I outro'd the two of them as: "Fred Astaire and Ginger Baker" which, once I'd thought about it, seemed completely appropriate.

Throughout the show, I watched as the sky behind the inn turned darker and darker. By the time we came out for the encore, the sun was gone and a cool wind was blowing. We played "Hash Pipe" (I was wearing my Weezer shirt), cut "Happy Together," and blasted straight into the "Good Time" Reprise. As we leaned into our final bow, the first drops of rain began to fall. As we bolted from the stage, the crew bolted *to* it—frantically maneuvering instruments and electronics to safety. I've never seen a stage torn down so quickly.

Once our soaked-to-the-skin crew had moved the T-shirt booth into the lobby of the inn, we settled in for our after-show meet-and-greet. I soon found myself engaged in a discussion with an intelligent guy—a PLC & HMI Automation Specialist, it says on his card—who was describing to me a meeting with his priest wherein they discussed the meaning of several Trooper lyrics. The priest, apparently had some strong opinions about what I had in mind when I wrote the songs and Bob wanted to know how close the cleric had come. Surprisingly, both Bob and the priest's interpretation were insightful and essentially correct at a level that rests a step below the face value meaning of the lyrics in question. I was moved that someone had taken the time to find a deeper import in the songs. Our conversation drifted to other topics. At some point, Bob brought up our mutual baldness. His was hidden under a ball cap, but the remaining hair, thin and scraggly, reached down to his shoulders—a hairdo that my son often refers to as a "Skullet." I joked that I had my buzzer with me upstairs in my room.

Fifteen minutes later, Bob was kneeling on the floor of my room, singing "Pretty Lady," as a small crowd of kids and band members watched clumps of tangled hair fall to the red carpet around him. There was a moment of indecision when Bob asked me to leave a long tail at the back. The kids all booed; his best buddy booed; Bob relented and the tail came off. He looked down at the pile of hair and said:

"That took me ten years to grow."

The bystanders cheered. Bob thanked me, shook my hand, gave me his card, and headed back out to the veranda with the kids behind him. I got an e-mail from him today, which said, in part:

"Thanks for the haircut, I've had a few compliments on it already :)"

Later that night, I huddled in the kitchen with Scott and Mark, one of the owners of the Inn. Mark is an incredible cook and was offering to make us anything we requested. He pulled out a block of Gorgonzola cheese to garnish a prawn dish for Scott. I told him I'd love to have Gorgonzola melted on something. "How about a T-bone?" he grinned. Later I shot some embarrassingly amateur pool with a couple of locals and overheard rumours that one of us (remember, there are eight of us including crew) had requested help with ejecting a naked woman from his room. It is still unclear how she got in, but a staff member routed her out of the bed (where she had decided to wait), and removed her from the premises. Sometime not long after that, Smitty played an acoustic set on a borrowed guitar—bringing the house down with a soulful rendition of "We're Here For A Good Time—Not a Long Time."

Wednesday, June 11, 2003
Toronto, Ontario

I have just finished watching *El Crimen del padre Amaro*. Besides loving this movie—I've realized that I also loved *Amores perros* and *Y tu mamá también* and that all three have two things in common—the amazing Gael García Bernal and the fact that they came from Mexico. Each of these films seethes with passion, humanity, and artistic bravery unmatched by anything I can remember seeing. While appearing spontaneously conceived by both director and cast, they look as though months have been devoted to the composition and lighting of every shot. Scenes play so naturally you become an eavesdropper rather than an audience member. There's sweat, pain, joy, honesty, brutality, and tenderness—and, most important, these movies are incredibly entertaining. Although I'm not recommending them for everyone (the dual diving board scene in *Y tu mamá también* comes immediately to mind), I felt the need to indulge in a short but enthusiastic evangelical moment.

We've had the day off in a hotel near Toronto International Airport. Most of us went to a big mall in the afternoon and spent a lot of money. There are thousands of cars and trucks and megatons of concrete out beyond my window. I've kept the curtains closed.

June 23, 2003
On The Road – Nova Scotia
Ontario Catch-Up

We're over halfway through our eastern tour, and driving, today, from Halifax to Sydney. It's a beautiful summer day and the green, verdant hills are rolling off into the distance on either side of the highway. We're listening to a CD by a band that opened for us in Mount Forest. We always accept CDs with foreboding because the bands want us to let them know how we liked their work, but thankfully this one, by Steve Dickinson, is really good.

I wrote an extensive, detailed description of the second half of our Ontario run the other night and, thanks to a combination of unparalleled stupidity (neglecting to save the original document) and Blogger's buggy-ness, the whole thing went up in digital smoke. It's been a long time since I've had an unrecoverable computer accident, so it's taken me a couple of days to stop believing that it was going to show up online once Blogger got their shit together.

Graffiti – London, Ontario

I celebrated my 53rd birthday in London, Ontario, with Patrick and Gary. We went out to see The Dwarves, a punk band famous for violent, sex-filled sets that often degenerate into self-destructive chaos after about fifteen minutes, at which point things are too fucked-up for the show to continue. After a couple of fun sets by two opening acts, the Dwarves hit the stage, the singer shouting, "Yeah, oh yeah, fuck yeah" after every song. He did this three times—I know this because they only played four songs, and then they... uh... fucked off. No violence, no sex—only the fifteen-minute set! It all seemed perfectly appropriate at the time. A good time was had by all... a great birthday party for me.

"My World, Your Nightmare" – London, Ontario

My favourite shows of the un-chronicled week were Montreal and Kingston. Montreal because it had been a long time since we'd been asked to play there, so we were thrilled to hear the crowd chanting "Trooper, Trooper, Trooper" as we changed our clothes backstage. Kingston is my favourite Ontario town for a lot of reasons, and Friday night was the best Trooper show there ever. Both shows were hot, sweaty, and passionate—for both the band and the audience. Other highlights of the week were the CAW (Canadian Auto Workers) Picnic in Oshawa, where we shaved Gary's head—in the style of Mr. T—onstage, while we played "Thin Brown Line"; the Mount Forest show, which was a very funny set that contained a cool version of the Doobie Brothers' "Takin' It to the Streets" and a great Trooper poem from our friends Dave and Jenny (part of which I delivered as a surprisingly convincing Eminem rap); another visit from the incredible Ontario Cookie Lady, who showed up in Whitby with a giant shopping bag full of cookies and fudge; and Frankie's solos every night, played on everything from kitchen sinks to beer kegs to beer boxes to pots and pans. In Montreal, Smitty brought up a big Hawaiian tiki statue thing, which turned out to be the best sounding drum of all.

Ontario is different from the rest of Canada. It's often beautiful, the people are great, but there's something unsettling about it for me, even after all these years. I think it may have something to do with too many people competing for not enough space, time, power, and respect. It's subtle, but it's often there in the background—cutting a thin, buzzing edge onto my days. As soon as we arrived in Halifax I could feel the change. Of course, we love it here in the Maritimes. We love the people, the places, and the culture. I feel more at home in downtown Halifax, where I went for dinner last night, than I do in downtown Vancouver.

Tonight we play at the Savoy in Glace Bay again. Glace Bay local, and Trooper fan, Steve Malloy, has been practicing Trooper songs in the shower every morning for the past week. I know this because I've been reading his blog every day since he started it, not long after I started mine. I know more about Steve than I know about some of my best friends. It's been surreal for me to read about his anticipation of the upcoming Trooper show. I'll also be seeing the well-known Cape Breton musician Robert Barrie again tonight. Robert and I also read each other's blogs, which is just so damn... interactive.

The Fortress of Louisbourg – Louisbourg, Nova Scotia

Tuesday, June 24, 2003
Port Hawkesbury, Nova Scotia
A Letter to Steve Malloy

Dear Steve,

Thanks for the awesome party last night in Glace Bay, Cape Breton! After reading your blog for a year, it was great to hang out with you, the lovely Lanti, Lawson, Bob, and what seemed like 30 other people at your communal apartment floor after the concert. I have read about your fortress of solitude... full of comics, posters, and comic statues—so it was a kick to actually be there, hangin' with you. Now, when I read about your daily adventures, I'll be better able to picture the settings... and some of the cast of characters. I forgot to tell you that I have an unopened figure of Spider Jerusalem, the protagonist of the *Transmetropolitan* comic book by Warren Ellis (of which I own books 1–43), so I was very impressed by your Dark Knight statue and your excellent Hulk figures collection.

Once again, your part of the set at the Savoy Theatre was the highlight of the show for me and, for that matter, the sold-out Glace Bay audience. Your rendition of "$100,000.00" was spirited and passionate, and "Thin White Line" (with Lawson singing backups) was also full of heart. I guess you know this by now, Steve, but the people in your town sure seem to love you. I'm convinced you got the biggest hand of the night. Maybe you should give up your gig at the tech support place and consider some kind of performance-oriented career. (No, you can't have *my* job!)

About the Atlantic Ocean thing, I thought you and Bob were really good sports to go into the water with the two buck-naked Trooper guys. In the glare of the headlights, the two of them were glowing bright enough to be seen with the naked eye (so to speak) all the way back in Sydney. Even though you left your shirt on, it was a better effort than the 20 of us who remained on shore, cheering and laughing. I suppose for you, swimming naked at two in the morning is a fairly common occurrence, but for at least one Trooper member on his first visit to the Maritimes, it was a very big deal to go for a swim in the Atlantic Ocean. Lanti, I'd like to officially apologize again if anything that happened last night made you uncomfortable—you, also, were a really good sport.

What a great bunch of friends you have, Steve. It was a pleasure for us to spend time with you all after the show. And if you see Robert Barrie, tell him he and his wife should have stuck around for the party!

Last night was the best possible "First Show in the Maritimes Party." As you heard backstage from the owner of the Savoy, it looks like we might be coming back for a big show in Sydney in August. We all look forward to seeing you, and your posse, there.

All the best,

Ra McGuire

Wednesday, June 25, 2003
Port Hawkesbury, Nova Scotia
Whoohoo!

I finished *War and Peace*. Good book.

Thursday, June 26, 2003
Isle Madame, Cape Breton, Nova Scotia
How to Make Friends

Three guys walk into a bar after work. Not just any bar; it's the "Island Nest" on Isle Madame, Cape Breton, Nova Scotia. It's a bright, fluorescent-lit, blue rumpus room of a place, with a bar, some pool tables, and about fifteen locals, including the two female bartenders, all of whom watch the three strangers carefully as they enter.

The three guys sit down, order some drinks, and start making tentative conversation with the local islanders. They order some wings—hot, mild, and honey garlic. The hot and the mild are the same temperature. They share the wings around. Locals move closer; the table expands. There's a guy with a suitcase—says his mother was awarded the Order of Canada for her poetry.

The locals start laughing. One of the three guys has smeared red wing-sauce all over the lower part of his face. He's eating his wings like he cannot find his mouth. Everyone is laughing now. He says,

"Oh, I've made a mess," and starts sticking napkins onto his face. Can't see his eyes anymore. Napkins stuck everywhere. Everyone in the bar is jabbering happily now.

Another one of the three guys gets up to go to the bar and does an exaggerated imitation of a co-worker who wears his pants very low. The two girls are particularly amused by this display of white cleavage. He puts an order bell down his pants and begins to dance. He rings when he shakes his legs. Not to be outdone, the guy with the wing-sauce face jumps up and, while standing close against the bar, lowers his pants... to the floor. More hilarity ensues. A few verses of "Barrett's Privateers" are then sung, locals and strangers harmonizing happily.

Before they leave, the two cleavage guys go to the men's room. Conjecture flies around the bar. Bets are on full nudity. The two bar staff girls are giggling nervously. The first guy walks out fully clothed—cause for both disappointment and relief in the room. He is followed (very closely) by the second guy, with his pants down around his knees, shouting, "Oh, Frankie, Frankie." More hilarity ensues.

Handshakes and hugs are exchanged between islanders and strangers before the three guys head back to their nearby hotel.

Isle Madame, Cape Breton, Nova Scotia

Friday, June 27, 2003
Yarmouth, Nova Scotia

We did a big ol' drive from Cape Breton down to Yarmouth today. I had more than seven hours to peck away at my trusty PowerBook and was able to write and organize all of my recent pictures.

Kevin Kelly is a guy I have admired for years. He was an important part of *The Whole Earth Catalog* with Stewart Brand and then went on to start *Wired* magazine, a must-have, cutting-edge journal of everything new and interesting in the world. Kevin is no longer the editor there, but continues to contribute excellent pieces to the magazine. One of his many current projects is a fascinating Web site called Cool Tools. Kevin asks readers to let him know about "things they love" and, after checking the items out, posts their recommendations. I wrote and said that I loved my Tom Bihn bag. He wrote back and said he loved my site, that I was the second person that day to recommend Tom Bihn and... could I tell him what it was I loved about the bag. I wrote a quick review. He wrote back and said it was "great" (blush), and could he "circulate it?"

Here's the review he posted:

Tom Bihn Brain Bag
Ultimate office and travel backpack

I spend 16 weeks a year touring back and forth across Canada. I work six nights a week—usually in a different city every night. My gear is in and out of airplanes and vans virtually every day. I have been a serious luggage fetishist for years (I've been touring for 30) and have gone through every conceivable combination of suitcase and bag.

For the last four or five years, I've been carrying a backpack. There were always obvious balance and hands-free comfort improvements with a backpack, but until a few years ago they were all made with hikers and outdoors people in mind. There was nowhere to put your computer, paper, and other essential toys. The Brain Bag is my second computer-oriented backpack.

I'm hard on luggage—even my guaranteed-for-life Tumi suitcase is starting to give out. My carry-on bags usually had a lifespan of less than a year. The Bihn bag, after two years, looks brand new. It's an organizational dream—obviously designed by someone who gives a shit. The computer (in my case a G4 Titanium) fits safely and snugly into a Velcro-closed, floating hard case in the back compartment. On top of it goes the "Snake Charmer," which is a two-compartment accessories bag with see-thru mesh sides that *perfectly* fits the remaining space. In the front compartment is an organizer for paper, files, etc. (the "Freudian Slip"), that can be removed from the bag easily. Each side of the slip is configured differently, so, depending on how you choose to use it, you orient it with the most useful side out. There are three big pockets on the front and a water bottle holder thing. Two of these pockets are subdivided inside for further organization.

All the hardware and material is first class and the thing fits so well that often, at airports or waiting at hotel reception desks for check-in, I forget to take it off.

I love the bag, not just because it's a great bag but also because it's an intelligently conceived, beautifully designed, and well-made thing. A rare find these days.

Wednesday, July 2, 2003
Toronto, Ontario
Heading Home...

I'm sitting on the floor here at gate 221 at Toronto International Airport. I've got my PowerBook plugged into the only AC outlet in the vicinity, right by the door to the ramp. Things are pretty quiet here right now because our flight doesn't leave for another two hours. We arrived at the airport over an hour ago with our fingers crossed. Our flight today was scheduled for 9:40 p.m., putting us into Vancouver at midnight. Smitty and Mike spent 20 minutes yesterday (after we arrived here from Halifax) wheeling and dealing with Air Canada staff trying to negotiate us a better leave time. Thanks to their efforts, we left Hamilton at six a.m. this morning on the promise of a 75 percent chance that we would fly sometime before noon. It's confirmed now that we will arrive in Vancouver 12 hours earlier than scheduled, which is a big improvement.

Misha and Dylan met us in Hamilton yesterday. They have been camping their way across Canada and planned from the outset to celebrate Canada Day with us. It was great to see them and fun hearing their often-hilarious road stories.

Canada Day in Hamilton was a giant family party in the expansive and beautiful Gage Park. Thousands of people partied with us on a warm Ontario summer night. The night before, we played the Casino in Halifax, outside under cover. It was one of the best Halifax shows I can remember and a great way to end the Maritimes tour. Our two nights at the Astor Theatre in Liverpool, Nova Scotia, were sold-out and really fun. The vibe of the crowd was overwhelmingly musical and supportive—perfect for the on-the-edge improv that ensued. I was riffing on the "Liverpool" thing, which led, of course, to the Beatles, which led, of course, to us playing four or five Beatles songs, which led, for no good reason, to "Smoke on the Water" by Deep Purple. The second show was as full of musical adventure as the first. Not all audiences will stay with you as you shimmy your way out onto a musical limb.

Since Liverpool was celebrating "Privateers Days" that weekend, we had some additional fun at the large, packed beer tent after our first show. Some of us danced like dervishes to the mostly acoustic bluegrass band that was thumping away in the corner. I made a brief appearance with them, singing the always dependable "Stormy Monday Blues." Marty Melhuish, one of Canada's best-known music writers, accompanied us to the beer tent. I had done a long, on-camera interview with Marty in the afternoon for an eight-part television series on Canadian music that he is directing. His film crew shot some of the Liverpool set for use with that interview.

White Point Beach, Nova Scotia

We stayed at the incredible White Point Beach Resort while we were in Liverpool. Twenty-five years ago Debbie and I stayed there after she did a Maritimes tour with me. The resort has grown and loosened up considerably since we were there in 1978. Then, a white shirt and tie were expected at both lunch and dinner. The atmosphere was both quiet and conservative.

White Point Beach, Nova Scotia

One night, those many years ago, after Debbie and I had returned to our seaside cabin after dinner, there was a knock on our door. One of the servers from the restaurant, standing timidly on our small porch, politely asked us if we would like to attend the staff toga party. On Saturday night, at the Astor Theatre, that same server brought me a photograph of Debbie and me, in our bed-sheet togas, on that magic night. In five or six hours, I'll be with Debbie again and can share that picture with her.

Sunday, July 6, 2003
Île-à-la Crosse, Saskatchewan
Ile X

After a long drive northeast from Vermilion, Alberta, we arrived, in the early evening, in Île-à-la-Crosse, Saskatchewan. Although technically not a reserve and technically not a first nation, Ile X is a predominantly Metis settlement, celebrating, this weekend, their 227th anniversary as a community. It is the second oldest settlement in Saskatchewan, and one of the oldest in Canada. There is only one accommodation in the town—the Northern Sunset Motel, one restaurant (part of the motel), and one store, which is a block away from the motel.

The Saturday night anniversary celebration consisted of a bright and noisy carnival, with rides set up in the middle of the main road, surrounded by randomly parked pickup trucks, and the Trooper concert, to be held adjacent to the carnival in the Ile X arena. Visiting a small, remote, northern community can be surreal at the best of times, but the Ferris wheel and barking carneys, planted rudely in the midst of this peaceful place, made for a strangely evocative scene.

Carnival–île-à-la-Crosse, Saskatchewan

On our arrival at the Northern Sunset Motel, we were greeted in the parking lot by some of the local people. We played in Ile X ten years ago, and we were welcomed back as though we were returning relatives. Winston introduced himself with a huge smile.

"We're glad you could make it back," he said with obvious emotion.

Another car full of people pulled in beside us. The driver got out and made his way over to me. He was in his 60s, brown and wrinkled.

Him: "I drove a long way from up north to hear the Troopers play tonight."

Me: "Aw, you wasted your time... they suck."

Him: (chuckling) "It was a good drive anyway. I picked up some hitchhikers." He extends his hand. "My name is Mr. Wolverine."

Me: (shaking his hand) "My name is Mr. McGuire."

Him: "Mr. McGuire... Pleased to meet you Mr. McGuire."

Me: "Pleased to meet you Mr. Wolverine."

Friday, July 11, 2003
Camrose, Alberta
Stage 13 Music Fest

The sun was beginning to rise as we kicked into "Raise A Little Hell" at the Stage 13 Festival in Camrose, Alberta, this morning. Thousands of diehard fans shouted the chorus—arms in the air—probably waking any sleeping campers in the nearby fields. I salute those people for waiting for our set and hanging in with us. I got back to the hotel at 5:30 a.m.

Months ago, the Festival's promoter booked us to open for Cheap Trick on the first night of the festival. Because we're playing Klondike Days in Edmonton next week, he pointed out that we were already in violation of the Stage 13 "radius clause." Radius clauses are included in most large festival contracts to ensure that bands playing won't be performing at competing shows nearby in roughly the same time period. The canny promoter offered to waive his radius clause... if the band would agree to play for less money than we would normally be paid for an opening set. Because we're already doing the Craven Festival and a show in Saskatoon this same weekend, making for decent routing, and because we liked the idea of opening for Cheap Trick at a "new music" festival, we reluctantly accepted his lowball offer.

Months later, our agents got a call from the promoter, asking if we would alter our agreement and play after Cheap Trick, who needed to leave the site early. Although this now put us in the headliner time slot (at one a.m.), there was no offer to improve our contracted fee. Over a barrel—it was too late to book anything else—we again reluctantly agreed. Although unhappy with the change, we secretly enjoyed the idea that it would now appear that Cheap Trick, a popular American band, and the real headliner, was opening for us.

Yesterday, our road manager called to tell me that Cheap Trick had decided to leave even earlier and that, rather than bumping our slot down so that we still followed them, the promoter had decided to put another band on between us. He reasoned that this would keep the crowd onsite, waiting for us to play.

It seemed to me that, it being the first night of the festival, we were going to have a pretty wasted audience: people who had spent the day packing, driving, and setting up tents, followed by some serious, first-night, heavy drinking. I couldn't imagine that this crowd was going stay pumped, or even, in some cases, around, during the intervening set. More important, our contracted deal was to either precede, or follow, Cheap Trick. With the order of the bands changed in this way, we were now clearly performing the role of headliner, but without either the appropriate pay or the advantage of having Cheap Trick warming up the crowd for us. Phone calls were made, threats were issued, and nothing changed. We could either play at one a.m. or forfeit the 50 percent balance of our already small fee.

When our driver delivered us to the site at 12:30 a.m.—half an hour prior to our 1:00 show time—our road manager was irate and perilously close to losing it.

"Fucking Cheap Trick's crew took *an hour* to get their gear off stage!! The other band hasn't even gone on yet."

I dropped my gear in the backstage dressing room and wandered to the side of the stage. I clearly had some time to kill.

"Hey, Ra McGuire..." a young, drunk, backstage person clamped his arm firmly around me. "Trooper is totally gonna rock the house tonight. The whole crowd was just chanting your name—it's totally gonna rock."

He introduced me to his friend, maybe 20 years old, wearing a Trooper laminate around his neck. "I work for Trooper," he told me—obviously confused, or drunk, or both.

An hour and a half later, just after two a.m., after the beer garden had shut down, we took to the stage... to the thunderous cheers of thousands of still-pumped, still-partying Albertans. It was a beautiful summer night/morning, and the stage sounded great. The drunk kid's prediction was on the money—Trooper totally rocked the house. Crowd surfing bodies floated toward the security pit in front of us, hundreds of arms reached across the metal barricade towards us, beautiful girl balanced on shoulders, flirted and flashed their breasts at us—and everyone sang along so loudly that I stopped singing in both "Good Time" and "Thin White Line" to let their voices take over. It was an all-round awesome show.

So there's the "business" of the music business—which often makes me crazy, and the "music" of the music business—which I love deeply.

And never the twain shall meet. Amen.

Saturday, July 19, 2003
Edmonton, Alberta
The Edmonton Randy Bachman Interview

I received an e-mail several weeks ago from a production company that's putting together a *Life and Times* episode about Randy Bachman for the CBC. They wanted an interview, parts of which would be included in the show. I had recently posted a rant called "Takin' Care of Bullshit" on the Trooper Web site, written after reading Randy's startlingly self-serving and, in Trooper's case, only marginally non-fiction biography of (more-or-less) the same name.

I wrote the lady back and told her I would be happy to do the interview. I had decided that regardless of the book's cavalier references to our band and the self-aggrandizing (and untrue) descriptions of how Randy taught us virtually everything we know, I was not going to let one silly book interfere with an opportunity to insert myself and my opinions into a national television special celebrating our mentor and former producer.

Out behind the stage at Edmonton's Klondike Days Exhibition on Thursday night, the interviewer prepped me for the interview. "Say what you feel. I don't want this to be a puff piece." According to him, a few important interview subjects have refused to talk at all. The nicest guy in Canadian music has turned him down. I tell the interviewer to have him call me; he *has* to be on this show. I want to explain my reasoning to him. Then the cameras are rolling.

Questions about our four-year working relationship evoke a surprising bittersweet ache that frequently leaves me standing thought-fully, but mutely, in front of the camera. I struggle for honest, appro-priate answers and find myself realizing, on camera, that I wish that Randy had become my friend, and that I was still sad that the many fun, intimate, and intense moments that we shared—moments that under normal circumstances would bond two people in a lasting friendship—remain only as disconnected anecdotes, hardly worth dredging up for the big-time TV interview.

"Could you describe Randy in one word?" he asks me.

"Enigmatic," I answer, after a very long pause. A passing truck obscures my voice.

"We'll take that again," he says.

"Enigmatic," I say again, with a catch in my voice.

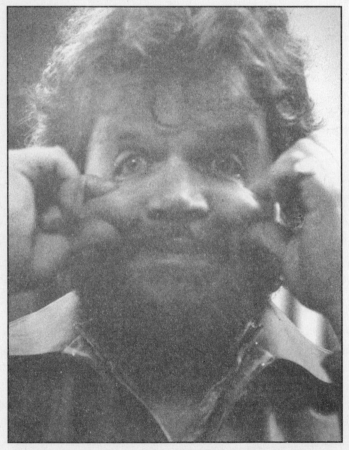

Randy Bachman, Phase One Studio, Toronto, Ontario, 1979

I tell my "Raise A Little Howl" story, the "Mormon Church Dance" story, the "Singing Every Beatles Song" story. They've been repeated hundreds of times since 1975, but there's not a lot of passion behind them. While I'm parroting them out, I'm thinking about Randy. The interviewer/director *really* wants to know about "Randy, the man," but the more I talk, the more I realize I don't have any useful answers for him.

The final question, strangely, was about friendship. Specifically, it was about how many friends Randy has, after a lifetime in the music business. I ducked what seemed like a set-up. I said that I was proud, after all these years of making music, to have become part of an excellent network of friends that in many ways has supported and sustained me and my band through the years. Then I said that I was sad that I couldn't count Randy as one of those friends.

It was the strangest, hardest interview I think I've ever done. We talked for a half an hour. I wonder what, if anything, they'll end up using in the show.

Saturday, July 26, 2003
Kapuskasing, Ontario
Update

K' so...

The Edmonton K-Days gig was awesome, albeit a bit stressful at the beginning because of the Randy Bachman interview thing, but once we started playing it was a ton of fun, partly because we played "Takin' Care of Business," "Let It Ride," and "These Eyes," during which I tried to work in the Maestro rap version ("seen a lotta highs and lows but that's just the way life goes"), which, I guess, the other guys have never heard, so what I was doing just sounded like a lot of disconnected gibberish, which was fine too, really. Then we had to get up at freakin' four a.m. to drive to the Merritt Mountain Music Festival where Pat (also known as Bob), Steve, Sarah, and Kelsey (our "Beer Girls"), Ben, and a few other old friends joined us for a hot, fun, and raucous afternoon set in a large field packed full of cowboy-hatted rockers. After this, because we had not eaten yet, we went to A&W, which was across the street from a cold beer store where Mikey went to get some and saw that Tommy Stewart—the drummer who played on all the Trooper hits—was playing with The Brent Lee Band in the bar next door, so we all went in, hugged and kissed Tommy, and played "Good Time." We had to leave right after, though, because Scott and Gogo were trying to catch an early ferry, which they didn't do because when they arrived at Smitty's house, and after some of the band and crew had consumed some of the aforementioned cold beer, they stayed for an impromptu pool party involving both nakedness and fully-clothed (including shoes) swimming. I got picked up by Debbie in Connor's wicked new ride and happily returned to White Rock, where, on my first day home, I did my best to help with the horror of house painting (something I now understand why we left so long to do again). On my second day home, Debbie, Connor, and I celebrated our dear friends Tom and Kerry's 20th Anniversary with the 20th annual traditional Anniversary picnic. Then, on my third day home, we all went to Larry and Sue's for the second annual BBQ and jam, where about a dozen of us had a great time sitting in a big circle playing guitars, mandolins, a trumpet, and a wash-tub bass, and singing every single song we could think of. On my fourth day home, we hosted a gala 70th Birthday Party for Debbie's Mom, Shirley, who at one point yelled out: "I'm having a great time—Happy Birthday everyone!", which means that she was having as good a time as the rest of us and then, like I never left the damn place, I was back at the airport again, strapped into my Tom Bihn backpack and dragging my big black suitcase covered in "Heavy" stickers, on my way to Toronto, where we spent the night in a boring airport hotel. I watched *Rush Hour 2* on my PowerBook and took many pictures, out my window, of the lonely Toronto night before falling asleep and waking up in time to head north on the highway to Kirkland Lake, Ontario, where, in the lobby of the Comfort Inn, a 30-something woman wearing gold sandals interrupted my conversation with the front desk lady and said; "*Ooo*, do we have a *celebrity* in the hotel then??!!" I replied, "uh, yes, I'm the singer for the band Trooper," to which *she* replied "Oh, good for you!" This was also where we were met in the dressing room by our now legendary (in *our* band, anyway) friend Sab, whose band opened for us and who has something (although none of us are sure what) to do with the promoter who's putting these three shows on. He single-handedly made it impossible to hear anything in our dressing room other than his gravel-flavoured voice shouting, once again—it's become a ritual—about the great sex he was going to have after the show, after which we hit the stage in the packed, echoing arena and played a tight, sweaty set that had the whole place moving like one big northern Ontario animal and where, among many other audience diversions, a young guy, in a misguided attempt to impress me, kept trying to pull down his girlfriend's dress to show me her breasts. After this, we slept and then left for a three-hour drive to Kaspuskasing, Ontario, during which we watched the first (and part of the second) episode of Ken Burns' *Jazz* and learned all about Buddy Bolden, Jelly Roll Morton, and my hero, Louis Armstrong (pronounced "Loowis" not "Loowey"), which we all enjoyed immensely, but had to put away when we arrived here. We had the perverse pleasure of beholding the strangest hairdo of the year on the nice front desk lady, after which I went for a long walk around this very unusual (and very muggy) town, taking pictures, stopping for a minute at the gate to the Lumberjack Festival outdoor activities, where I was told it cost $25.00 to get in, but that this would also grant me admission to the Trooper concert tonight. (This is interesting, because Sab told us that tonight's show was sold-out, and how could that be if they were going to sell me a ticket.) I turned down the offer and walked on to a video store and rented *Mulholland Drive* and *Spun*, which I just watched and enjoyed a lot. Then I got to thinking that I hadn't updated my blog, and how the fuck was I going to cover everything that has happened, somehow imparting a sense of careening through the days without really taking the time to stop and catch my breath.

Kaspuskasing, Ontario

Monday, July 28, 2003
Mattawa, Ontario
My Mouth Organ

On Friday night, in the noisy Kirkland Lake dressing room, I pulled a broken mouth organ from my bag and considered, out loud, throwing it into the audience after playing my introduction to "Baby Woncha Please Come Home." Gogo quickly suggested that, rather than tossing it, I give it to him—which I did. I explained to him that at least two of the notes were stuck and that several soaks in hot water and some detailed probing of the reeds with my Swiss Army knife had failed to resuscitate it. As well, the tiny screw was missing from one side, leaving the thin metal casing shifting around dangerously close to the lips. Regardless, Gogo was thrilled with this new instrument and began making tentative music with it, quietly blowing and sucking wide clusters of notes as we prepared for the show.

After playing with it for a few minutes, he asked me for a lesson.

It's been a very long time since I've given any thought to mouth organ technique; my interaction with the instrument has, for many years now, been limited to playing the solo for "Good Time" and the intro for "Baby," both of which are so deeply carved into my onstage groove that I now hardly see the process as "playing." Because of this and because I've never really seen myself as a "player," I was momentarily nonplussed by this talented musician's request for instruction.

For two days before this we had been watching a documentary on Jazz featuring the amazing Wynton Marsalis who, in segments interspersed throughout the show, demonstrates the trumpet techniques of some of the great Jazz practitioners. Marsalis is a truly inspirational musician, and his contribution to the show was affecting all of us. We found ourselves trying to talk like him, using phrases like "musical conversation." Gogo's interest in the mouth organ may have had something to do with the prevailing Jazz vibe in the band. It was also inspiring me, as we talked, to reconsider my relationship with the instrument.

I pulled another harp from my pocket, making jokes about how anyone could do what I do and, after some thought, ran through the few basic licks that I know: isolating notes, bending notes, trilling notes, staccato notes, and "double stopping." These are some of the bits that, strung together properly, make up a credible harp solo. Gogo asked when I began playing.

My Dad plays the mouth organ. He can play the rhythm and the melody simultaneously in an amazing juggling act of notes and percussive playing—the melody peaking through holes in the broken rhythm, the tongue and mouth negotiating a complex interplay of movements that I've never been able to duplicate. To the great delight of kids and adults alike, he could also play a tiny mouth organ that he would hide completely in his mouth, the notes and rhythm emanating clearly from his lips. A mouth organ was with him in the Army, handy in his pocket. It would come out at home, on Muirfield Drive, at parties and golden backyard campfires (as would my mother's accordion). He would play and sing songs like "Ivan Skavinski Skavar" and the hauntingly beautiful "Lili Marlene." My first mouth organ was one of his.

As a teenager, I used to hitchhike a lot. I traveled all over western Canada and as far south as Los Angeles. A mouth organ was always with me, handy in my pocket. I began playing solos with it in Winter's Green, in the late 60s, a band that would dive fearlessly into long jams, parts of which included free-form improvisations on my harp. I play "cross harp" style, I explained to Gogo in my brief lesson, as opposed to "straight harp," which is the style my Dad used. In cross harp mode, the key is determined by the "suck" notes (the notes that will bend) while straight harp is played in the key of the "blow" notes. So, for instance, in the key of A ("Here For A Good Time"), I play a "D" harp.

Gogo pointed out to me, mid-lesson, that I was overly humble about my abilities on the harp. He gave me several compliments on my playing, the value of which I don't think he realized. Chuffed and bolstered, I decided to throw a solo into the middle of "Baby" that night.

The Kirkland Lake arena was packed. After five days off, our show was tight and energized, and the crowd totally locked in with us. I forgot to do the harp solo.

The next day, Gogo carried the discarded harp with him everywhere. Working hard at isolating notes, bending them, and building complex rhythms with breath control. In the sweltering Kapuskasing dressing room that night, he proudly showed me his progress. He encouraged me again to include the harp in the breakdown section of "Baby."

There were 5000 people pressed tight into the Kapuskasing arena that night. It was so hot that halfway through the first song my hands were too sweaty to pick up my mic stand. The air was so thin that it took five songs to settle into a breathing pattern that would supply enough air for singing while avoiding an oxygen-starved blackout. The mostly French-speaking crowd was delightful, and the show soared. My first improvised solo in roughly 20 years was less than spectacular.

Last night, in the makeshift dressing room below the Mattawa Museum (which was behind the large outdoor stage we were to play on), Gogo continued to encourage me. Frank, Scott, and Gogo were enthusiastic about the idea of a solo, and Gogo, particularly, championed a more open section for me to play over. I wandered the dark museum basement chugging solo ideas.

The Mattawa show was outside, totally SRO, and like a homecoming. The Voyageur Days promoter told us we are the first band that they have booked for a second time. The crowd welcomed us back with an excellent summer evening party. My solo, worked up a bit and presented over a pared down, more percussive background was a lot better.

After the show (and the "Raise A Little Hell" fireworks display!), Gogo dropped Scott, Frankie, and me off at the local bar on the small main street. The place was filled with people from our show. We were welcomed repeatedly as we moved through the room. The three-piece band was jumpin'. We danced, signed autographs, swapped stories, and made new friends. Soon we were up on the small stage, jamming. The guitar player knew "Good Time," so we played that. Scott pounded out the groove for "Mustang Sally," so we did that, the stage crowding with locals singing the "ride, Sally, rides," I sang "Stuck In The Middle With You" phonetically since I only know three or four of the actual words in the verses—it worked fine.

Then Scott yelled across the stage: "You got your harps?"

I grinned and reached into my pocket. "Blues in A," he called to the guitar player.

The little PA system distorted perfectly giving my harp a traditional bluesy edge. Lost in the press of the happy crowd, eyes closed and oblivious, I merged with the little plastic and tin instrument between my lips. It stuttered and growled, it moaned and cried, and I disappeared into the music I was making.

I have Gogo to thank for that.

Tuesday, August 5, 2003
Toronto, Ontario
Catching Up...

I'm junk. Useless. Exhausted, sleep deprived, unshaven, and barely able to use my brain for anything more complicated than checking, every five minutes, to see if my boarding pass is still in my pocket.

I'm at the airport in Toronto. Our flight leaves at 15:40, three hours from now. My alarm went off, in my motel room in Geraldton, Ontario, at 06:00 this morning. I had slept, at that point, for less than three hours. An hour later we were racing down the highway on a three-hour drive to Thunder Bay. Our driver, who had bragged about not having slept in several days, woke us several times as he abruptly swerved back into his own lane. On one particular high-speed corner, the 15-passenger van came close to lifting onto two wheels. Gogo began making conversation to help keep him awake, and I told him, quietly, from my sleepy haze, to slow down. We were dropped off at the Thunder Bay airport about three hours ago. The good news is that, partly as a compensation for losing some of our bags when we flew in from Newfoundland, Air Canada let us upgrade to executive class, or as they bombastically refer to it: Super Elite.

The day before yesterday we woke up in St. John's, Newfoundland, after less than three hours sleep, and flew for four hours to Toronto, waited two hours, then flew two hours to Thunder Bay, where the same driver had picked us up and driven us the three hours into Geraldton—in time, basically, for a quick shower before the show. We are all running on empty.

Six days ago, we played at the beautiful Club 279 above, and part of, the Hard Rock Cafe on Yonge Street in Toronto. The show was an incredible sold-out success in spite of (or possibly because of) the massive Stones-AC-DC-Guess Who-Rush-SARS-fest scheduled for the following day. Every member of the Toronto audience seemed to know every word to every song. The whole night just rocked.

Graffiti – St. John's, Newfoundland

The next day, we flew to St. John's, Newfoundland, my favourite city in Canada. I hooked up there with Dylan and Misha who had made their way to The Rock since we had last seen them in Hamilton, Ontario, on Canada Day. Our day together involved some sightseeing, a radio interview, and lunch at Nautical Nellie's on Water Street. Returning to the hotel we met up with old friends Dave Allen and Boink, both of whom were working with the band 54•40 at the George Street Festival that night. Guest List activity ensued, and later that evening, ten of us walked into the friendly madness that is George Street.

George Street is a large, happy party surrounded by bars, bands, and pizza joints. After 54•40's set, the street stayed full of wild but friendly partiers. The Trooper entourage started the night in a blues bar with a great band and then moved to a more mainstream place a few doors down, where I was asked to sing "General Hand Grenade" and "We're Here For A Good Time." In fact, I hardly needed to sing at all: the packed club was singing along so loudly, I doubt that any one heard me. My favourite moment of the night came not long after when I was coming down the stairs from 54•40's dressing room, where I had been visiting. As I descended into yet another nightclub featuring live music, I could hear the band playing "We're Here For A Good Time." I reached the bottom of the stairs and con-tinued walking right up onto the small stage, where I stopped at the bass player's microphone. At first he seemed about to shoulder me away from the mic, but when I began to sing, his jaw dropped. It was the scat thing I do at the end of the song, a pretty distinctive part. The rest of the band, who hadn't noticed my arrival, nearly stopped playing. Big grins filled the stage as I finished the song with them. When the song ended, and after exchanging high-fives and hugs with the band members, I wandered back out onto the crowded street. I love moments like that.

St. John's, Newfoundland

The following day we drove to Grand Falls-Windsor and played a hot, sweaty set for a club full of mostly young, very animated Newfoundlanders. We drove the five hours back to St. John's the next day.

Our return to the Bay Roberts Klondike Festival was a triumph. We had played the show two years earlier, backing up Big Sugar, and the Newfoundland favourites: Great Big Sea. This year, we were headlining the show, backed up by Loverboy, Streetheart, and, ironically, Randy Bachman.

The dressing room trailers were set up as a circular compound backstage. Our friend Mick Dalla-Vee, who plays in Randy's band, greeted us as we arrived. "Randy wanted to stay and sit in with you, but..." he said. Soon, the true gentleman of Canadian rock, Kenny Shields, joined us. Kenny's had some health problems lately, and it is an inspiration to see him back on the boards. Kenny and Fred Turner are my two favourite Canadian rock guys.

Loverboy finished their set and rolled into the compound. Soon we were all huddled in their trailer, checking out Paul Dean's PowerBook and geeking-out like Steve Jobs groupies at a MacWorld Convention. Doug Johnson, a fellow White Rock resident, and I discussed the new recording studio being built mere blocks from our respective homes.

Twenty minutes later, we walked onstage to a thundering roar from 20,000 cheering Newfoundlanders. As both Mike Reno and Kenny Shields had told me before we went on: the people in Newfoundland love our band. That reciprocal love was evident for the duration of our two-hour-and-twenty-minute set.

I had arranged earlier to have Frankie "screeched in" onstage. "Screeching" is a traditional Newfoundland initiation that involves very strong rum (the "screech"), some complicated linguistic exercises, and, finally, the kissing of something — usually a codfish. I was "screeched in" in 1977 at a bar owned by, and named after, a well-known Newfoundland wrestler named Sailor White. My particular screeching involved kissing Mr. White's large and unattractive ass. Frankie delighted the crowd with his attempts to mimic an old time Newfie accent and finally, with coaching, mastered the required phrase. The brown mickey bottle was produced and handed to Frank for his ritual shot of screech. Joking, Tom, The Screech-er told him he had to drink the entire bottle. Taking him at his word, Frankie had glugged down half the mickey before the shocked DJ could pull it away from him. The crowd, of course, roared. Frank became an honorary Newf seconds later when he kissed, not a cod, but an attractive girl brought on stage for that purpose.

During our last visit to Bay Roberts, our friend Steve Bradbury had arranged a boat trip for us. We spent the afternoon with Bob and his son touring Conception Bay. Afterwards, we visited Bob's father who was building a large boat, by hand, in his garage. The day left a deep impression on all of us, but Scott was so moved that he wrote a song about the life he had imagined the senior boat builder had lived, there on the coast. At the show on Saturday night, we pared down to acoustic guitars and a tambourine and sang "Bay Roberts Boy From Newfoundland." It was only the second time we had ever played it (we had done it the night before for practice), and I think the audience could tell how stoked we were. They responded overwhelmingly as Scott grinned happily.

I had told Dylan and Misha that the Bay Roberts concert would probably be the highlight of our touring year—and I was right. I am very thankful to the people of Newfoundland for their kindness, generosity, and unbounded spirit. I won't forget that show.

St. John's, Newfoundland

Last night we played the Geraldton Jamboree with our Scottish brothers, Nazareth. A crazed crowd of young fans had bubbled right up onto the stage by the end of our show, terrifying the few security people on hand. The festival-sized crowd roared through our too-brief 70-minute set. We left the stage feeling as though we were only half finished the gig.

Which brings me back around to here, the Toronto airport, where I'm sitting at gate 227 in a little cubicle with a card phone and an AC outlet. We're all exhausted. We go home for three days and then, on Thursday, we fly to Nova Scotia to headline the Rock-the-Dock festival in Sydney, play a bar in Bridgewater, and then fly back to Newfoundland to play the Blueberry Festival in St. George's.

Then we'll have a much-needed two-week holiday...

Friday, August 15, 2003
White Rock, BC
Sydney, Bridgewater, St. George's...

I'm on summer holiday right now: Not answering the phone, not calling anyone, hiding out.

But...

I wanted to at least jot some notes about last weekend so I don't forget...

Rock the Dock—Sydney, Nova Scotia:

Thousands of people in parkas and under umbrellas. Same big beautiful stage as the Bay Roberts show. Missed Reckless—sorry Robert. Laurel Martel, who played before us, sounded awesome from the dressing room. Excellent security guys dug Subway Steve out of the front row and brought him back to sing. Steve was his usual Steveness—introduced me as "quite possibly my hero." Damn, maybe next time I'll be "for sure" his hero. Sang "Thin White Line" very well. Scored excellent "SECURITY" hat after getting security chief's permission.

Classic's—Bridgewater, Nova Scotia:

Uh, Bridgewater, ya... uh... Nice people—maybe a little shy. Thirty-five smackers per person, ferfucksake!

Blueberry Festival—St George's, Newfoundland:

Got picked up by a 70s limo, bottomed out on dips in the highway. Hour-and-a-half drive to Stephenville from Deer Lake Airport. Our driver was Ed, who has a Strat. The room service girl (who told me she had looked up our room numbers ahead of time) was so excited to meet me that she was shaking. Gave me two things to sign. Autographed them both. After she left I realized that one of them was the bill for dinner and that I had neglected to tip her.

Fred Penner was at the gig; he had been playing the same show that day. We first met Fred in Rankin Inlet, Nunavut, where he taught us several phrases in the local language to say onstage. He wrote it out phonetically for us. Fred came out and participated in Frank's drum solo, holding a galvanized garbage can and dancing and grooving like no one would ever guess that Fred Penner could dance and/or groove. All right, there's a third Winnipeg guy that I *really* like. He left a note at the front desk of the hotel suggesting we get together for a longer hang next time. I'll be there, Fred.

It was an excellent show all round. They had planned for 2500 people, but had to take down their fence to accommodate what looked like more than 4000.

Our dressing room was the back room of a four-lane, five-pin bowling alley. After the show, they turned it on for us and the eight of us, plus the guy who hired us (my extreme bowling partner, the 60-something Elton White), and some of the other show people, played the most astonishing game of bowling I've ever seen. Thirty minutes of solid, almost hysterical, laughter! Two balls at a time. Five balls at a time. Two bowlers at a time. No taking turns; if you have a ball, throw it. Guys sliding on their belly down the lane after hurling their ball. One frustrated bowler (OK, me) ran down the lane, crawled under the thing at the end, and knocked the pins down by hand. Jesus, it was just the funniest thing. Elton and the rest of the local boys invited us back next year for a tournament. They mentioned maybe doing this one naked.

Then... the next day—driving and flying and flying and flying, all friggin' day. This was the day that Toronto International Airport was a network news item. Did you see us there, running (actually running) from one gate to another in the chaos caused by the Air Canada layoffs? Arrived home at 11:00 p.m. Started David Adams Richards' amazing new book, *River of the Brokenhearted*, in the morning and finished it two minutes before we touched down in Vancouver.

Back to my holiday now.

CHAPTER EIGHT

August 30–December 22, 2003

A Songwriting Conversation, Canadian Music,
The Irish Terrorist's Memorial Service, Uncle Jack,
A Large Grey Blanket, A Changing Face, Managing the Band Etc.,
My Wonderful Wife, Reviews of Five Favourite Movies,
The Middle of Nothing in Particular, Technical Advice,
On Songwriting, Cornering Phosphenes,
David Gates on Songwriting,
Our Van Blows Up, Highway Hero, Home Life, Fake Ra McGuire,
Other Fake RMs, Crazy Talk, Our 32nd Wedding Anniversary,
Connor's Fake Punch, Lord of the Rings, Merry Christmas!

Saturday, August 30, 2003
White Rock, BC
A Conversation

Me: "'K', so you should write a song today. You've really been feeling in the mood for writing lately: poetic, thoughtful."

Me: "I'd rather work on my blog. Maybe work on the Web site redesign. I should also be designing a new T-shirt... and the poster's getting old now... I've got some good ideas for the poster."

Me: "You've got a full day of sitting in the van. You should write a song."

Me: "I've also got eight movies in my bag. I'm thinking of watching *The Player*, directed by Robert Altman, two thumbs up."

Me: "What's the fucking problem here... why are you ignoring me?"

Me: "I'm not ignoring you."

Me: "Then why don't you write a song?"

Me: "What about?"

Me: "Huh?"

Me: "What should the song be about?"

Me: "It doesn't matter... just start writing... something will shape up."

Me: "Oh ya, right... a song about nothing."

Me: "'K', well, uh..."

Me: "Aha..."

Me: "No wait... write about how it feels to be away from home and wishing you weren't. That's what you're feeling today."

Me: "Oh yeah, very original. A lonely road song. So... you want it to be a country song kinda thing... like 'Thin White Line'?"

Me: "Shit, I don't care... just start working on the words. Do the music later."

Me: "I've gotta have some sense of the music while I'm writing the words... different rhyme schemes work with different grooves. And any time I try to write a narrative kinda thing, it screams to be a three-chord song. Just what the world needs, another three-chord song. Jesus..."

Me: "Some of the greatest songs ever written were three-chord songs..."

Me: "So we just stopped the van for a piss stop. We pulled off the highway into the overgrown yard of an old abandoned gas station, windows boarded up, weeds climbing the walls. So there we all were, lined up across the front of this broken old building at the side of a northern Ontario highway... pissing into the cool afternoon air..."

Me: "Hey..."

Me: "At the gig last night in Sudbury, people backstage were telling us about a popular band (that we know quite well) that trashed the dressing room trailer, to the tune of three thousand dollars, and left behind used needles. Which explains why _____ was looking so skinny and haggard last time we saw him. Gogo made a joke that they were just knitting needles and that the trailer trashing consisted of a bunch of half-finished afghans laying around."

Me: "Quit changing the subject."

Me: "This is my blog. I want to write something."

Me: "Write a fucking song."

Me: "I'm going to watch a movie now."

Me: "Wus."

Me: "*The Player*, directed by Robert Altman. I wonder if he's got his audio thing working any better? His early movies had terrible audio—you could never hear what people were saying. *Nashville* was really bad for that."

Me: "Fucking chicken-shit."

Me: "Fuck off."

Me: "You fuck off."

Thursday, September 11, 2003
White Rock, BC
Canadian Music

Why is it that Barenaked Ladies are so famous and The Weakerthans (who I saw last night with Connor and Simon) aren't?

Monday, September 15, 2003
Gibsons Landing, BC
Loss

Shadow was hit by a car a week and a half ago. He had been part of our small family for 11 long years. A quarter of our family is now gone. It was heartbreaking. It still is. I had no idea just how much I loved him.

Shadow was an Irish Terrier. When people asked, I would say; "Irish Terrorist." He had that terrier overabundance of energy that, when we took him to the dog park, fuelled a circumnavigation of the entire park in the time it took us to walk down the first short trail. He could run faster backwards than most dogs could run forwards and often did, taunting the lagging dog, face to face. He loved everybody... and fully expected everyone to love him—and play with him... as soon as possible.

We often wrestled. He would bare his teeth and growl threateningly and I, on my hands and knees, would do my best to do the same. I would slap at his face with my hands while he snapped and leapt at me with his legs and feet, sometimes spinning 360 degree circles in front of me. He would catch my hands and wrists in his teeth and never, ever, bite down on me. Even in the heat of a full-on war, his flashing teeth would grab onto me gently, barely touching my skin. He would play 'til one or both of us was out of breath. Usually, it was me.

Having Shadow in our house was like having a perpetual toddler to care for. Our early efforts at training him were only partly successful. In the yard, he barked loudly at passing cars, people, and dogs and, of course, made a total mess of the grass and the garden (until we fenced it in). If the front gate was inadvertently left open, he would make a run for it. The local pound brought him home once, suffering from an afternoon of play in Semiahmoo Bay where he had obviously consumed a large amount of salty ocean water. Once, during a party at our house, he bolted past an arriving guest and out into Adventureland. I hurriedly excused myself from the party and spent the next hour following him through the backyards of my White Rock neighbours, as he sniffed and pissed on every exciting new object he came across. We met some of those neighbours for the first time after they called to tell us that they had brought Shadow into their house after finding him playfully jousting with cars in the street.

This time, when Debbie and Connor found him, he was sitting in the middle of the road looking confused. Blood was coming from his mouth. The rest of that night was spent at the Emergency vet. They called me, in Regina, from there. For the next three or four days I couldn't think about him without crying. Being on the road when it happened was really difficult for me. Things got a bit better once I was finally able to talk about it with the band.

People have been really sweet about it. We've received sympathy cards and many kind and thoughtful e-mails—for which we are very grateful. I have been unable to write anything since that night. No subject seemed important enough to warrant the effort. I realized a few days ago that I needed to write this... before I could write anything else. So, this is Shadow's memorial service. I will miss that damned dog.

My Dad's older brother, my Uncle Jack, died the same night that Shadow did. He'd been living in the Cariboo for many years and I hadn't seen him for about ten of those. Prior to that I have only childhood memories of him, his 1953 Studebaker Lowboy and his wonderful black lab, Mark. My Dad told me last week that Jack was the nicest man he ever knew. That's high praise from the nicest man I ever knew. My heart was, of course, broken, again—mostly for my father's sake.

The sense of loss... and the cold, dark idea of loss... enveloped me like a large, grey blanket for about a week. I'm feeling better now, sitting in a ferry terminal outside of Gibsons Landing, waiting to go home. Writing this has helped.

Monday, September 29, 2003
Victoria BC
A Monday One-Off

The room was nice. It had a comfortable, swivel-able, tilt-able, leather chair with casters (like the one he had at home), a desk equipped with an AC outlet and two phone jacks built into its surface and—a treat for a working musician—blackout curtains.

He was tired, but he felt the need to write. As he typed, glancing occasionally at the mirror in front of him, he noticed for the first time that the two crevices that cut down his face on either side of his nose were not symmetrical. The one on the right started above the nostril, right where it rolls into the nose, while the one on the left started almost at the bottom of the nostril and continued down the face a good half inch further than the other. Each time he looked up from his computer screen, he was again struck by how strange this looked and how odd it was that he had never noticed something this obvious.

I had been traveling since noon. It was six o'clock. To help kill the time in the terminal parking lot, I watched an episode of *Family Guy* on my PowerBook. I also answered 14 of the 23 e-mails in my Inbox, leaving the longer, personal ones for later.

There had been a couple of difficult ones that afternoon. One was from a band that had, apparently, given me one of their CDs to listen to at a show somewhere in Ontario. They wanted to know how I liked it. I wrote that I could not find their CD ("how rude is that?!" I wrote, honestly embarrassed), and did they have any of their songs online for me to check out? It was a lame response. My only consolation was that it was, at least, honest.

A songwriter had written, asking about his producer's involvement with his songwriting process, and at what point did the producer's suggestions constitute collaboration. I wrote a long response, maybe still feeling guilty about the lost CD, telling the songwriter to sit down with his producer and talk honestly with him about "who's doing what and who gets what."

I answered another e-mail from an enthusiastic guy I had worked with in Regina, who was asking, again, for a job, either as the band's merchandise man or, since he'd heard that job was taken, any other work there might be with any bands on the coast. "My bags are packed. Please reply." Although the response was short, it took a long time to compose.

Another e-mail requested permission to use a band T-shirt in a TV series being produced for the Sci-Fi channel. "Sure," I wrote, "on the condition you send copies of the shows."

A fellow King's X fan from Texas wrote offering condolences over the recent death of my dog. I received at least 30 e-mails, from people I did not know personally, expressing their condolences. Touched once again, I wrote thanking the man for his kindness.

I responded to a quick thought from one of my best friends, a music critic, commenting on a conversation we had been having regarding Universal Music's recent CD price drop and the subsequent, and far less advertised, return to regular pricing.

A friend, the sound man for a couple of popular Canadian bands, wrote saying how good it had been to hang out on George Street in St. John's, Newfoundland. He sent best regards from one of the bands. An easy one to answer...

I sorted through 30 photos that had been sent to the Web site and forwarded, picking two for myself. I wrote two or three e-mails that were part of an ongoing conversation with our Web meister about an upcoming Web site redesign and a couple of particularly difficult Frequently Asked Questions and how they should be answered. The Web meister called as I was packing up my computer and the van was pulling into the bowels of the giant white ferry.

The previous two weeks had been a blur. Debbie and I were renovating our 12-year-old home. Painters hung from ladders, staining the high, shingled walls, as the two of us prepared and painted the walls and windows on the two south-facing decks. Painstaking, detailed, and rewarding work that turned hours into minutes. A series of five appointments with a new chiropractor—a last ditch attempt to deal with chronic back pain—and three long visits to the dentist, in preparation for long overdue bridge work, had taken some of that time. Driving lessons with Connor had taken some as well. Overall, I was deliriously happy to be home.

He checked the time on the corner of the screen: 8:04 p.m. Show time, at the Empress Hotel in Victoria, BC, was 9:45, lobby call at 9:15. It was time to get ready for work.

After hitting "command S" and pushing his swiveling chair back from the desk, he made his way to the bathroom. There in the fluorescent brightness, he leaned in to the mirror. The lines on either side of his nose were perfectly even.

Thursday, October 16, 2003
White Rock, BC
Some Movie Reviews for Dave...

My friend Dave has asked me if I'd review my five favourite movies for a new Web site that he and two friends have started. Since I've spent part of the first travel day of this two-week tour to write the reviews, I've decided that I should post the fruits of my efforts here. So... here they are:

Ra's Reviews:

If it were easy for me to pick five favourite movies, I wouldn't be a true movie fan. A partial list of favourites that I compiled for my Web site contains 132 titles. As I was counting them, just now, I thought of five more.

The following list of five favourite movies has come to mind today. A different list will come to mind tomorrow, so I should probably bear down and finish this as soon as possible. These are films that I would happily watch right now, basking in their complete and engulfing power. Two of the movies are wildly popular, two are not, and one represents my favourite movie category: the documentary.

Fargo (1996)

Supposedly based on true events, *Fargo* is the story of a bad idea that slowly and inexorably spins completely out of control. Frances McDormand's Marge Gunderson ("I'm a police officer from up Brainerd investigating some malfeasance.") is one of the greatest, albeit most improbable, movie heroes of our time and one of the most fully realized characters I can remember seeing on screen. Jerry Lundegaard (William H. Macy), the incompetent and overwhelmed car salesman who instigates the disastrous chain of botched events, is painfully hilarious in his inability to either control the falling dominoes or, at the very least, save his own guilt-ridden skin. Steve Buscemi's small-time hood—over his head in an escalating nightmare of problems brought on by his own lack of nerve—is also brilliant.

The movie was filmed on location in Minnesota and North Dakota during a hard, grey winter. The low-key and detailed characterization of small-town mid-western life had me grinning repeatedly in recognition and is, in many ways, the real appeal of the movie. Everyone in Brainerd speaks in a clipped American patois that sounds like the McKenzie brothers brought up in a second generation Scandinavian home. Anyone who has seen the movie can do the oft-repeated "Oh, yaaaaa" perfectly.

Fargo was, and is, such an unusual movie that it could easily have gone off the tracks in the making. Watching it, I am still awed by the courage of the Coen brothers, the film's creators and directors. The movie's impressive balance of comedy, suspense, and believable violence contains no easy stereotypes—every character and situation is unique, yet totally recognizable—and no moments of formula movie-making—every scene is a complete surprise. With *Fargo*, the Coens have made an endearing and entertaining movie that is both unique and recognizably human.

Something Wild (1986)

Seventeen years ago, in the first half of Jonathan Demme's *Something Wild*, playing Lulu, a reckless dare of a woman who burns up the screen with over-the-top mischievous sexuality, Melanie Griffith rocked. Her performance, though, was only a small part of what I think is one of the most overlooked and under-appreciated movies of the 80s.

The extravagantly adorned Lulu meets the timidly conservative Charlie (Jeff Daniels) when she catches him dining and dashing on his downtown lunch bill. She offers him a lift. Rather than returning him to his office job, she takes him on a ride that will, ultimately, last the length of the movie. The awkward interplay and erotic tension that sparks between these seemingly opposite characters fuels the first half of the movie. It's sexy, funny, and engaging. At about the halfway point, Ray Liotta shows up and the movie makes a hard right turn while at the same time putting the pedal firmly to the metal.

Jonathan Demme is now a famous director with both *The Silence of the Lambs* and *Philadelphia* to his credit. *Something Wild*, an earlier movie, is a far less formal production than either of those. Opening with a blazing salsa track by David Byrne (I bought the soundtrack), the movie rocks, careens, and dances. It's a colourful, funny, occasionally horny, exciting, and fun ride.

Sling Blade (1996)

I guess everybody knows that Billy Bob Thornton is a genius and that he wrote, directed, and starred in *Sling Blade*—his masterpiece. Most of my friends have heard my Carl impersonation and/or showed me theirs. I attended a recording session once where everyone talked like Carl. "Umm hmmm," we all said at every opportunity. "I reckon I got no reason to kill no one. Umm, hm."

I came to love Carl as he made his way back out into the world after spending a lifetime in a mental institution for killing his mother and her lover with a "sling blade." Thornton's creation of Carl, both in the writing and the characterization, is a triumph. Obviously mentally challenged but wise in ways that most would not have the strength for, Carl finds friendship with a young boy and his family. John Ritter is also brilliant. Dwight Yoakam is surprisingly good as the asshole Doyle, and one of my favourite actors, Robert Duvall, does a powerfully understated cameo as Carl's estranged father.

Sling Blade is sometimes painful, sometimes uplifting—sad and hopeful at the same time. It's a movie about doing the right thing, and determining what that right thing might be. It's also a movie about people being good to each other and the outside limits of what that can sometimes mean.

Shower (2001)

A large percentage of my favourite movies list is made up of non-American movies. *Talk to her*, *Yi Yi*, *Amélie*, *Quitting*, *Crouching Tiger, Hidden Dragon*, *Amores perros*, *Y tu mamá también*, *The Princess and The Warrior*, *Va Savoir*, *Vidocq*, *Princess Mononoke*, *La Cage Aux Folles*, *Gallipoli*, *Ghost in the Shell*, *Il Postino*, *New Waterford Girl*, *Cinéma Paradiso*, *Run Lola Run*, *The Full Monty*, *The Sweet Hereafter*, *My Left Foot*, and *Beijing Bicycle* are only the few that I can remember now...

Shower is a Chinese movie about tradition, family, and change. It takes place in a small-town Chinese bathhouse that will soon be torn down as the town is "revitalized." The owner of the bathhouse and his beloved, mentally challenged, son are visited by his second son, who is a now a successful businessman from a large city.

Shower is a bittersweet comedy full of love and kindness. There's nothing particularly unique or challenging about it. As light as it appears, though, I've been drawn back to watch it three times. Beneath its charming humour, it quietly considers many good and valuable things often left behind in the wake of progress.

Genghis Blues (1999)

The legendary physicist Richard P. Feynman has been my hero since I watched a PBS documentary about his life 20 years ago. An amazing and complex man, Feynman's greatest appeal to me was the fact that, despite his great brilliance, he was a straight-talking, down-to-earth guy who, for instance, took endless joy from his trips to South America, where he played conga drums in a neighbourhood street band. He wrote two books about his life and several books (including one called *Genius*) have been written about him. I have, of course, read them all. One of his many adventures involved a tiny country in the dead centre of the Soviet Union called Tannu Tuva. Almost on a dare, he and a friend traveled to Tuva where they were welcomed as warmly as visiting royalty. Part of their curiosity about Tuva came as a result of hearing recordings of Tuvan throat singing—a mysteriously generated style of singing that produces two distinct notes, simultaneously. The effect is similar to that of a bagpipe with its droning low note accompanied by a melody played (or, in this case, sung) over top.

Last year, in a copy of *Utne Magazine*, I saw an ad for a documentary called *Genghis Blues*. It described a blind San Francisco blues singer by the name of Paul Pena who, after managing to record some throat singing from a rare Russian short wave broadcast, had studied the technique, on his own, for years. He translated the lyrics using two Braille dictionaries—the first, a Tuvan to Russian, the other from Russian to English. Totally self-taught, he slowly became the only throat singer not born in Tuva.

After Richard Feynman's death, Ralph Leighton, the friend who had accompanied him to Tuva, arranged for a troupe of Tuvan throat singers to visit San Francisco. At that performance, in the lobby at intermission, Paul Pena throat sang for the leader of the troupe, a man named Kongar-ol Ondar, revered in Tuva as "a cross between John Kennedy and John Wayne." Kongar-ol was astounded by Pena's earthquake-like throat singing style and invited him to Tuva for an upcoming throat singing competition. This is the point at which this remarkable documentary begins.

I love documentaries because the truth is so often more fascinating than anything a writer could dream up. This is truly the case with *Genghis Blues*—a movie about dreams, friendship, determination, and the way that music can erase boundaries, both real and imagined.

Sunday, October 19, 2003
On The Road in Alberta
High Level, Alberta to Edmonton, Alberta – 780km

The fog settled in thick this morning. The cinderblock Greyhound station across the street was disappearing as I did my last check around the room. Before we went on last night we did our usual leave-time negotiation. Not surprisingly, everyone wanted to leave early. It's 11:00 a.m. now and High Level is an hour behind us. Although technically this is a day off, most of the day will be consumed by driving from here to Edmonton.

It's cold, grey, and monotonous out there. We're the only vehicle on a dumb-straight road cut through the middle of nothing in particular. The trees are cut way back from the pavement so you have time to see the moose coming. We've seen a couple of coyotes and a deer. I could not live in High Level.

I have a song by the tail. I heard the whole thing in the shower last night. I have only a few of the first lyrics and a title I like a lot, but the idea behind it, the underlying point, is a good one. I'm still fighting my skittishly stubborn internal editor for the words and images. He/it seems to think that nothing I do is good enough, but I've had some recent successes at convincing him otherwise.

Monday, October 20, 2003
Edmonton, Alberta

A Conversation with my ISP's Internet Accounts Representative:

Me: "If you had the usual recorded message at the beginning of your tech support routine, saying that the connection problem I'm having was the ISP's fault, I wouldn't have had to sit here waiting for forty minutes to find that out from one of your tech support guys."

(Obviously Asian) accounts representative: "Making one of those messages takes a long time for them to provision."

Me: "Sorry?"

Accounts representative: "Making one of those messages takes a long time for them to provision."

Me: "To... 'provision'?"

Accounts representative: "Yes. It would take them a long time to provision."

Me: "I'm not understanding you here. What does that mean?"

Accounts representative (after pausing and collecting himself): "It would take a long time for them to... **DO**."

Me: "I've never heard the word provision used in that way."

Accounts representative: "What's the matter—don't you speak English?"

Tuesday, October 21, 2003
White Rock, BC
Joe Henry and Songwriting

Once, long ago, in the summer of 1996, I copied and pasted a piece of my six-chapter unfinished novel into my primitive new Web site. It was about the unhappy relationship between the novel's protagonist and his uncooperative muse. "Ned Freeman" was having trouble writing songs. I'm still having that trouble. I tried at the time to convey some sense of the delicate and precarious dance of muse, editor, and ego that is the challenge of songwriting, but succeeded only at illustrating one small part of that dynamic.

I bought Joe Henry's new album (*Tiny Voices*) yesterday in Edmonton and was reminded of a review of his last album (*Scar*) that began with a perfect description of the songwriting art. I looked it up and have it here, ready to paste. First though... here's what I wrote in '96:

"Inspiration (or what seemed as though it might pass for inspiration) flashed for only an instant in the swirl of his mind before it was rudely blown out by a cool wind of insecurity. Nothing was allowed to settle long enough to take root. Everything was quickly dismissed as unsuitable for reasons even less well formed than the ideas being rejected. Grasping and holding onto an idea before it was hustled quickly and unceremoniously out the back door of his consciousness was often impossible.

As a child Freeman had played a game with the microscopic threads of cells that floated mysteriously on his eye-

balls. They were difficult to study because they were in constant motion. The trick was to maneuver the cells into a delicate balance by focusing further along their trajectory and then to observe them peripherally until they began to move away. Freeman had always thought of this technique as "sneaking up" on the cells.

Sometimes he succeeded in sneaking up on songs; feigning disinterest in order to subvert the instant-editor. This approach required a fearless lack of concentration that Freeman was usually unable to muster."

Now here's the first bit of the *Scar* review, written by David Gates:

"Every serious musician—hell, every serious artist of any kind—knows the work would be impossible if you ever stopped to think about it. You're not allowed to imitate yourself, but at the same time you have to stay true to yourself. All it takes, basically, is every bit of your intuition and your intelligence—and some third faculty to keep the one from strangling the other."

Yes. That's it exactly. That's the gig, all right.

Friday, October 24, 2003 – Near High River, Alberta

Saturday, October 25, 2003
Barrhead, Alberta
Mark Underwood

We were about five kilometers outside of Carstairs, Alberta, when the engine of our brand new van started making a strange knocking sound. We pulled off the highway onto a gravel country road, and debated what to do. We decided to call Ben, the guy who rents us all our west coast vans and trucks, to see how he thought we should proceed. After hearing a description of the noise and guessing that it was an electrical problem, Ben told us to drive on to Airdrie, where there was a GM dealership that could have a look at the motor. We pulled back out onto the highway.

A few minutes later, the knock got dramatically worse and Smitty reported a significant drop in power. Growing increasingly uncomfortable, I began packing my things into my backpack, wrapping up cables and gathering any belongings from the front of the van.

Then the motor exploded. A thunderous bang followed by what sounded like breaking glass and mangling metal. As Smitty struggled to guide the van to the shoulder (the power steering and power brakes were gone), I watched as a fireball lit my rear view mirror.

"We've got flames over here. We're going to have to bail."

White smoke obscured the view out of the back window. Frank and Scott were making their way up the inside wall of the van as it jerked to a stop. Doors flew open as we all leapt into the brown grass of the highway shoulder. A pickup truck had pulled over with us. The driver jumped out, grabbed a fire extinguisher from the back of his truck, and ran toward the front of the van, spraying down the flames.

According to Mark Underwood, our Good Samaritan, he heard the bang from inside his cab and watched as a sheet of flame shot out from under the back of our van. After extinguishing the fire, Mark piled us all into his crew cab, our gear in the back, and drove us to the Airdrie GM Dealer. Jammed tightly together in the pickup cab, the six of us laughed and jabbered like drunken teenagers, reconstructing what had happened. A fire truck, with siren blaring, passed us, heading toward our van. I called 911 and filled them in.

We gave Mark, a 20-something former resident of Pictou, Nova Scotia, lifetime guest-list privileges for any Trooper show—anywhere, any time. He helped us out with the kind of commitment and selflessness that assumed that there was just no other way that you should deal with this kind of situation. Mark works for Champion Technologies; he's their Drayton Valley Area Representative. He lives in Edson, Alberta. He's a good man.

Monday, November 24, 2003
White Rock, BC
Ketchup

White Rock Pier – White Rock, BC

Last night I was coughing uncontrollably in bed. I broke free of the manic, breathless cycle for a few brief seconds and sat up. I applied my best brainpower to the question of why I couldn't stop coughing. I came to the confident conclusion that each cough was a physical effort to peal away a thin layer of... uh... something... and that because the layers were so thin, and because they were at "such a high resolution," I was unable to deal effectively with the layers one at a time. A hopeless situation... and one that clearly necessitated continued out-of-control coughing.

I've had this cold for a week. I got it the day the tour ended. My guess is that I was in the process of getting it for a week or so. The Prairies tour, although successful and enjoyable at every level, was tiring and at times overwhelming. It took all my energy to pull off. Once again, I'm very glad to be home with Debbie and Connor.

The cold has given me a good excuse to lay low, which would be better if laying low were something I was good at.

I've been working on the graphic design for a large and complicated Web site. It's taken up a lot of my brain. It's a creative and rewarding project, but it thrives on the obsessive compulsive part of me and often leaves me with little energy or inclination for anything else.

My fucking computer blew up the night before I was to leave on the tour. I stayed up 'til three a.m. cadging together a working operating system and enough apps to get me through. I left for the airport three hours later. I worked on the Web site on the plane. I also watched an episode of *Family Guy*.

I missed the Three-Minute Film Festival, where my submission, *Hotel Room Windows*, was shown. Debbie and Connor attended and showed their films: *Imagine Silence* and *Floor Cloth Fun*. They reviewed the event for me on the phone. It was a hoot. Cindy and Monty, who put the festival on, had us over a few nights ago to re-cap the evening. That was a lot of fun. Then Debbie got this same cold.

I took Connor, Dylan, Simon, and Derek to see the Interactive Media campus at the Vancouver Film School on Saturday. Stephanie, the Admissions Director, gave us the talk and the tour. Dylan's thinking of attending and the other three would probably love to— although Connor still seems more interested in the straight-up film campus.

We watched a two-hour series premiere of *Da Vinci's Inquest* last night. It's the best thing on TV.

I will recuperate now. Later, I will write something... better.

Wednesday, November 26, 2003
White Rock, BC
Still Sick

We've finally decided to just stay in bed all day. But we have failed to be successfully bedridden. We came downstairs to eat and are staying online for "a few minutes."

I'm reading *Shakey*, a biography of Neil Young that was given to me by my pal Lance Chalmers. It's fascinating on many levels. So far (I'm half-way), I'm very happy that I'm not Neil Young. It's an excellent book to be bedridden with, though.

A guy named Dwayne in Ottawa is pretending to be the former singer for Trooper. He's telling people there that he took over the job for three years in the 70s while I went into rehab. I exchanged several letters this week with a concerned friend of someone at the losing end of this con. We've had other letters from other cities about this Dwayne guy. It's a little unnerving, but not something I'm un-used to.

In the actual 70s, a man was arrested for rape after pretending to be me. He picked up a girl at the bar and took her to the beach, where he perpetrated his crime. I found out when a local newscaster called me for comment. In the 90s, I got a call backstage at a gig from a girl apologizing for not being able to make it to the show. I told her I didn't know who she was. She reminded me that we had gone out together only a few days before. I told her that she had better come and have a look at me. This other Ra McGuire, Lead Singer For Trooper, had wined and dined her in his Lincoln Continental. He had asked her, ahead of time, which of his many expensive cars she would like to go out in. She had picked the Lincoln.

My most disturbing encounter with this mercurial Ra McGuire took place the day I received a large parcel full of documents and a letter from someone describing himself as my twin brother. According to the letter, we had been separated at birth. The critically important purpose of the letter was to make me aware of the fact that the two of us had been robbed of our birthright. The voluminous documentation in the parcel proved conclusively, he contended, that he and I were destined to be the dual Kings of Canada.

I've just received a complimentary copy of *Cool Tools 2003* from Kevin Kelly. It contains my review of the Tom Bihn backpack. Kevin Kelly is the coolest.

I also received an e-mail from Bob Colebrook inviting the band to the remote and beautiful Nass Valley to play for the Nisga'a people. I had to compose a response that simultaneously said I'd be honoured to play there *and* it will cost a whack-load of money—a good job for a Gemini.

I have to listen to the MP3 of "Crazy Talk" by Chilliwack that I downloaded last week so I can sing it with Bill Henderson (who wrote it) this weekend at the Salt Spring Island/Fulford Hall gig. When I wrote to Bill about playing with us he wrote back that a jam would be "essential to our enjoyment." I'm looking forward to this show. I *did* write Randy Bachman, who also lives on the island, inviting him to come out and hang. I got an e-mail back from his manager saying that Randy would be in Victoria "looking after his wife." I hope Denise is OK.

Salt Spring Island, BC

Monday, December 22, 2003
White Rock, BC
Merry Christmas

I'm not sick any more. I'm happily hunkered down in White Rock enjoying a much-needed rest. On Saturday, our 32nd wedding anniversary, Debbie and I re-watched the first two *Lord of the Rings* movies back to back. That's what I call relaxing.

Connor is now recovering from a broken nose, four fractures in his cheekbone, three stitches under his eye, and trauma to his eyeball that caused it to bleed for two days. All this from one punch, delivered by accident while filming a scene for a project he wrote and was directing and starring in. The guy was supposed to *pretend* to punch him in the face. It was a very scary couple of days in Emerg. We are so thankful that he's OK.

As I slowly wind down from last year's action-packed schedule... 2004 is opening up as a bright and hopeful vista ahead. There will be some big changes in the way Trooper does business next year. I have also begun a few creative projects that will unfold by the Spring.

I am happy and hopeful.

Merry Christmas everyone.

Wednesday, December 24, 2003
White Rock, BC
Magic

All respect to Peter Jackson for his dedication to perfection in the making of magic.

Saw *The Return of the King* tonight.

I am speechless, but, luckily, I have found a review of the movie that can speak for me. In his brilliant review of the film, "Mr. Critic Takes a Holiday," *LA Weekly*'s Chuck Wilson said that for those hours watching *The Return of the King* he was "just a guy who sat down in the fifth row with one of his best pals... stared hopefully up at the screen, and was granted the one thing he needed most in the world—a sense of wonder." That sense of wonder is a rare and very valuable commodity for me these days. Mr Wilson goes on, eloquently, to say: "...this epic, aching film reminded me that I haven't seen everything after all; that movies are miraculous; and that within me, still, is the kid who used to pull his legs up under him, to be taller, to see more of the screen, who wondered, 'How did they do that?' and at the same time didn't care, being grateful, simply, that there were shadow makers who knew the trick for taking him out of his body, out of his world. Which felt, then and now, like an act of salvation." Amen.

Light on the Bay – White Rock, BC

CHAPTER NINE

January 2–March 15, 2004

Fifteen Songs!, The Blues Album, Dad's 84th Birthday,
Mom and Her iMac, Alex's 75th Birthday, Con's New Song,
"You Might Think It's Easy But It's Not," Dylan/Weezer/Wilco,
Hal David and the Bridge, Our New Agent,
"Where Do Songs Come From?",
The Room with the Spring-Loaded Door, How to Start a Song,
A Song's Progress, "I'm Not Prepared to Say That Something's
Lost," Alchemy, Steve Allen Rocks, The "Instant Editor,"
Chasing the Moving Finish Line, All the Paraphernalia,
Gear Slut Geek Spaz, The Hat on the Beat Before the Snare,
A Reason to Celebrate, Song Number Two,
Bad Day for Songwriting, Excuses?, A Poem, Shine Like You Do,
Another Conversation, The Math, My Tools Are My Instrument,
My First Guitar, When Right Is Wrong, The Winter's Green,
Two Ex-Hippies Get Married, Applejack, Not "Rock" Enough?,
Two for the Show – Randy and Me, Song vs. Arrangement,
The Digital Player Piano, Composing AND Arranging,
A Miracle of Modern Technology, Song #2 Technically Finished,
An Artist Like My Dad, The Trooper Web Team,
Out of the Closet

Friday, January 2, 2004
White Rock, BC
15 SONGS

I want to write fifteen songs.

More to the point, I want to write 15 good songs—which means, based on my not inconsiderable experience, that I need to write 30 songs—half of which will be good and half of which won't. Over the course of my four-decade career in music, I have written or co-written about two hundred songs—half of which were recorded... and half of which weren't—so, in theory, 15 more shouldn't be a problem.

The thing is, though... I've been thinking about writing those 30 songs for nine years and have only completed three of them. If I continue on the same schedule (an average of one song every three years), I'll have my thirty songs finished by 2085. I will be 134 years old. It better be a blues album.

Ninety-eight of the songs I've written or co-written were recorded and released, and about a dozen of those songs were hits. Most of those songs enjoyed an impressive run in the Canadian top ten—a rare feat that most songwriters can only dream of. Despite all of this songwriting success, I have too often found myself unconvinced of my ability to write another great song and, as hard as it is to admit, too afraid to try.

It's January 1, 2004. I'm 53 years old. I'm going to write and record 15 good songs this year.

Sunday, January 4, 2004
White Rock, BC
Happy Birthday, Dad!

It's my Dad's 84th Birthday today. Mickey McGuire is an unbelievably talented artist, craftsman, and perpetual seeker. He is also one of the kindest people I know. I'm proud to be his son. We went to visit him and Mom today. We delivered birthday presents and disassembled their Christmas tree. I shoveled the recently fallen snow from their driveway. Mom made lunch and we all had a few laughs. I showed Mom how to e-mail MP3s from her 17" iMac. She's cool too.

Then we shopped for a family gathering we're hosting tomorrow to commemorate Debbie's Dad's 75th Birthday. Alex still strongly resembles Mr. Clean and the current Pope in his younger days. He spent his life fighting crime and, for the ten years prior to his retirement, he sat at the helm of the Coordinated Law Enforcement Unit, a joint effort of the RCMP and the Vancouver City Police to fight organized crime. It's like having Eliot Ness as a father-in-law. He is uncomfortable with celebrations in his honour, so we're trying to keep this event low key. He's been one of the good guys all his life, and he deserves a party.

Connor was working on a new song today. He recently finished a "trailer" for the film he's doing for school. He's been having a personal renaissance over the Christmas holidays and it's been inspiring to watch him. He says that the new song is going to have a falsetto part in the chorus. I didn't know he could sing falsetto.

This is still about songwriting. It's about my life and how I'll need to fit the creative time into a life I wouldn't change. Last night I wrote half a song, specifically the verse. I suppose, since writing a second and third verse is much harder than writing the first, I wrote slightly less than half a song, but, coming up with verse lyrics, chords, *and* melody is a big step. The song is vaguely about right now. The first line is: "You might think it's easy but it's not."

I recorded it with the built-in mic on my PowerBook, into a barely sussed copy of DP4 (*Digital Performer 4*). I broke a string while doing it. The recording sounds terrible, but the song sounds good.

This morning I asked Connor what kind of music I should be writing. He thought for a minute and said: "Bob Dylan." We talked about Dylan and artists that sound like him. Wilco came up. Connor also said that I could do songs like "O, Girlfriend" by Weezer. He has amazing taste and a great ear for what works and what doesn't. It's unlikely I would have had the focus to hone in on the Dylan/Weezer/Wilco groove this early in the process, but I think that, had I somehow managed to successfully think it through, I would have landed there, or somewhere very close. It gives me important additional context to think ahead to the arrangement stage of these 15 songs.

Monday, January 5, 2004
White Rock, BC
In the Midst of a Third Verse

Did you know that it took Hal David three years to come up with the bridge for "What the World Needs Now..."?

("We don't need another mountain...")

All Burt had to do was move his fingers around on the keyboard...

Monday, January 5, 2004
White Rock, BC
Later that Verse

Jesus...

E-mails from our booking agent and his assistant knocked me right the fuck off course for the last hour. Talk about a change of mental direction.

I *had* to respond to them because it was the very first correspondence from our *new* agent (and agent's assistant) since our introductory meeting with them in December.

Okay, back to the task at hand. I have two good verses, a really good B-verse, and a vague sense of the chorus' melody...

Tuesday, January 6, 2004
White Rock, BC
The First Song Progresses...

Every now and then, someone will ask me:

"Where do the songs come from?"

My songs come from a place deep inside me that I have still not found a dependable way to connect with. They're in a room equipped with a door that is often impossible to open. Sometimes, when I least expect it, the door just opens on its own, allowing concepts and fully blown phrases to flow out and into my consciousness. More often though, the door—when I can find it—requires a significant effort to coax open. Over the years I have cajoled, bribed, begged, wrestled, and attempted to seduce the door. Nothing works consistently. Even if I succeed in opening it, the door is spring-loaded... and pulls hard against me. It can slam shut after allowing only a brief and tantalizing glimpse of a song to escape. Sometimes that's all I get.

I started writing a song five days ago.

I began, this time, by playing and singing something that just felt good. I sang words that made no sense but rolled easily off my tongue. After playing this way for an hour, the shape of a song began to emerge. Its hills and valleys revealed themselves. Afraid that the melody would drift from my consciousness, I launched a program called *Audiocorder* and made a quick and dirty recording, through my computer's built-in microphone, of what I had. A string broke on my guitar just before I hit the record button. The recording sounds terrible, but I have referred back to it several times—careful not to lose the spark.

The next day, the melody was still with me. Had I woken up and not remembered the melody, I would have started the day discouraged. This is a traditional derailment moment for me, and I am very easily derailed.

I sang the melody over and over, much of the time silently, throwing it repeatedly at the door to my muse, my room of inspiration. The door bounced open with the first line:

"You might think it's easy, but it's not."

It fit the melody and phrasing perfectly and was one of those great first lines that invite you into a song. I answered the line from my conscious mind:

"Frankly, this is taking all I've got."

The two lines—one from my subconscious and one from the very top of my head—banged around in my mind for the next few hours. Together they presented an accurate snapshot of my mental state. I searched the vast mess of my mind for further images. I knew what I wanted to write about, and needed passionate images— phrases that sang on their own—before I put my voice to them.

"all the false bravado...
all the fare-thee-well"

That was the door opening again. I grinned. Busted! Here was my muse ridiculing me. I hung up on the last line for several hours.

I tried a few things that seemed forced. I typed brackets around the space where the two lines should be. Like this:

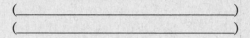

That's how I've always done it. If something does show up, I scribble it in there.

The second verse came on the second day. I was playing and singing the first, incomplete verse and sang right on in to the second:

"I have been here many times before"
"All dressed up and waiting at the door"

Interesting, huh? Guess what door that would be...

The difficult thing about second and third verses is that I feel obliged to mimic the rhyme scheme and phrasing of the first verse. It's something you'll see in virtually everything I've written. It's a habit I'm planning to break a few times within this batch of songs. The image of myself "dressed up and waiting" collected colour in my mind. Later that day, perfectly mirroring its first verse brother, this appeared:

"armed with good intentions,
eager as a child"

The last, still a little awkward, line came quickly:

"I know I will be waiting here a while."

That was it for the day, but I was happy with the way the song was gathering itself together.

A full day passed without songwriting. The music lingered in my head. This morning my groove was more fully on. I played through, and then past, what I had recorded that first day. I pushed out and up from what had become the verses and explored places where a more passionate section might exist. Soon, I had three equally interesting possibilities. Rather than choose one, I went back to the lyrics. My plan, a technique I have used before, was to keep the musical direction that best supported the most inspired lyric. I danced back and forth between the lyric and the melody (and the supporting chords) for an hour.

I had been writing the lyric in a program called iOrganize that auto-saves at five-minute intervals. This morning I found myself moving away from the PowerBook and scribbling notes on a lined pad. My favourite line of the song came next. As the key and my voice lift upward, I sing:

> "I'm not prepared to say that something's lost
> But I want it back, no matter what it costs"

It was a shock to me to read this brutally candid line that perfectly encapsulated my feelings on this return to songwriting. Exhausted, I stepped away from the writing to help Debbie un-decorate our house.

I began to think specifically about the point of this song. What were these unconscious flashes describing? How should I tie this up? I needed to aim my thought processes in a more focused direction. I willed myself into a one-man brainstorming session. One of the participants (I swear that's what it felt like) brought up the fact that what I was trying to do was like alchemy. I was trying to turn everyday random thought into a jewel of concentrated imagery. I carried boxes of Christmas decorations to the basement and riffed on alchemy. "Trying to turn (   ) into gold" uh... "before I'm too old... trying to turn (what?) into gold." I dropped into editor mode, something that should be avoided when trying to create.

"So this will mean that you're writing songs so that you can get a gold record" he/it screeched, "...that you're a mercenary craftsman just trying to make a quick buck."

I made some lunch and tried to forget about songwriting altogether.

Someone told me yesterday that Steve Allen, the creator of (according to legend) more than seven thousand songs... dreamed his songs. The songs were ready for him, full-blown, in the morning when he woke.

Jesus...

Wednesday, January 7, 2004
White Rock, BC
The First Song Winds Up

Tuesday's Adventures Continued...

It took an hour or more to disengage myself from the critical screech of my instant-editor. There is no profit in arguing with it/him—he/it is much smarter and cagier than I could ever hope to be. The only respite is to completely ignore the critical barrage coming from that end of my brain. This is difficult and takes time.

I returned to the song after a long lunch, still embracing the general concept of alchemy but convinced that "gold" would play no part in the afternoon's poetry. Making a not-too-difficult leap, my conscious mind soon landed on "water into wine." It was too pat—too quick and easy a solution. I also didn't like the Jesus-ness of it – the biblical gut grab that I didn't really deserve. Despite my reservations, I let myself continue to float in its vicinity. The difficulty in turning-something-into-something-better was the point of the song. I felt very close.

I went back to the beginning of the B-Verse/Chorus section. Early on I had sung the lyric:

"And the days go by," drawing out the "daaaaaays" because it felt good to break out of the verse phrasing.

The problem was, I have sung that line hundreds of times while working on lyric-free songs. I just enjoy singing those words. The line nearly didn't make it to the song for that reason. I was going to replace it, as I always have in the past, with a more considered, more appropriate collection of words. Instead, I caught myself and sang it again, working thoughtfully toward the next line, which became:

"While I chase this moving finish line"—a chunky, emphasis-on-every-word line containing an appropriately discouraging image.

The second line cemented the first. I was very happy. I began singing the section from "and the days go by" to the end of the unfinished second half. My mostly unintelligible mumblings often concluded, for lack of anything better, with the words: "into wine."

A good hour later, after drifting in and out of the songwriting zone, I sang this straight through:

"As the days go by
I will chase this moving finish line
'Til the stars align
and I turn this lukewarm water into wine"

Some conspiracy of my conscious and unconscious mind had delivered this gift. The independent lines had become a single, beautiful sentence. The religious overtone had softened, and the "lukewarm water" metaphor mirrored my reluctance to return to songwriting.

Buoyed by this small success, the last verse came quicker than the first two. Once again mimicking the first, I wrote:

"You might think it happens naturally
that may be true for others, but not for me
All the paraphernalia
All the rock and roll
cannot help me disinter my soul"

"All the paraphernalia" was one of the first phrases I had written on the lined pad. I loved it and was hoarding it for the last verse. It refers, of course to the ever-growing pile of computer gear and recording equipment that I buy in the hope that it will, some day, some time in the deep dark of night, produce a finished song without me. I have been trying in vain to assemble a working digital equivalent of Steve Allen's brain.

"Disinter" is the word I wanted, suggesting an "un-burying" of my soul—but it took some time for me to get past "exhume" and "resurrect"—the former being disgusting, the latter returning Jesus to a song where he clearly wasn't welcome.

The phone rang. Connor was leaving school and bringing his film and television team to our house to shoot the last few scenes of their film project. The dining room table, where two of the scenes were to take place, was covered in Christmas decorations. That was the end of songwriting for the day.

Songwriting – White Rock, BC

TODAY...

Today I drifted in and around songwriting. For the little I feel as though I did, it seems like I may be finished writing the song.

This morning, I was at the point where I needed to scope the entire song and consider what, if anything, to do next. I played what I had over and over. This exercise revealed that there were a few rough parts that I repeatedly stumbled on. The obvious problem area was the last two lines of the first verse, the other was the phrasing of: "I will chase this moving finish line."

I purposely left the odd timing of this line. I wanted to break away from the phrasing in the verses. I was hoping for a choppy, staccato delivery, but when I played it, it just seemed awkward. Because I knew what I was looking for, I bore down on making it work. After a while I had added two extra chords under the line, each one pushed a bit to emphasize the staccato feel I was looking for. It made a big difference.

I played the song for Debbie several times. She said she "loved" the song and helped me find a tempo that worked better with the words. She told me that when I played the song at this slightly slower speed, and sang it a little less aggressively, my voice made her "go all Jell-O-ey." Debbie is my perfect audience. I told her that if no one likes these fifteen songs but her, I would still consider the project a success.

Although I didn't realize it at the time, the very last thing I did to the song was to add the last line to the first verse. It turns out that I had a much better sense of the song after finishing the B-verse/Chorus and the completing line fell out of my lips while playing through the song. Here's the last bit now:

"All the false bravado
All the fare thee well" (which I had for four days)

"All this lying does not serve me well" (the final puzzle piece.)

After adding those words to the song, I still had a nagging feeling that something else was needed. For one thing, I was convinced that the song was only about a minute and a half long. After buck-rigging a mic clip for my little mini-disc mic with a blue rubber band, I fired up *DP4* and recorded just the guitar track. Without a space for a solo the song was three and a half minutes long. It took half an hour for me to accept that I might be done.

Anything can happen to a song. It might be re-worked when it's being arranged or when it's being recorded, but the fundamental personality of the song has to be fully formed so that, if I did want to make changes later, I wouldn't have to repeat this five-day process to get my groove back on. I backed away from the song cautiously.

After adding a slight chorus effect and a bit of EQ to improve the recording of my amateur guitar playing, I record-enabled a second track in *DP4* to sing on. The program threw me an alert box informing me that I could not proceed and that I should try removing some effects from the tracks. This knocked me seriously off course. Pissed-off that I was unable to complete the most basic of recording tasks, I logged on to Digidesign's site to investigate *Pro Tools LE 6.2.2*, a likely alternative to DP4, which I was beginning to blame for my problems. Over an hour later, when I had wound down from a serious A-Type geek-out, I remembered that I had a small digital recorder—a Roland BR8—upstairs. Connor uses the thing so much I had forgotten I owned it. The BR8 is the perfect songwriting tool—simple, quick, and dirty. I ran upstairs to do the recording. All the Shure mics and mic stands were at Nikhil's house, where Connor's band Anger and After rehearse. The little mini-disc mic wouldn't work. My beautiful $1000.00 AKG mic wouldn't work either because of its XLR jack.

I packed it in for the day at 3:00 and went back to investigating the new version of *Pro Tools*, which, I was surprised and happy to see, now supports *Rewire*—an interface for the amazing *Reason*, a "virtual studio rack" and recording environment that I have been experimenting with lately. I then did some research on *SampleTank*, a virtual sampler that contains more than 1500 patches and plays nice with *Pro Tools*. This software would let me turn a midi keyboard into at least that many different instruments. I feel as though a visit to the Annex/Pro shop is imminent. This, by the way, is *far* more dangerous than a visit to A&B Sound.

Thursday, January 8, 2004
White Rock, BC
A No-Songwriting Day

Today I did no songwriting.

Debbie and I drove into Vancouver this morning and had some fun. Debbie went to Chintz & Company, arguably the best fabric store in the city, while I went to the Annex/Pro audio shop where I enjoyed an audio geek-out with Bryon Low, arguably the smartest audio geek in the city. My plan was to purchase an upgrade to *Pro Tools 6.2.2*, which I did, and to look into buying *SampleTank*. Bryon is going to NAMM next weekend. NAMM is a huge trade show hosted by the International Music Products Association and attended by thousands of musicians and audio freaks every year. Some day I'd like to go. Bryon suggested that I wait 'til after the NAMM show to make any gear decisions, in case something new and amazing is announced there. I also went to a downtown Mac store where I purchased a Macally keyboard, a Kensington Expert mouse (which is actually a trackball), an iCurve Plexiglas laptop stand, and a USB hub. These purchases will effectively turn my laptop into a desktop and make long hours of either typing or digital audio shuttling much easier on the wrists and back. Debbie and I then met up at Chintz and made our way back to White Rock. I have spent the rest of the day installing software and generally geeking in a satisfied and contented manner. New gear always makes me hopeful.

Connor worked on *his* song today, sitting beside me here in the den. He's got *Reason* up and running and was working on a string line in the Matrix sequencer. It's taking him some time, but he's shaking the program down pretty well. The finished product sounded great.

Tomorrow I will hook up the Mbox to *Pro Tools* and record my new, as yet untitled, song.

Monday, January 12, 2004
White Rock, BC
Monday Morning Coming Down

The weekend has been difficult, thanks to the return of the flu/cold that showed up right at the end of the last tour. My brain is not functioning in any useful way—my eyes won't stop watering and there are piles of Kleenex everywhere I look.

On Friday, I successfully installed a whack load of software and, despite my congested nose and throat, recorded a workable version of the new song.

Connor is often sitting beside me as I work at my computer. He has been working on an arrangement for a new song—a moody, angst-ridden love song called "Bleed the Runway." I installed *Pro Tools* on his machine as well and, between us, we worked out inter-face glitches and other potential roadblocks. These moments of shoulder-to-shoulder, real-world cooperation with my son bring me a lot of joy. Watching his talent unfold and being able to participate in the process, even in a small way, is a gift I will always be thankful for.

Friday evening, Debbie and I began our weekend film festival with *Out of Time* (dumb but fun) and *Seabiscuit* (wonderfully old-fash-ioned and moving). Connor worked at the computer, watching the movies through the den window. After *Seabiscuit*, I rejoined him in the den/recording studio, where he helped me with a drum groove that I started building in *Reason*:

"Wait... there's an open hat there on the beat before the snare."

On Saturday, Debbie went out shopping, looking for off-season bargains on outdoor furniture, leaving me to rest and hopefully shake my cold. I decided to surprise her by installing the new Panther operating system on her PowerBook. Two hours later, I was still trying to return her computer to working order. The installation had stalled-out... seizing up in the middle of a process that left me with neither a new or old functional system in the computer.

Connor continued work on his song, adding digital audio recording to the imported *Reason* track. That night, while Connor entertained Megan and Anna downstairs, Debbie and I continued our weekend film festival with *Northfork* (beautiful, quirky, and affecting) and the amazing *Assassination Tango* (I *love* Robert Duvall). After the movies, I hooked up the Oxygen 8 keyboard to the M Box and interfaced it with *Reason* for the first time. *Reason* is the most amazing music-making tool I've ever seen. In one straightforward program it offers a collection of tools and resources that would otherwise require massive amounts of time and money to assemble. All of the samples seem useful, which is not the case with other sample collections. I found an organ that went well with my drum groove and fooled around with some chords. When I added some shimmering strings to the organ track, Connor looked over.

"That sounds awesome," he said.

It sounded like a song by a band from Britian, "Spiritualized," almost religious in its solemn beauty. I played it over and over, liking it more and more. It's what I will try to develop today.

I spent a very happy Sunday visiting furniture stores with Debbie. We later met up with Connor, Simon, and Derek, who were returning from downtown, and went for green curry and Pad Thai at Leila Thai here in White Rock last night.

This morning I made some notes about the crashed computer and sent them to the tech at the local computer store. I just called and found out that I can't bring it in until at least tomorrow. They suggested that I try "zapping the P-Ram"—so I'll try that.

I feel like shit and am not much in the mood for creating, but these are the kind of obstacles that I must learn to overcome.

Monday, January 12, 2004
White Rock, BC
Bad Day for Songwriting

Computer software tools are not like their analog counterparts. In the digital world, your tools can change (or lose) their ability to function without exhibiting any obvious signs of having altered. This can happen at any time, without warning. It happened to me today.

Everything worked perfectly on Saturday, but not today. Nothing had been moved, changed, or damaged. When I set up to do some singing, I could see the bouncing volume meters but could hear nothing.

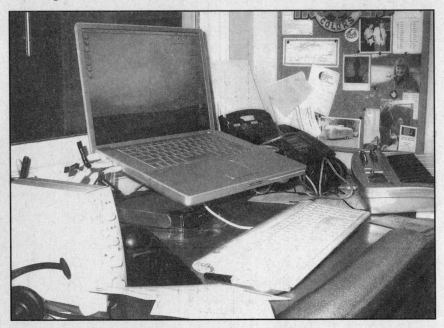

My Recording Studio – White Rock, BC

In the morning, I had noodled out a very cool melody for the "Spiritualized" idea that I started on Saturday night. I was excited about singing the part, but when I fired up the necessary software, I hit the above-described brick wall.

I tried everything to get things rolling again. This was one of those computer glitches that often turns out to have been caused by operator error, but I was damned if I could figure out what mistake I had made. I patched and re-patched, double-checked the mic and the hardware, and tested each piece of software independently. I narrowed the cause down to either cabling or software. Since the cabling hadn't been touched, the software seemed the likely culprit.

Hours went by without success. Finally, embarrassed, but forced to suck it in, I called Bryon. I explained to him what was happening.

His response was quick and authoritative:

"I have no idea what that is, Ra. You're going to have to call Digi about that one." (Digi is Digidesign, the California company that makes *Pro Tools*, my digital recording software) "Give me a call back and let me know what it was, OK?"

On my own again, but oddly happy that Bryon was also stumped, I unplugged everything from my computer and hooked it up to Connor's to see if it would work there. I fired up his copy of *Pro Tools* and the incoming microphone blipped the bright green line in the meter. Everything was working as advertised. I then plugged everything back into my PowerBook, turned it all on, and found that everything was now working perfectly!

I don't know why it worked with those same cables in place on Friday and Saturday, or why it stopped working today. As a result of my day's efforts, all I have learned for sure is that there is some serious USB voodoo that I should keep a close eye on. By the time I had finished with this digital hell, it was past four o'clock. Connor was home from school, Debbie was back from shopping, and I was completely exhausted and pissed off.

Saturday, January 17, 2004
White Rock, BC
Excuses?

Almost a week has gone by and I have not finished another song. My real life has risen up and consumed the time and brain-space that I had hoped to use for songwriting. It's my tendency to gravitate away from the writing at the slightest excuse, but I'm convinced that at least 70 percent of what I've been doing was necessary.

The most recent focus of my energy has been the return of the Trooper touring machine. It has lumbered awkwardly out of hibernation and has begun stumbling, with increasing strength, toward the Spring tour. We begin 2004 with a new west coast agent. Although we still work with the SL Feldman and Associates agency (SL himself being the band's manager for years), our responsible agent has changed. This change has necessitated twice the work I would expect to be doing at this time of the year. We are starting over at many levels. Change, as always, is both exciting and exhausting.

I'm forced to think in depth about Trooper again, and being reminded of its importance, I exhumed a complex Trooper-related project that was put away in early December. I have spent the last few days sitting in front of this computer, wearing my telephone headset, talking, typing, and preparing the band for another successful year of touring.

I have not used all the intervening time for business. Some of it—the best part—went to my family—a not-unselfish agenda that brought me the most joy.

The melody that I began in the last post is still with me. It has developed a second section where the chords double up and the structure suggests an R&B approach. I've been singing it to myself and have sat down with the acoustic guitar a few times to flesh it out. I have all the melody and chords, and I may have found the perfect verses in my pile of lyrics. I am hoping that a chorus-like lyric will develop soon. I know it will contain the word "miracle," but that's all I know for now...

Wednesday, January 21, 2004
White Rock, BC
Song #2 Rounds the Bend

This morning I kicked around the house, occasionally revisiting the new song, and coming up with absolutely nothing. I loved the music I had put together in *Reason* but was drawing a blank on the words. The word "miracle" had popped up a few days ago and it seemed appropriate to the music, so I figured I had a good starting point. As the day rolled by, I realized that I was wrong. Any actual discussion of miracles, no matter what direction I approached it from, seemed overblown and stereotypical.

It is disturbingly easy for me to sink into a writer's-blocked state of self-loathing and hopelessness. During these achingly painful interludes, I am absolutely convinced that I have never written a good song and that any effort expended on writing a new one is a total waste of time. Brain functions scramble. Any semblance of orderly thought is subverted. I find myself thinking in half-thoughts, quarter-thoughts, even. My instant-editor not only hates the ideas as they come, he hates the place they come from. As I wandered, aimless, from room to room, I could feel my creative mind seizing up.

I decided to have a shower. Knowing for certain that I was escaping the creative pressure cooker took the edge off. Clarity returned. My first revelation was that I needed to lay back on my approach to the lyrics. The song has a relaxed swing to it, and the words and concepts I was throwing around were too tense and structured. I needed something more loose and natural. Before I left the den, I looked up a poem that I had sent to Debbie on a recent tour. One of the approaches I had been considering for the word "miracle" was "you are my miracle." The lyric was to be for Debbie, but I couldn't wrestle it down. Still on that train of thought, I read the poem. I could feel that it would work: not the words in the poem, but the idea of it. It's about being away from home and trying to fill the empty space of her:

I gather the few small moments that define my day

A glimpse of colour here
a reflected glow there
Or, sometimes, the rare, surprising yellow-gold of pure light
A smudge of understanding,
Or the fragile flame of faith

I assemble them carefully at the temporary centre of my life
And with that unwilling kindling
I try to coax a flame

I add what I can from my dwindling reserve of passion

I fan it hopefully

I pay so much for such a small return
I can make a spark but I can't convince it to burn

Nothing can

Shine like you do
"Shine Like You Do," although not intended as one, is a great

title for a song. "Shine" might be even better. As the hot water beat down on me I sang those words to the tune I had been imagining. I relaxed into it. The whole thing was working as a piece. Clean, I returned to the *Reason* track. I sang some of the poem's words, trying to drop them comfortably into the groove. "I pay so much for such a small return" became "I pay so much for nothing." Soon I was a songwriter again. When Connor arrived home from school with Simon, I couldn't wait to sing it to them. Later, Debbie smiled broadly when she heard it.

"It sounds a bit like R&B..."

"Yeah," I said happily.

Sunday, January 25, 2004
White Rock, BC
An Essay and Another Conversation

A study released on December 23, 2003, by the Ottawa-based Canadian Policy Research Networks (CPNR) concluded that Canadians work an average of 1,790 hours per year. I was away from home, on tour with Trooper, for 112 days in 2003. That's a total of 2688 hours—898 hours more than the Canadian average.

"So what the fuck is this?"

"Not sure."

"Looks like the start of an elaborate excuse."

"No, I don't think so."

"What else could it be?"

"It's... it's an exercise."

It could be argued that 672 of those hours—a number arrived at by multiplying an average of six hours of sleep by the amount of days away—should be subtracted from my total working hours. In response, I could point out that, since that "average sleep time" usually begins at three a.m.; not at home with my wife and son, but in a different hotel—in a different city—every night, and is usually interrupted in some way—at the beginning of the rest of the world's conventional workday—four hours later, whether I like it or not—and since some of that average sleep time is accumulated in two-hour increments—that some, if not all, of that 672 hours should also be counted as time on the job.

But for the purposes of this exercise, I'll subtract those 672 hours—leaving 2021 hours of touring work in 2003. By the end of my touring season, using this equation, I have already worked 231 hours more than the average Canadian.

"Oh, ferfucksake."

"No, seriously... I just want to do the math and see how it works out."

"You've spent over an hour on it already!"

"I'm really bad at math."

"Right... so what's the point?"

"Well, if I work more hours than the average guy just while I'm on tour..."

"Uh huh, yeah... and...?"

That same average Canadian, after work and six hours of sleep a night, is left with 4780 hours a year to devote to his family, his home, his friends, and himself. After my time away from home and the six hours of sleep a night when I'm at home, left with 4554 hours (226 hours *less* than the average Canadian) to devote to my family, my home, my friends, and myself... and the business of managing and overseeing the business that is Trooper.

A conservatively estimated four hours of Trooper-related business a day subtracts 1012 additional hours a year from the time I have for my family, my home, my friends, and myself, bringing that total to 3542 hours—1238 hours less than the average Canadian.

"You get it now?"

"Too many numbers."

"The point is, everything that I have to do, my whole life that isn't my touring work, has to fit into the spaces left between the tours. And when I figure in all the other Trooper-related work, I end up with 2721 hours less than the average guy. No wonder I can't find time to write!"

"Feeling sorry for yourself?"

"No—okay, maybe, but there's a serious point to it though. It's not just whining."

"I know."

"You do?"

"Yeah, now get back to work."

Wednesday, January 28, 2004

White Rock, BC
Excellent Day

An excellent day of writing. Love the song. Nearly done.

Friday, January 30, 2004
White Rock, BC
Progress

The melody, chords, and arrangement for "Shine Like You Do" are done. The lyric could be done if I wanted to settle for what I have at this point, which I don't. It's down to three lines that I cannot seem to nail. Have I mentioned that Hal David took three years to come up with the lyric for the bridge of "What the World Needs Now"?

Sunday, February 1, 2004
White Rock, BC
My Tools Are My Instrument

There was a guitar in our house on Muirfield Drive. It wasn't an expensive guitar and it retained the same set of dead strings for its lifetime. I would pick it up occasionally and plunk hopefully. The first song I learned on it, at 14 in 1964, was "The Rise and Fall of Flingel Bunt" by the Shadows. I played the whole song (more correctly, that part I had learned, which was just the introduction) on the first four notes of the big E string. Soon I had worked out "Ferry 'Cross the Mersey" by Gerry and the Pacemakers (years later I interviewed Gerry Marsden on TV) and "Get Together" by Jesse Colin Young and the Youngbloods. These songs had chords and were, subsequently, more challenging. I'm not sure if I knew at the time that I was learning these songs "left-handed." From the start, I had picked up the guitar and strummed naturally with my left hand, making the chords with my right, which was wrong.

My right-handed younger brother, Gary, began playing the guitar and, within a week or two, left me behind in the musical dust. At the time, I was singing in my first rock band, and I soon forgot whatever I had learned on the instrument. It wasn't until three years later that I had the audacity to purchase a Gibson SG Jr. and a huge Ampeg amp from Bill Lewis Music on West Broadway and begin playing "rhythm guitar" to Brian Smith's lead guitar in The Winter's Green. My short-lived guitar-playing career was a massive fake-fest. I learned only enough to get by and barely managed that. Nonetheless, there I was one evening in the 60s, onstage in the Agridome (the largest venue in Vancouver prior to the construction of the Pacific Coliseum), backing up the Beach Boys—and playing electric guitar.

It was not long thereafter that I dropped out of straight society, and The Winter's Green. I took an acoustic guitar along on the road with the"Traveling Arts and Crafts Faire," a mobile version of the hippy-centric Renaissance Faires that I co-organized with my friend, graphic artist Ron Sayer. I played a bit of guitar at the Faires—mostly three-chord country songs. Near the end of the traveling Faire, my traveling companion and I concluded that the hippy life was not for us and decided to get married.

I hooked up with Smitty again once the hippy dream had tarnished. We put a band together that featured Norm Roth (the guy I sold my Gibson SG to) on rhythm guitar, so once again I was just a singer. From then on... through High Country, Applejack, and, finally, Trooper... I played no guitar in the band and very little guitar at home.

Occasionally, throughout my Trooper years, I would hammer out a song in my living room and bring it to the band. Most of these self-penned songs—presented to the band on an acoustic guitar as I struggled amateurishly with the chords—were turned down cold. Others received a quick and half-hearted arrangement and were played live a few times before they were quietly dropped from the set. The criticism was usually that the songs weren't "rock" enough. These criticisms mostly came from Smitty. Since the two of us wrote most of Trooper's songs together, he had the weight of history behind his approach. In fairness, my songs may have sucked: it's difficult for me to know. At any rate, I was never convinced enough of their value to fight him on that point.

The exception to this general rule was "Two for the Show." I presented this song at a rehearsal that Randy Bachman was attending as our producer. He loved it and actively participated in the creation of its arrangement. He had heard through my limited guitar technique and recognized the bones of a good song. He strapped on one of

Smitty's guitars and worked out some interesting arrangement details, leading the band through the process. When we recorded the song, Randy created and played the signature lead guitar solo. The song was the title track of our second album and became a big hit.

There's the "song" and there's the "arrangement" of the song. It's a very important distinction, and one that I make to new songwriters all the time. "This Flight Tonight," as recorded by Nazareth, was written by Joni Mitchell. Her version, with its sparse acoustic arrangement, presents the tune as a witty and wryly humorous folk song. Nazareth's arrangement of the song transformed it into a powerful rock and roll hit record. "Love Hurts," as recorded by Nazareth, was written by Boudleaux Bryant, for Roy Orbison, in the 60s. The original recorded arrangement is entirely different from Nazareth's, but both songs were hits: one, a thunderous Big White Rock Ballad; the other, a tender lost-love lament. How the song is presented is critical to its perception and acceptance by the audience, even when that audience is your own band.

The music that supports and "frames" the song—the arrangement—conjures atmosphere and associations and triggers instinctive and cultural responses. It is an important part of what the listener ultimately "hears."

My primitive guitar skills produce the kind of playing you may have heard on early Hank Williams records. I strum well—in a folky, country way. A good example of this strumming shows up on "Thin White Line," the only other Ra McGuire song to be recorded by Trooper. Although Smitty actually plays the acoustic guitar part on that record, you can hear the only kind of playing that I can manage convincingly.

With neither the time nor the inclination to purchase and learn to play a guitar set up for a left-handed player, with the strings strung in the opposite order to that which I had grown used to over the years, I was frustrated in my songwriting. For a while I pretended that I was going to learn piano, but got no further than my first set of finger exercises. Then, in the mid-90s, I bought my first digital sequencer.

A sequencer is the digital equivalent of a player piano: those pianos that appeared to play themselves, but in fact were powered by a foot pump and an ingenious paper "piano roll." Player piano rolls were "cut" by a pianist who performed on a special piano that cut holes in the paper roll that corresponded with the notes he or she played. When the player piano played back these rolls, the holes triggered and played the appropriate notes.

A sequencer (which is a piece of computer software) allows you to "cut the roll" digitally, but, more important, it allows you to track multiple performances of what sounds like virtually any instrument: piano, strings, organ, drums, guitar, sound effects—and manipulate those performances, with the help of the computer, until you are satisfied with them. Suddenly, I was able to record a complete band arrangement for a song *while I was composing it*. The computer allowed me to create credible instrumental performances that were limited only by my patience and the time it took to carefully manipulate the digitally generated notes.

It has taken 'til now for this dream to become a serious reality for me. I wrote "Cold Water," a beautiful song that Trooper performs regularly in its set, using Opcode's *Vision* sequencer and Digidesign's *Pro Tools*. I presented the band with a finished arrangement that is virtually the same as the one we play live. Although the presentation and rehearsals were not a total slam-dunk, I had more support for this song than any other I've presented.

I have graduated now to the combination of Propellerhead's *Reason* and a much-improved version of *Pro Tools*. What I have been doing is creating the arrangements while the song grows: I began this latest song ("Shine Like You Do") by building a drum track. I knew the groove I wanted; I picked out the drums and decided when and how they would be hit; I added a melancholy Hammond organ to the finished drum track playing simple three note chords; I used *Reason*'s sequencer to move the misplayed notes into their proper places. I then created a soaring string line that I copied and pasted into the appropriate locations. The opening melody—my favourite part of the song—was picked out casually with my little Oxygen 8 keyboard balanced on my lap. I played it over and over 'til I loved all the notes. Then I moved a few of them around 'til they were positioned perfectly. I sang all three of the background vocal harmonies in *Pro Tools*; I cut and pasted the results. I have sung a few "scratch" vocals and it sounds great. The words could be a bit better—more spontaneous-sounding. They need to sound like I just thought of them, but they don't—quite—yet. When I'm done, I'll have a complete arrangement recorded for the song.

Although this approach extends the time needed to complete the songwriting, it dramatically reduces the time that was once spent arranging and recording the finished track. Most of the important creative decisions are made by the time the song has revealed itself. More important, as the track develops an atmosphere, the song is encouraged to follow on in that direction.

In the old days, I would self-consciously present my songs, strumming feebly on the guitar and singing hopefully. Now I can play someone an MP3 that sounds very much like a finished recorded track. It's a miracle of modern technology.

Monday, February 16, 2004
White Rock, BC
Big Day

Ah, yes... two whole weeks of near-frantic activity, only part of which was songwriting.

Today, though, I'm going to finish "Shine." I'm going to put the pants on this turkey.

But first, I have to call Trooper's new travel agent about the fax I got back from the Air Canada Group Express Leads Desk about the possibility of working with the Conventions Desk to upgrade our suddenly restrictive travel booking situation, and fill out and send in Debbie's Mom's rebate form for the new printer we got her on the weekend, and eat my McCann's Irish Oatmeal, and have a shower.

Tuesday, February 17, 2004
White Rock, BC
LATER...

I am technically finished the song—all the lyrics, melody, and chords. Whoohoo! I have sung a serviceable vocal track and invented a cool orchestration for the bridge, which is also now recorded in *Reason*. The bridge was one of the things that ground me to a halt a week ago. I have one now. I still need to add a guitar part or two, maybe some big chords at the end. The track is a great amalgam of things I love.

Tomorrow I'll be hooking up Shirley's ADSL for her and showing her how to send an e-mail and surf the mighty Web. I'll also probably continue today's long conversation with my partner about our 2004 touring schedule. I hope I also have time to write and record some guitar...

Monday, March 15, 2004
White Rock, BC
More Ketchup...
Morning – White Rock, BC

There's a strong possibility that the redesigned "Official Trooper Web Site" will be launched in the next few days. This giant project has been in the works for many months and, since the only acknowledgements on the site will be tucked away on the "Credits and Site Submissions" page, I'd like to sincerely thank Heather Uhl and her husband, Brian, for their untiring and brilliantly successful battle against php, http, and a veritable mountain of Trooper-related data. Recently, the two of them have been virtually sleeping under their desks, trading sleep for more time to wrestle with the large and often uncooperative digital beast. The rough plan was to launch the site at the beginning of the first Trooper tour of 2004. Technically speaking, this is still the beginning of that tour. Thank you, Heather and Brian, the new site is awesome.

Eight years ago, Tim Hewitt and I started playing around with html. At the time, in 1996, the only people online were geeks and freaks. There was no Google, no eBay, no Amazon.com. Web pages took so long to load that it was smart to plan a collection of small non-computer-related tasks so there would be something to do while you waited. You could brew a cup of coffee in the time it took to load the first Trooper site that Tim and I constructed. Making that first Web site was difficult work in a strange new medium full of geek-speak and voodoo, but the process was rewarding, and it was exciting to pioneer a completely new, and not a little exotic, frontier. We watched as other bands fired up their own sites. The "links page" became an important lifeline between these new, often isolated, outposts as they came to life on the Web. I created hundred of GIFs and JPEGs—I loved working with the convoluted hypertext interface, but most of all, I loved making the graphics.

I have always wanted to be an artist like my Dad and slowly, over time, my secret Web site work brought me the skills I needed to qualify me for the "Graphic Designer/Art Director" job that I was never technically hired to do. My partner, Smitty, came to understand the value of the Trooper site, and began to appreciate the work I did to make that site look good. His support, and the work that Tim and I put in, got the Official Trooper Web Site off the ground.

Just at the point where the maintenance of the site became too much for Tim and me, we fluked on the perfect Web meister. We had no way of knowing at the time that Heather could handle a job as big as the site's management had become, but she agreed to take on our fledgling site and with incredible patience, careful planning, and a lot of hard work has turned it into an impressive online focal point for all things Trooper. With the help of a small and changing staff, she has hammered together a site that will now stand with the best online. I am proud to say that I have been part of that small staff.

For the past few months, I have been corresponding daily with the team about the look and feel of the new site—FTP-ing graphics and assembling a real-time, but offline, mock-up. I was always unhappy with the design of the current site, but at the time of its creation I was overwhelmed with other Trooper work and it became merely the best Trooper site that time would allow. This time around, I suggested that we start planning months in advance so that we could give the design the attention it deserved. For all our preparation, we were all still surprised by what an enormous job it became.

My mother wrote me an e-mail today, excited about the imminent launch. On the subject of my involvement, she suggested, sweetly, "Credit should be given where credit is due." So I'm coming out of the closet on this "Graphic Designer/Art Director" thing this morning. I do get a mention on the "Credits and Site Submissions" page, as "Photoshop God" and, for people who visit the site, that's all they need to know. But, thanks in part to my Mom's encouragement, I decided that those of you who have been following along with my "2004 Songwriting Adventure" deserved an honest explanation for the month-long gap in my writing. The new site has been a rewarding collaboration—it's work that I love and I'm very proud of what we have all accomplished. Now I'm going to try to relax for a few days.

Sunset over the Pier – White Rock, BC

Sunset over the Pier – White Rock, BC

CHAPTER TEN

March 22–October 18, 2004

Fred Penner Sings with Trooper, Peter Jordan,
The Singing MLA, Sardines in Saskatoon, Throat Trouble,
Dazed and Confused in Ottawa, The National Gallery,
Going Walkabout, The Wok Inn in Kingston,
Shwartz's in Montreal, A+A's White Rock Show, Un-Sexy Women,
The Southern Shore of Nova Scotia,
With Our Scottish Brothers on The Rock,
Eighty Pounds of Lobster, Annoyed and Aggravated,
Grounded in Edmonton, The Writing Room, The F-Bomb,
The Fredericton Fiasco, F-Word Update, 11 Hours Sleep in 4 Days,
110,000 People Since June, A Trooper Resurgence,
Debbie and I and the Temptations, Dad Visits Hospital – Twice,
Harry Clarke McGuire, A Turn for the Better,
Love-Fests and Sell-Outs, Ra & Myles Sing the Blues,
The Kuujjuaq Trip, All You Can Drink for Free,
Maclean's Photo Shoot, Lederhosen, Mikey Leaves the Group,
Plane Party, Truck Break-In

Monday, March 22, 2004
Driving Across the Prairies
Heading Home...

We met Fred Penner in 2001 in Rankin Inlet, Nunavut, where we participated in a two-day high north concert with him, Kim Mitchell, and Farmer's Daughter. Fred taught us phrases in Inuktuk, so that when we walked on stage I could say: "kovia sook peecee," which means "are you having fun?" Two years later, we met again at the Blueberry Festival in St. George's, Newfoundland. That night he came onstage and rhythm-jammed with Gogo and Frankie on, among other things, a galvanized garbage can. We parted that night promising to get together the next time we were in Winnipeg.

Last Friday, in Winnipeg, we met with Fred in the afternoon and worked out a rock arrangement of "The Cat Came Back." In the middle of our show, we brought him on and the sold-out crowd, for whom his appearance was a total surprise, went ballistic. Every single person in the audience instantly became an uninhibited child, blissfully singing through a large and guileless smile. During and after the song, the room shook with a roar of love and respect. Once again, Trooper was experiencing one of those transcending moments that make the work we do so magical. The big fun for me, and the rest of the band, was hanging out with Fred Penner in the dressing room after the show. I am very happy to report that he is exactly as you would hope him to be: a sincere and thoughtful gentleman with a great love of people of all ages. I am also happy to say that he clearly had as much fun that night as we did.

We met Peter Jordan in Edmonton, Alberta, last year when he was filming a segment for his award-winning TV show *It's a Living*. The interaction between Peter, a charmingly unassuming guy with a great sense of humour, and the boys in the band made for some hilarious moments that became part of an hour-long special episode that may be up for a Gemini Award this year. On Friday afternoon, in Winnipeg, Peter came by with a film crew to shoot footage for his final show. Once again the sparks flew. Although we were supposedly working from a prepared script, we all drifted into some pretty funny territory. As always, we'll have to wait 'til the show airs to see what got kept and what got cut. I hope they keep the part where Peter turns around and says: "Oh look, it's Fred Penner!"

Last night we played the huge "Kamoniwannalaya" party in the Prairieland Exhibition Centre in Saskatoon for a sold-out crowd of 3000 of the drunkest university students we have ever had the pleasure (and occasional spine-tingling terror) to see accumulated before us. This was the Brahma Bull of audiences—so over-clocked on alcohol, drugs, testosterone, and estrogen that it required serious wrestling and superior balance to keep on top of it. The intense energy and unabashed adulation translated into a crowd that teetered on the razor's-edge of chaos. At the front of the stage, I was pushed, pulled, stroked, and caressed and, looking out into the throng, I could see that energy telegraphing back into the darkness. Afterwards, collapsed in the dressing room, I recalled the final scene of a brilliant novel, wherein the disgusting and totally unlikable protagonist mixes up a scent that engenders love in all that smell it. After an intentional over-application of this perfume—our hero is literally torn to pieces by an adoring crowd.

Rear view—Near Melfort, Saskatchewan

We've been out for eleven days in western Canada. We played nine shows. Canmore, the first one, was once again a sold-out, jam-packed party of a gig. Back Alley in Calgary the next night was not jam-packed but still fun. Our triumphant return to Reds at the West Ed Mall the next night was another SRO love-fest, during which a local MLA joined us onstage to sing a short version of "Raise A Little Hell". The whole bit was hugely funny and filmed by the local TV station, CFRN. I got an e-mail from the MLA yesterday saying that the piece they aired was "hilarious." Thanks to Graham Neil for putting that together. And thanks to the amazing Edmonton fans for another night of rock and roll nirvana. The next night, we played the *over*-sold Briar 2004 show at CNH Place in Saskatoon, Saskatchewan. Hours before show time, the hall was filled to capacity with 5000 people, while another 2500 waited outside in the sub-zero weather. Since the unlucky overflow snaked right around the building, blocking *all* of the fire exits, the show's organizers decided to let them in too. Packed like sardines into that incredibly humid hall, the roaring crowd ebbed and flowed like a syncopated sea against the stage. It was an amazing show.

I woke up on Monday with a bad cold, exacerbating already troublesome throat problems caused by the extremely low humidity on the prairies at this time of year. Typically I can work through this dryness by running my hotel room shower for steam, and by doing extra vocal exercises through the day. A cold, though, adds an additional, and uncontrollable, element to the problem—leaving me powerless to do anything but watch and wait for the symptoms to pass.

My voice suffered noticeably in Lloydminster that night and two days later in Regina. Thanks to the cold's unwelcome interaction with my vocal chords, those two nights were difficult and painful for me. My only memories are of fighting with a throat that I no longer controlled. I coughed and hacked and moaned vocal exercises in every moment that I wasn't singing. By Brandon, Manitoba, my voice was coming back to me. The sold-out crowd helped to push me back into the groove and my mid-range finally, and thankfully, returned to me. The next morning, I was on the phone with Fred Penner, organizing our Winnipeg rehearsal.

Prairie parking lot

I've written this as we make our way west, homebound across the still partially snow-covered prairies. Tomorrow is the first day of spring, but it was -20 in Winnipeg the other night. I'm very happy to be returning to White Rock, "the Fish and Chips Capital of the World," and the place where my wonderful family waits for me.

Saturday, May 22, 2004
Ottawa, Ontario

It started raining just before I did my live TV interview this afternoon. The interview was outside, next to the big outdoor stage we're playing on tonight. I was told that if there's lightning, the show will be canceled.

On the road again.

I'm dazed and confused—comin' and goin', not knowin' where my groove is yet. Not here, not there. The usual. Show's at 9:30—gotta jet.

Sunday, May 23, 2004
Leaving... Ottawa, Ontario

We went to the National Gallery this morning before lobby call. The Group of Seven, Claude Monet, Alex Colville, Pablo Picasso, Vincent van Gogh, Peter Paul Rubens. It is, of course, a world-class gallery with world-class art. As always, the visit has lifted my spirit and restored my soul. Last night's show was incredible too. Big, pro stage; thousands of people going nuts. There was also some action-packed Trooper golf-cart action on the site after the crowd had cleared. I'm calmer today, and happy.

Tuesday, May 25, 2004
Kingston, Ontario
Going Walkabout

I don't shave. Truthfully, I don't shower either. I get up, gather a few things and then walk out into the city—sometimes aimlessly, and sometimes with a vague purpose: a lanyard for my new laminate, some DVD media, a book, a CD, a movie. I can fill a day wandering and watching, taking the faint pulse of the world.

"Going walkabout": I've called it that for years. I've wandered lost, a gold-card vagrant, through every major city in Canada and many of its towns and municipalities. I walk down streets and lanes, cutting kitty-corner, as-the-crow-flies across parking lots and unfenced abandoned spaces. I walk quickly where only cars are allowed, on thin dirt paths next to roaring concrete overpasses. I consort with street kids and Holt Renfrew Sales Associates. I am nothing and, especially, nobody.

A disturbing thing happened today. I carefully grazed three bookstores and two music stores and didn't buy a single book or CD. I'm going to have to think about what that means.

I ended today's cruise of Kingston at the Wok In. The warm glow of my "dinner number 1"—tender chicken in a sweet Cambodian red curry sauce with basil, lemon grass, lime juice and, I think, anise—is still with me back here at the HoJo.

Last night, our first night off, I rented two excellent movies from the ever-dependable Classic Video shop down the block. *Before Sunrise* and *Man on the Train* were both brilliant in their own way. Tomorrow we go to Montreal.

Everywhere is walking distance if you have the time—
—anonymous

Saturday, May 29, 2004
St. Stephen, New Brunswick

We are one hour away from St. Stephen, New Brunswick. We've left the rain behind, and our big, white, rented GMC Yukon is tracking confidently down the sunlit highway. Frankie is driving; Smitty is curled up, fetal, in the seat behind him, sleeping. Gogo sleeps beside him, his head and neck bent painfully, and I can see Scott's bare legs propped, feet against the back window, in the visor mirror. I am, as always, in my perpetual shotgun location, my lap warm from my PowerBook.

We left the sold-out show in Kingston this morning at three a.m.

We returned to the hotel, slept for three hours, and then headed out for Toronto. I logged another two hours' worth of upright sleep on the way. On the plane to Halifax, I slept for another two or three, upright, hours. So, in broad theory I have had seven hours' sleep. We waited in the Halifax Airport for an hour while Mike and Smitty sorted out the rental vehicles. We drove away from the airport in the pouring rain and have been driving now for four hours. I wrote and answered e-mails for at least one of those hours.

On Wednesday night the band and crew went for dinner at the amazing and legendary Schwartz's Hebrew Delicatessen in Montreal. It's been many years since I have been there, and I'm happy to say that nothing has changed except the age of the waiters. The 60-year-old, poker-faced, wisecracking servers that I remember from the 70s have been replaced by their 30-year-old, poker-faced, wisecracking sons. Otherwise, the smoked meat was still the best in Canada, the open flame steaks were still awesome, the kosher pickles perfect, the fries amazing—the traditional cherry Cokes delicious. Like the Bamboo in Toronto, one day we will return to Montreal and Schwartz's will be gone, but until then it was a joy to revisit that uncompromising hole in the wall where great food rules.

The Bourbon Street show in Pointe Claire was another rock and roll triumph as was our first visit to the large and seriously rocking IronHorse in Kingston.

Connor is playing his first show in ten months tonight in White Rock. I am *so* pissed that I can't be there.

Sunday, May 30, 2004
Fredericton, New Brunswick

There's a four-hour difference between St. Stephen, New Brunswick, and White Rock, BC. I asked Connor to call me after his show last night to let me know how it went—and then reconsidered when I remembered that the call would come in at 5:00 a.m. my time. I dreamed about the show and woke at 7:30, unable to take advantage of our 1:00 p.m. lobby call. I went online hoping for news. In my mail there were two letters, one from my friend Pat Glover who was at the show and reviewed it for me, and one from my friend Monty Sheldan, who reviewed the show and sent three excellent photos (he's a pro photographer) of Connor onstage. Encouraged, I surfed over to the Dylan Industries site where I found five still shots from the show... and two short videos!! Five hours after the show had ended, I sat watching my son on stage—in a hotel room in a small town at the other end of the continent.

Debbie's e-mail came in an hour later with more details of what seems like a very successful show all-round. Connor not only played the show, but was instrumental in its conception and promotion, so its success was a coup on many levels for him. I am, as always, achingly proud of my boy.

The Trooper band and crew were very tired when we arrived in St. Stephen yesterday at eight p.m. After a quick shower and some food from the Sobeys across the street from the hotel, we were off to the sold-out arena for our second St. Stephen Concert/Party. As successful as the show was, I had a difficult time keeping my groove on. At various times during the set, as I moved to the front of the stage, I would suddenly feel a hard tug on my pant leg. When I am balanced tentatively at the front edge of the stage, usually with one foot up on a wobbly monitor, this can be a dangerous scenario. When it first happened, I looked down to see a very drunk woman winking at me and moving her tongue in what she must have thought was a seductive manner. Another woman repeatedly worked her hand up under my pants. Another tugged at the drawstring at the bottom of my pants, throwing me off balance *and* succeeding in undoing it—leaving it trailing around for me to trip on. I did my best to avoid them, but staying back from the front of the stage kept me isolated from large parts of the crowd. It required a serious act of will to rise above the evening's unfortunate onstage circumstances, but I managed to keep smilin' for the whole set.

"Can't let one or two bad eggs..."
–anon

Thursday, June 03, 2004
Bridgewater, Nova Scotia

Cloud rested thick and unrelenting on the upper branches of the dark scrub forest. A line of slow-moving cars, headlights lit at three in the afternoon, moved determinedly along the narrow Nova Scotia highway toward a grey and indistinct horizon, a film of misty rain spitting in the wiper-blade intervals. The temperature-controlled, leather-clad, interior of the new rental vehicle was warm and, at the moment, quiet, but for the monotonous and, increasingly, tedious sound of wheels on road.

My torn baseball hat—the one with the embroidered skull-and-cross-bones-on-a-shamrock patch—was pulled down so low on my face that viewing the road ahead required me to thrust my stubbled chin high in the air. Having just done so, I wondered again at the effort. Everything looked much the same as it had looked for the past five hours.

Although endowed with one of the most beautiful coastlines in the world and a charming road that follows it faithfully, Nova Scotia also offers a more expedient travel route, carved straight and unimaginatively through the middle of the stunted forest, for those either unconcerned with charm and beauty, or who are simply in too much of a hurry to care. Today, making their way from Saint John, New Brunswick, to Bridgewater, Nova Scotia, for an 8:30 show, Trooper fell squarely into the latter category.

The baseball hat—which was purchased new and pre-distressed at an Oshawa, Ontario, mall, but for which I was half-seriously considering a new story that involved a visit to the Temple Bar district in Dublin, Ireland—blocked both the unappealing view and what daylight there was left from interfering with the blue-tinted liquid crystal display of my sleek, silver computer. A portable and foldable plastic cowling, clipped ingeniously to the screen, blocked the rest. The closing credits of *Autumn Spring*, a sweet, melancholic movie from Czechoslovakia, had just rolled across the screen and I shifted uncomfortably in the passenger seat.

"Even these seats can be a butt-breaker, eh?" Frankie grinned from the back, folding up his headphones.

Sunday, June 06, 2004
Stellarton, Nova Scotia

Happy 17th Birthday, Connor James McGuire...
I love you (and miss you) very much.
Dad

Thursday, June 17, 2004
Toronto, Ontario

It's been a long time since we were out this long. It'll have been a month and four days once we're home. This has been a particularly exhausting run, with short days full of more work than usual. Happily, the shows have all been very successful.

We're driving from Owen Sound to Toronto, where we play tonight at the Hard Rock Cafe on Yonge Street. We're all pretty quiet today. I'm often asked if I ever get tired of doing this. The generally truthful answer is no, I don't. Today, though, I am tired of doing this.

Since my last post we've done an eight-day tour of Nova Scotia and Newfoundland with Nazareth.

Triton, Newfoundland

It was a lot of fun—and a lot of work. All of the shows were early, which left us little time, after traveling, for ourselves. We bonded heavily with our Scottish brothers this time and, as a band, made a valiant effort to keep up with them in the party department. Our failure at this was so dismal that I am embarrassed to discuss it at all. The Nazareth band and crew party (and drink) harder, longer, and more passionately than anyone I have ever met. My favourite of several Trooper/Nazareth gatherings took place last weekend at two o'clock in the morning in St. Anthony, Newfoundland, in a private room in the local hotel. It was the end-of-tour party *and* my 54th birthday party. Both bands and their crews sat down at a long table and tried, unsuccessfully, to consume 80 pounds of fresh-cooked lobster (and an endless supply of beer) that had been organized by the tour promoter, Jack Livingston. It was daylight when I left the table. There was another large Nazareth-centric party on the ferry back to Cape Breton the next night, but I chose to stay in my stateroom and watch *Winter Sleepers* on my PowerBook. Apparently, at that party, there was some friction with the ferry staff, which I'm not sorry I missed.

All of the Trooper/Nazareth arena shows were sold-out and particularly successful for us. Going back to Newfoundland felt almost like returning home, and we were welcomed like favourite relatives visiting from "away." I wish we'd had more time there.

St. John's, Newfoundland

The last two nights here in Ontario were plagued by technical problems onstage that made pulling off a convincingly focused

Trooper show a serious challenge. From all reports, though, we seem to have succeeded. The Hard Rock has been a extremely fun gig for us, so I'm looking forward to tonight, and the "Great Canadian Fly In" in Sarnia tomorrow night sounds like it might be a hoot. I'm looking forward to that too.

At the moment, though, I'm tired, professionally and personally frustrated, annoyed, aggravated, and missing my family. The only positive blip on my present mental radar is the renewed conviction that I need to write enough good songs to fill a CD. I'm half-finished a giant book called *Songwriters on Songwriting* that contains in-depth interviews—with all the usual suspects—about the deeply mysterious process that I have committed myself to. It's been reassuring to see that even the greatest songwriters in the world have suffered as I have in pursuit of their muse.

Sunday, July 11, 2004
Edmonton, Alberta
A Few Days Ago

The captain of the plane just announced that the cell containing the lightning has moved right over the airport. His announcement coincided with the start of the heavy rain that is still pounding the tarmac outside my window. We left Yellowknife at 7:30 this morning, followed by a five-hour layover here at the Edmonton airport. We've been sitting in this grounded plane for more than an hour now.

I'm playing soundtrack music through my PowerBook speakers. Scott's sitting beside me reading *The Power of Intention*. Frank, Stobey, and Craig are standing at the back of the plane, keeping the flight crew in stitches. It's not an altogether bad day. In fact, I have been appreciating the time to myself to catch my breath and gather my thoughts.

I was very tired when I wrote my last post. I felt better the next day. The final three shows of the tour were beyond excellent. The Hard Rock was packed and rocking again; Sarnia was a big stage show, marred only slightly by the bad weather; and the Dragon Boat Festival in Vancouver was beautiful in every way.

Debbie and I have been converting our upstairs guest room/music room into a writing room where I can meet with my muse without distraction. All of the songwriting documented here took place in a room that is directly in the centre of our main floor family life. Phone ringing, doorbell chiming, and all the distractions of everyday life were the backing track to my creative endeavours. Soon I will have a beautiful blood-red and silver lair in which to wrestle with my craft.

Our work was interrupted by an e-mail alerting us to an article in the *Province* newspaper about my use of the F-word at our Canada Day show in Port Moody last week. I was reminded once again of the crushing power of the press.

Years ago, the Fredericton "no-booze, no-show" story (that claimed that we walked out on a show because we couldn't get free drinks) was circulated after we bailed on a gig when it became clear we weren't going to be paid. Nonetheless, the Canadian Press ran the story across Canada without bothering to fact-check with us.

This time, the writer did call me for comment. I did not, however, receive his message until after the story ran. A black lump churned in my stomach as I read the description of the "hundreds of face-painted families." In fact, there were 6000 people there—crammed against the stage—rock-show style. There is no indication in the story that the "G-rated family Festival" show began at ten o'clock at night, and of course there was also no mention that the band was called back to the stage after a tumultuous, end-of-set encore. I did use the F-word, for which I have apologized officially. It was a stupid mistake, and I am truly sorry that I lost the "all-ages" plot that night. The story, though, spun just slightly, painted us in a terrible light—as swaggering, careless, immoral, rock star jerks—the polar opposite of the image we work so hard to maintain.

"Please stow all your belongings, lock your tray tables, and put your seats in their full and upright position."

To Be Concluded...

Thursday, July 15, 2004
White Rock, BC
F-Word Update

There's a small blurb in the *Vancouver Sun*, the other (less sensational) Vancouver newspaper, today with a (more flattering) picture of me, and a more balanced story about my Port Moody F-bomb. My mother received a call from a writer at that paper who asked her if he could do a story about *her* reaction to all this! Thankfully, she declined.

Also, I have received an e-mail from the guy who made the original complaint that started this whole controversy. He has accepted my apology and said that he and his daughter will continue to enjoy our music. We appear to be on good terms.

I don't have time for a real post... but I wanted to keep track of this as it happens.

Tuesday, July 20, 2004
Driving Home from Nakusp, BC

There's nothing like a successful weekend full of summer festival shows to clear your mind and refocus your perspective. I am, once again, in the passenger seat of a rented van, rolling down the highway with my four compatriots. Scott, Frankie, and I just watched *The Last Samurai*—an excellent movie—and now I've got some homeward-bound time to kill.

The F-bomb aftermath has eased off a lot, and I'm no longer thinking almost constantly about the F-word and its significance. The newspaper printed part of the apology I posted on the Trooper site ("I goofed, admits Rock Star") and a big colour picture of the band. I think the whole affair was well-handled. I have mentally composed several essays on the topic since, but written nothing down. There is something very important about that handful of common, occasionally vulgar words that George Carlin identified as not suitable for television, and I am strangely reluctant to leave them behind, although common sense would suggest that as the best course.

Over the last three days I've slept, only 11 hours in a bed. Long drives and early show times have left us little or no time for much other than the work. Happily, all three shows (Quesnel, Cold Lake, and Nakusp) were extremely successful, full of love and celebration. The summer has been incredible so far. We determined yesterday, in a moment of van boredom, that we've played for about 110,000 people since the beginning of June. We figure that, by the end of September, we will have doubled that number. Debbie told me that a friend heard on the radio that Trooper is having a giant resurgence. If that's what this is, I'm in favour of it.

We have only two days off before we play in Red Deer with our pal Bill Henderson and Chilliwack. Our agents are still putting the final touches on another two-and-a-half week run through Ontario and the Maritimes that will follow a week later. I'm feeling very good about my life. The writing room is nearly ready. Many good things are on the horizon.

Monday, August 2, 2004
Port Colborne, Ontario

Last night was my first sleep in a bed since Friday night, three days ago. Those three days have been a blur of remote prairie highway, Toronto concrete, and noise-canceled airplane emptiness. We've played two more love-filled shows and added another 14,000 people to the summer's rapidly growing tally. In case it wasn't abundantly clear on the nights in question, I again send my thanks and love to the people of southern Saskatchewan and Port Colborne, Ontario, where, despite numerous real-world difficulties, nothing could go wrong.

Since we last spoke, Connor's band, Anger and After, won the "Rock Stock and Skate" battle of the bands (sharing a suspense-ending tie with their friends Rio Bent), which will take them, once again into the brilliant Rock Beach Studios to record. We celebrated Tom and Kerry's 21st Anniversary with the 20th Anniversary Picnic—an excellent party on a beautiful White Rock afternoon. Debbie and I spent a euphoric evening downtown at the beautiful Orpheum Theatre with the still-mighty Temptations and the (somewhat-less-mighty-by-comparison) Four Tops. The Temps maintain a level of performance excellence that completely blew us away. It was an inspiration to me to see a show so perfectly conceived and executed.

I also spent some time at the Langley Memorial Hospital, where my Dad was obliged to visit for a few days because of pneumonia-induced shortness of breath. I'm happy to report that he has returned home now where he can wander free of the tubes and wires that tied him, unwillingly, to his hospital bed.

There were also several brief business-related skirmishes that came and went with a minimum of aggravation—mucked-in (awkwardly as always) with the ebb and flow of my everyday family life. That family life remains my favourite part of my time at home.

A full night's sleep has restored me. I'm ready to rock. We are out for two weeks of what looks to be a run of fun summer shows. I'm ready for whatever adventures await us.

Tuesday, August 3, 2004
In the Air
Sleeping

I'm on another plane. This one's taking us to New Brunswick. This will make three provinces in three days: Saskatchewan, Ontario, and New Brunswick. There was a powerful, non-stop lightning storm this morning on our way from Port Colborne to the Toronto airport. We had a 4:15 a.m. lobby call—I don't think I slept last night. I'll sleep in Saint John.

Wednesday, August 4, 2004
Saint John, New Brunswick
Damn

My Dad's had to go back into Emergency.
Please send him your love.

Thursday, August 5, 2004
Sydney, Nova Scotia
Dad

I've been thinking about my Dad a lot since he went into the hospital.

I have realized that he's still my hero, after all these years. He is an intelligent, wise, wildly talented, and unbelievably kind-hearted man. He's a true warrior-poet—balancing his depths of creative talent against the passionate heart of a "man's man." Give him a pencil and he will draw for you whatever you can imagine. Give him a hammer and, up until recently, he will build for you whatever you need.

He was a boxer. He was a biker. He was a hunter. He is a painter, conjuring in his paintings a world of kindness and beauty. He's a poet—the first person I ever saw write a song lyric. He raced stock cars. He "crashed the flaming wall" on his motorcycle. He could, up until recently, design and build anything. He and my Mom were the first musicians I ever met. He played mouth organ, including a little one he could play inside his mouth. He's a sign painter and graphic artist. He's a great singer. He's a sculptor, a furniture maker, and a model builder. He made puppets—marionettes, actually—the kind with strings attached to their joints. He put on puppet shows, acting out the children's book he wrote. He once had a fist fight with a big and burly neighbour—and, to my everlasting pride, he won. He is a human library stocked with the thousands of books he has read. He made toys for my two brothers and me: a rifle with a real metal barrel, a microphone on a stand. He has worked very, very hard all his life.

Beyond all of his accomplishments, though, he is probably best known for his kindness. He has always been incredibly generous with both his time and his talent. He is smart, funny, and humble. He embodies that which he admires most in a man. He is a "good egg."

He is also a great father, and I love him very much.

His name is Harry McGuire—Buddy (or "Uncle Buddy") to his family and Mickey to his many friends. So... now that you know him a little better, could you take a minute to send him your love?

Monday, August 16, 2004
Kingston, Ontario

Another highway, this one leading to Kingston, Ontario. The tour's been going well, and Dad seems to have stabilized somewhat. He's still in the hospital, and they're still doing tests to determine why he's lost so much weight, but the major infection and the stupidly low blood sugar seem to have gone away, which is encouraging. I swear he took a turn for the better after I asked you to send him your love. Thanks, everyone, for the many kind and thoughtful notes. Your positive energy has helped sustain the highest energies we could manage through these very tentative days.

The vibe is extremely high in the band right now, which has also helped me to deal with this long-distance family crisis. Most of the shows have been love-fests of unparalleled proportions. Most have been sold-right-out. We've covered a lot of ground and are resting up tonight and tomorrow before covering a lot more. On Tuesday we fly up to Kuujjuaq, Quebec, for another northern adventure. Kuujjuaq is right at the top of Labrador, across the water from Baffin Island. Although it's not the most northerly place we've played, it may turn out to be the most remote. We go from there to St. John's, Newfoundland (by way of Montreal—don't ask), and from The Rock back to Brantford, Ontario, the next night. The *next* afternoon we play in Darrington, Washington—at the opposite edge of the continent.

There have been some excellent parties so far. The post-boat-ride fresh-caught-gourmet-salmon-fest in Liverpool, Nova Scotia, comes immediately to mind. The most notable, for me, took place after the show in Saint John, New Brunswick, where I found myself onstage in a small bar singing and playing blues and R&B songs with Myles Goodwyn from April Wine. Myles is a notoriously introverted guy, and I've spent years trying to get to know him at backstage hangouts all over the country. I have never seen Myles anywhere but backstage, so this was a serious breakthrough of some kind and a ton of fun in the bargain.

Thursday, August 19, 2004
Kuujjuaq, Quebec

4:30 a.m.

5:05—5:06—5:10—5:12—5:12...

He forced his eyes to remain open. He was sure he had slept since he last looked, but the clock seemed to have stopped at 5:12. He waited, watching. A red '3' blinked into place. He rolled out of bed, taking one step across the small room and landing awkwardly, naked ass to cold leatherette, on the chair in front of the glowing silver laptop.

His eyes remained slit-like, prepared for the screen's glare. He opened the lid and bathed the room in blue light. He fumbled the cursor to "check now" and watched as a single e-mail—subject-line: "Visual"—appeared in his Inbox. The body of the message contained only a URL:

http://trooper.com/TEMP/hellweek.jpg

A double-click yielded a browser window full of a map of Canada with thick blue lines describing the routes we would be traversing this week. Coast to coast, top to bottom. I looked through the rest of my Inbox: CNN—nothing of interest; Connor—no post for several days, busy with his summer film class; B@B—the same one about the new computer; Macintouch—too early for the day's post; Die Puny Humans—Warren Ellis is in Vancouver visiting the set of his new TV show. Something interesting—good.

Not much to pack because I had been careful not to take too much out the night before. Everyone else was paring down to one bag—leaving the rest in the van in the Montreal hotel's parking lot. Long ago I decided that it was easier to throw everything into my giant Tumi roller than to sort out a day's worth of gear and re-pack it. A rolling bag is a rolling bag regardless of its weight.

The hotel room alarm-clock radio blasted to life loudly at 5:45 a.m. This was the correct time for my wake-up call, but, mysteriously, I had not set the alarm. While I was turning it off, the phone rang. Lurching across the bed and, lying on my stomach, I picked up the receiver and then dropped it back on the cradle. Back at the computer, I Googled "Kuujjuaq" and came up with a surprising number of hits, including *www.nvkuujjuaq.ca/en/* where I read about the remote, high north Quebec town and the festival we would be playing there. My phone began chirping an adrenaline-inspired staccato melody: my backup wake-up.

Bathroom. Dress. Wrap cables. Zip up. Backpack on. Suitcase up. Dummy check. Flip the "Please Do Not Disturb" sign. Down to the lobby. The sun just clearing the horizon. "Good mornings" exchanged. Airport shuttle. Can't stop singing "Come On Eileen" by Dexy's Midnight Runners, especially the part that goes "toora, loora, toora, too loo rye-yay, Eileen." Brain bombed at least two days ago.

Much of Dorval International is old and sprawling and chaotic. Pieced together like a Sao Paulo slum, it resembles, in places, the first few levels of the *Blade Runner* city. As I straggled with the rest of the band through this seething landscape and toward the First Air gate, the noise began to subside until, arriving at gate 36, at the tip of a mile-long, fluorescent-lit finger, a calming quiet settled over the small collection of Kuujjuaq-bound travelers.

Nine hours later I sat on the single bed in my Kuujjuaq hotel room with my laptop, at 90 percent battery, resting on my out-stretched, naked legs. The room had no air conditioning and was prickly, sweaty hot. I tapped the keys, remembering the day's events. My first unpleasant duty upon arrival at the airport in Kuujjuaq had been to remind at least three of the enthusiastic, and otherwise instantly likable, committee members that our contract stipulated five hotel rooms and that "billeting" the band and crew was not an acceptable option. I could see the hurt look in their eyes as they repeated their heartfelt welcomes and insisted that we would be "treated right." It broke my heart to play hardball with them, but, as I suspected, hotel rooms did turn up.

But not before a Keystone-Cops-in-slow-motion series of musi-cal chairs pickup truck rides from the airport to the gig and the only two hotels in town... dragging luggage from one truck to another, swatting at the clouds of merciless mosquitoes and blackflies, in hopes that someone would take the reins and bottom-line our accommodations for the evening. Ida Saunders rose heroically to the occasion and, after getting us roughly squared-away, took us on a tour of her beloved town.

Ida was a wonderful woman — no-nonsense, highly intelligent, charming, funny, and the perfect host. As part of our tour, she took us to her home to meet four of her six children. It was her oldest boy's birthday. One of her daughters was celebrating a pre-school graduation that afternoon, so, as well as touring us around, she had also to attend the grad and bake a birthday cake before the evening's show. She took us to one of the town's two stores to buy ingredients for our dinner. The Co-op Hotel, where we were staying, has a large kitchen and dining room for its patrons. At the store, Ida showed us the rack of fox pelts. The fur is very popular for lining parkas. Three hundred and twenty-nine dollars for one of the unbelievably soft, white ones.

Fox pelts – Kuujjuaq, Quebec

The town consists of a scrambled grid of virtually identical, characterless buildings that are the duplex homes that most of the people live in, interspersed with utilitarian boxes that are the bank, the store, the hotel, and the school. According to Ida, there are private homes scattered around, but these "Social Homes" make up the bulk of what we saw. The town is obviously expanding and the new school and the state-of-the-art theatre we were to play in were their proudly displayed symbols of progress. Ida took us to the beach where we watched a large silver boat turn and begin making its way toward us. This was one of the community boats—there are fourteen communities up and down the coast from Kuujjuac—and they are used for, among other things, transporting large community walrus-hunting parties to a nearby, uninhabited island.

Kuujjuaq, Quebec

Although the town is small, Ida mused that she had once picked berries in an area where there were now homes. She laughed as she pointed out a small yellow house and explained that its owner had purposely built far away from the village to ensure his privacy. He was now surrounded by new neighbours. "We all feel sorry for him," Ida said wistfully. It took me some time to realize that her sense of scale, perhaps also in things non-geographic, was dramatically different from mine. Less than a quarter mile from her current home, she pointed out the first house she had lived in and said that driving by it was a "trip down memory lane."

As we sat in the Co-op Hotel's spartan dining room, eating canned soup, crackers, and cream cheese, Scott and I discussed the fact that it's not about the houses and buildings. Scott believes that the people here are fundamentally closer to "the Source." Their freedom from competitive consumerism leaves them able to live more full and connected lives. This may be one of the reasons why we like it so much up here.

It's the day after the Kuujjuaq show. I am once again on a First Air plane—headed, this time, back to Montreal. There is great adventure in this life I lead, and an opportunity to connect with cultures and communities in a deep and moving way. Our farewells at the airport were like those experienced by family members leaving home for a year. Hugs and handshakes, kisses and last-minute photographs.

I slept in this morning, missing the four-wheeler adventure and the boat trip. I was happy, though, cocooned in my room—maybe a bit overdosed on being an accessible part of the perpetual centre of attention. After the show, we were surrounded for at least an hour by a crowd of delightful, elflike children who returned again and again for another autograph—on a different part of their body or clothing. The committee in charge of the event joined us backstage afterwards. It's rewarding, in a situation like this, to be as good at what we do as we are. We hold up our part of the bargain impressively, and afterwards, with the people who hired us, there is a sense of satisfied completeness. Our new friend Akpic (his nickname, which means "cloud berry" and is also the name of the festival) drove us the few blocks back to the "auberge" in his pickup. Scott and Gogo and I settled in front of the lobby TV that was showing *The Song Remains the Same*, a Led Zeppelin live concert video. We laughed and talked and quietly wound down from a long and eventful day.

He sits uncomfortably in his tiny airplane seat with his Bose noise-canceling headphones on and his silver laptop jackknifed awkwardly, at a 70 degree angle, between his stomach and the fold-down tray table. He types from the sides of the keyboard, its underside growing hot on his belly.

His computer now carries a collection of photos of Kuujjuaq, but he knows already that, rather than revealing the true heart of the place, most people will see only a motley collection of rundown buildings, dirt roads, and old rusting cars. The plane is going to land in Canada's largest city. And he is going to move on... to Kingston for the night... and then to St. John's, Newfoundland.

Monday, September 20, 2004
Edmonton to Vancouver

I'll see how much I can write between the Edmonton International Airport and the Vancouver International Airport. This amount will be determined partly by time and partly by battery capacity. I'm starting at 52 percent because I forgot to plug in my AC adapter on the way from Hanna to Edmonton.

Last night, at three a.m., Frankie wanted to show us how fast he could run on a treadmill. He had only just gotten up to speed on the Hotel Fitness Centre's treadmill when Scott tried to join him in a run-in-progress. Scott tumbled to the floor and the treadmill lurched to a stop. After the ensuing hilarity, we realized he had fallen on the plug, dislodging it from the wall. Shortly thereafter, we, very wisely, chose to go to our rooms and sleep.

Last night was the $125.00 per ticket Hanna, Alberta, show. It was an all-you-can-drink-for-free event—the first we've ever played. Let your imagination run wild for a moment, conjuring the state of the audience. The show was a rocking, small-town house party with all the expected drama and action. The night before was an Oktoberfest event in Calgary. Todd Korol, an ace freelance photographer who shoots for *Sports Illustrated*, *Time*, and *National Geographic* met us at the Sun Centre to shoot our half of a four-page photo essay—featuring Trooper and April Wine—that will run in *Maclean's* magazine on October 4. Todd was there to document another average Trooper performance, this one featuring a *Playboy* Bunny and Yours Truly dressed in a complete Oktoberfest lederhosen outfit. Todd shot literally thousands of photos at the sound check, my hotel room, the dressing room, and the show. Once again, it will be interesting to see what makes it to the magazine.

My Dad is out of the hospital and extremely happy to be back at home. I am convinced that his arguably miraculous recovery had a lot to do with the concentrated best wishes of a lot of people he does not know. Thanks so much to those of you who took the time to send him your positive energy.

Mike Pacholuk is no longer our tour manager and sound man. He gave us two weeks' notice just after we finished the Darrington, Washington, show. It's been a bit of a scramble but we have, in customary Trooper fashion, landed firmly on our feet. Our old friend (and former road manager/sound man) Paul Cloutier filled in this weekend and we have been talking to a highly recommended candidate who has toured both the US and Europe with big-time US groups. In a stunning example of the power of intention, we called him at a point where he was "between engagements" and seemingly keen to work with our band. This sudden change in our daily business has instigated a fresh look at many of our on-the-road procedures and practices and will, ultimately, bring about many improvements to our lives out there. There is a new and extremely positive focus developing around that side of our work and, although it's been difficult and time consuming, I'm pumped about the new road ahead.

In many ways, I'm sad to see Mikey go. He'd been with us for six and a half years and had become part of the family. His Dad has also been sick lately and the experience of running back and forth across the country to look after him had slowly been bringing Mike down. The burden of sadness, added to the hard work of one of our busiest summers ever, has probably had something to do with his departure. I, of course, wish him the very best.

I'm tired, both physically and mentally. Spiritually, I'm feeling good, but all of my other functions are down, running on the dim, minimal light of emergency power. I need a rest and am committed to a two-week escape plan that I will institute when this plane lands in Vancouver. I will do no Trooper work. I will take no business calls. I will obsess about nothing.

Except... I have to dig up and scan archival photos for the *Maclean's* article, and maybe an interview or two for the Commodore show on October 1, and I guess I have to help bottom-line that New Year's offer from Lloydminster—but that's it... I hope.

I just changed batteries. I had forgotten the spare I carry in the bottom of my amazing Tom Binh Brain Bag backpack. I'm mid-flight to Vancouver now. Smitty just bought the boys a drink.

OK: so here are your cultural assignments for the coming month. You must rent and watch *City of God* and you must read William Gibson's latest book, *Pattern Recognition*. These are the best movie and book, respectively, that I have read and watched in a very long time. Fresh as hell, intense, and unbelievably entertaining.

The entire emergency door row is out of control. Paul, Craig, Gary, Smitty, Frankie, and some big guy with a ponytail are laughing and waving their arms around. The flight attendant seems remarkably unconcerned and may, in fact, be complicit. She has spent most of the flight either with them or off getting more drinks for them. She's enjoying the attention. My noise-canceling headphones are currently feeding me a Radiohead soundtrack for their antics.

"Please store your bags under the seat in front of you or in the overhead... yada-yada-yada..."

Monday, October 18, 2004
Edmonton, Alberta

Someone broke into our crew truck tonight. The truck contains thousands of dollars worth of equipment. They stole cookies and beer.

CHAPTER ELEVEN

October 19, 2004–July 4, 2005

Doug Bennett (cool with no regrets), Christmas 2004,
Goodbye Dad, Flickr Crack, The Wired Life,
Singing Snowbird on the CBC, Spock Days, Live in Calgary,
Connor Graduates and Ra & Debbie Celebrate,
The *Globe and Mail* Writer Will Live with Us,
14,000 People Sing Happy Birthday to Me, Atikokan,
High Rise Threat in White Rock,
The Tour – Written in the Style of Mr. Cheney's Two-Page *Globe
and Mail* Story, A Good Gig

Tuesday, October 19, 2004
Red Deer, Alberta
Doug Bennett

I'm not dealing well with Doug Bennett's death.

I was in the West Ed Mall on Sunday when I got the call from Mikey Pacholuk. I was in a clothing store, a surreal setting for that kind of news. My first unfiltered thought was that there was now a large, un-fillable, Doug-shaped hole in the world.

Doug Bennett was a smart, funny, and thoughtful man who had long been an important part of the world I live in. I always admired his intelligence, tenacity, humour, and fierce independence. We were not close friends, but we were quick to settle into a comfortable camaraderie whenever we were together. We played the Commodore together two weeks ago. He looked terrible, but did a great show.

I didn't sleep last night. I woke up every five or ten minutes, thinking about Doug. I linked off an online story about him this afternoon and found myself at "obituariestoday.com" where I read 14 pages of condolences and reminiscences, many of which were from friends of mine in the biz. I was deeply touched, and felt obliged to contribute, if only for Nancy's sake, but could not muster the words, could not get a bead on what it was that hurt so much. I was crying when I heard a quiet knocking on my hotel room door. It was a writer from the Valleyview newspaper wanting to do an interview. I tried to explain to her what was going on and failed miserably... much as I am now.

I'm sad and brutally conflicted, about many things tonight. This is rough prose, and I know it, but I needed to write something.

I'll miss you, Doug. I sincerely hope that you are still "cool, with no regrets."

Sunday, October 24, 2004
Campbell River, BC

my fumbling hands overflow with souls, promises, and pledges
all eight arms fail
a cacophony of voices deafens—pulling and pushing

I will be standing over here for a while...

Monday, March 14, 2005
Prince Rupert, BC

Harry Clarke (Mickey) McGuire – January 3, 1920–December 1, 2004

My father died on December 1, 2004. The loss I feel is boundless—the sadness, while intermittent now, can still be as powerful and as painful as it was on that heartbreaking winter night. Before he died, we were blessed with a month-long opportunity to talk intimately with him, sharing our love and saying all those things that often go unsaid. It was a good, and beautiful, death. He lives on in me, Debbie, and Connor, my brothers and my mother, and the many, many people whose lives he touched with his kindness, his generosity, and his endless depths of talent and imagination.

Sunset – Prince Rupert, BC

Tuesday, March 22, 2005
Canmore, Alberta—Some Kind of Purgatory

Flickr has just announced their liaison with Yahoo, so, my guess is, everyone and their dogs are logging on for the first time, or have simply been reminded to check their "your photos/recent activity" page again for "recent comments." I've checked mine several more times than necessary already today, wondering, like a science-fair schoolboy, about reactions to my heavily Photoshop-ed picture of a craggy Camrose, Alberta, mountainside taken after arriving at the Drake Inn yesterday afternoon. I had immersed myself in their creation, my computer giving me the power to show what I saw and—this is the seductive part—present the results to the world. Brigit, a seemingly lovely lady from Hamburg, commented on my mountain photo this afternoon, voting in favour of art and forgiving my Photoshop adventures. (There was a long thread at Flickr Central about "Flickr crack" and, although I contributed to the lighthearted "you know you're addicted to Flickr when..." posts, I am beginning to see that this seemingly benign Web site is consuming far more grey-matter real estate than is healthy.)

Out my hotel window – Canmore, Alberta

In spite of this, though, the computer that seems to grow from my fingertips is the undeniable focus of my waking life—on the road at least. On my lap in the rented black Yukon XL, or set up with speakers and sub on hotel room desks and tables, I can breathe art, entertainment, music, business, and family life through its portal. Connor's new recordings arrived at two in the morning. The mp3s had the word "rough" attached to the titles, which made me smile. The final date and time for Wednesday's recording session arrived this afternoon. It's going to be odd to sing "Snowbird" on the CBC. The Yahoo Finance site revealed the continuing steady climb of Apple stock, a topic of happy discussion with Debbie during our morning call.

The blog. That was the reason I sat down in the first place. I have left it so long, languishing, and probably hit-less, my last few posts dark and sad, negotiating the difficult subject of my father's death. I hope now to carry on in a more positive vein. My life, in fact, has been good, but the best-laid plans have once again gang agley...

Monday, March 28, 2005
Sylvan Lake, Alberta
Flickr/Blogger Integration

I'm sitting in a motel room in Sylvan Lake, Alberta, trying to organize the integration of my Flickr photo pages and my Blogger Blog. This is one of three accoms on this tour without high-speed access and, if I remember correctly, the last time I posted I was on dial-up as well. Every time I set this up wrong, I'm punished by a five-minute wait—two and a half on either side of the post. Half to get it up and half to delete it. Hopefully this one will work, because my eyes are starting to cross...

Friday, June 10, 2005
Calgary, Alberta
A Day Off at the Delta Bow Valley Hotel

The Delta Bow Valley reflected – Calgary, Alberta

Mike has e-mailed the Vulcan Spock Days promoters, requesting five pairs of ears. It occurred to me last night, during my cab ride home from the downtown Calgary Irish pub, that it might be tricky wearing them over our new in-ear monitors. Some modifications may be necessary.

The Spock Days show is tomorrow. The Calgary Q107/MaxTrax live radio broadcast was yesterday. Today is a seemingly eternal gift of freedom from responsibility—24 solid hours of rare time alone. I'm sitting at a large black oval desk, surveying Calgary from my vantage point 24 storeys above the swollen and rapidly moving Bow River. I am at peace and happy.

The live radio performance felt good. We played like we had just been let out of a cage. It was our first show after a month off and you could feel the excitement onstage. Frankie was gasping for air as we returned to the dressing room.

"Fuck, that was fun!" he said.

Last week Connor graduated from high school and celebrated his 18th birthday, while Debbie and I celebrated the end of a 12-year feigned commitment to an educational system we do not entirely support, and our son's official (by our standards) entry into adulthood. All three of us sense a dawning of a new day, full of promise and adventure.

Two months of virtually solid touring stretch out before me. The band is tight and in great spirits. The itinerary looks like a total hoot. It's summer again.

View from my room – Calgary, Alberta

Friday, June 10, 2005
Calgary, Alberta

Rain Dance

From the 24th floor of the Delta Bow Valley Hotel – Calgary, Alberta

I decided to go for a walk. I turned around when a few large hailstones struck my unprotected head. I reached the hotel as the skies opened up. I took this picture from the 24th floor.

Sunday, June 12, 2005
Vulcan, Alberta

Peter Cheney, a writer from the *Globe and Mail*, is meeting us at the airport in Thunder Bay. He'll be with us for five days, after which he's writing an in-depth story about the band.

Walking slowly into the Thunder Bay airport baggage area, straining under the weight of his over-full backpack, Ra McGuire looks tired and old. The once skinny and longhaired singer is now overweight and bald. His dull

eyes have the bloodshot glaze of a man who's had only three hours sleep. It's six o'clock in the afternoon. The band is scheduled to perform their headliner set at seven.

I've read some of Peter's stuff. He's an excellent writer. The pieces I've read seemed more like chapters from a novel—deep, thoughtful, and detailed.

There is pandemonium in the Trooper dressing room. Empty Corona bottles litter the floor as Frankie Baker, his white and naked body still glistening with sweat, leaps on Scott Brown's back.

"Oh, Baby," he yells. "Give it to me... give it to me now!"

Peter will be there for my 55th birthday party, which will start officially at midnight tonight, in Thunder Bay.

Monday, June 13, 2005
Thunder Bay, Ontario
My 55th Birthday

So much has happened that I couldn't hope to document it all. It's my birthday today. I cannot believe that I'm 55 years old. Last night 14,000 people sang "Happy Birthday" to me. Brilliant.

Patricia is driving us from Thunder Bay to Atikokan, where we play tonight. Peter Cheney is in the van with us. He is telling amazing stories. He was in Afghanistan during that war. He has worked with and written about a Canadian porn star, serious cold-blooded killers, and an infamously incestuous family from Nova Scotia.

Nothing strains my throat more than full-out laughter. After the show last night I didn't stop laughing for more than a couple of minutes. I can still see Frankie standing in the aisle of the bus, doing his pornographic impersonation of a flight attendant's seatbelt and mask speech. There were four flight attendants on the bus with us. One of them was standing at the front of the bus, delivering the whole speech, word for word—perfectly. The rest of us rolled in the aisles.

Thursday, June 16, 2005
Oshawa, Ontario

I saw only six Trekkies at Spock Days in Vulcan, Alberta. There were hundreds in town, apparently, but we missed them—their rubber foreheads and crisp red suits returned to starships, battle cruisers, and shuttle crafts in preparation for the sold-out, blow-out Trooper party at the Vulcan Culture and Recreation Centre. It took us nearly the full duration of our intro music to get through the tightly packed crowd to the stage. It was an excellent show to begin the tour.

Near Vulcan, Alberta

The following night's show, in Thunder Bay, was a passionate and beautiful communion with a rolling sea of 14,000 people. After only four hours' sleep, and several hours of driving and flying, we hooked up with Peter Cheney at the Thunder Bay airport. It took only a few minutes for him to become one of the boys, often shaming us with his war stories (real ones) and humour. Prism met us backstage at the Fort William Park site. Al Harlow is Canada's Dick Clark—an ageless true spirit—happier now than I've seen him for a long time. It was a pleasure, and an inspiration, to see him on the eve of my 55th birthday. Chris, the promoter of the three-day Rock the Fort Classic Rock Festival, surprised me onstage with a birthday presentation that featured Big Bird, 55 helium balloons, and, the best part, 14,000 people singing "Happy Birthday" to me. The level of warmth and honest affection from that crowd was very moving. Other old friends backstage included the infamous Debbie K Debbie, Toni D from BC, and Greg Malo and Frank Baratta—who have taken some of the best live photographs of this band that I have ever seen. I have documented part of the hilarious busride back to the hotel previously. A short party at the T Bay Casino ensued, with members of Prism and Harlequin also in attendance.

Patricia Lambkin, an independent filmmaker, political activist, and an excellent traveling companion, picked us up the following morning. She drove us the two and a half hours to Atikokan, Ontario. Storytelling, now grown to full-blown, semi-competitive stature due to the presence in our midst of a national media professional (with possibly better stories), fills the 15-passenger Ford with laughter. We are taken to a placid resort at the water's edge, 12 miles out of Atikokan. As I enter the lobby, the lady behind the desk says;

"Hello, Ra, Happy Birthday!"

The people we met and partied with in Atikokan were kind, extremely fun, and shared a seemingly communal depth of character that is rare these days. The show was, after some relocating of the exiled "dry" side of the arena, a total rock and roll hoot. The party afterwards, though, was much better. Gogo sat down at a standup piano and banged out every song you could hope to sing. At one point 20 or more of us gathered in a tight mass with our arms reaching up, our fingers touching in the centre, singing loudly:

"reaching out
touching me
touching *you*..."

I have been calling home three and four times a day, partly because it's early in the tour and the connecting cord is still achingly strong, and partly because there is a drama unfolding in our beautiful hometown of White Rock, BC. Monday night was the City

Council meeting that determined the timeline for the approval of a monstrously inappropriate high-rise development proposal for our presently idyllic seaside town. Debbie and I have worked for weeks to oppose this development and had hopes that this meeting would see a public turnout that would fill the Council chamber's 50 seats and show the Mayor and Council that the citizens of White Rock were serious.

When I returned to my room early the following morning, e-mails and phone messages alerted me to the fact that 250 "boisterous" protesters had attended the White Rock council meeting! From all accounts, it was a stirring, overwhelming success. Only a few hours later, I awoke, unable to sleep, and logged on to the *Peace Arch News* Web site where the Mayor (a former proponent of the high-rise development) was quoted as saying that the developers should "go back to the drawing board." The lead line of the front page story was: "Bosa Properties' high-rise proposal has been dealt a major blow, with Mayor Judy Forster speaking out against the plan." Many phone calls home and happy e-mails followed.

For some of the Trooper entourage, the party continued until the sun came up. Not long thereafter we were back in the van with Patricia, making our way back to Thunder Bay for our brutally turbulent flight to Toronto. Our arrival in the Big Smoke was followed by a visit to an amazingly good Thai restaurant, from which we watched a massive thunderstorm in relative safety (our baggage was delayed at the airport because of a "code red" concern about wind spouts touching down). As we downed the last of our Singha and paid our bills, the rain abated and the sun returned.

Today we've traveled to Oshawa, Ontario. I should shower now.

Monday, July 4, 2005
White Rock, BC
The Tour—Written in the Style of Mr. Cheney's *Globe and Mail* Story

The bark of a lone dog echoes sharply though the village. Mr. McGuire rubs his eyes and rolls from the bed. Laughter fills the nearby kitchen. The owner and proprietor of Winnie's Cozy Corners Bed and Breakfast has prepared a huge and delicious breakfast, and as Mr. McGuire enters the dining room, he joins the rest of his band, Trooper, and their crew, crowded around a long food-covered table.

None of the eight-member entourage has slept for longer than four hours, but lack of sleep has had no effect on their morning good spirits. Stories from the previous night are shared over plates of bacon and eggs, sausages, toast, and cups of strong coffee. Winnie hovers like a mother, enjoying the easy banter and contributing significantly to the contagious humour that fills the room.

Eight hours earlier, Trooper took to the large concert stage erected in the heart of Gingolx village, welcomed loudly and lovingly by a crowd of 800 children, teens, adults, and elders, to perform the final show of the second annual Gingolx Crab Festival.

Mr. McGuire surveys the beaming crowd from the centre of the stage.

"Am awillinah," he shouts.

"Am!" the crowd responds, delighted.

The people of the Nass Valley and the Nisga'a Nation have converged on Gingolx, on the shore of the wide and mighty Nass River, for a three-day festival that features Prairie Oyster, Doc Walker, Lisa Brokop, George Leach, Chilliwack, Trooper... and the best Dungeness crab in the world.

Served from ice-filled green garbage cans, the hours-fresh crab is the hit of the VIP lounge, across the muddy road from the large festival stage. Sitting at a crowded table in the corner of the jam-packed room, Chilliwack's amiable drummer, Jerry Adolphe, shares his crab-eating knowledge with Trooper's Mr. Smith and Mr. McGuire, dipping thumb-sized morsels of white meat into small bowls of garlic butter. Mr. McGuire's black T-shirt is splattered with white crab shrapnel as he is introduced to local dignitaries, shaking hands and signing autographs. All of the assembled performers are overwhelmed by the warmth and depth of the welcome they are receiving in this remote First Nations community.

Gingolx, BC

Trooper's show, finally initiated at 1:30 a.m., is received with a sustained roar from the stage-crowded audience, their combined voices obscuring Mr. McGuire's in the set's opening song, "We're Here For A Good Time." The band plays with passion and commitment, cheered on by an appreciation they can feel. Mr. Baker's back steams white smoke into the cool night air. The crowd sings "Thin White Line" accompanied by Mr. McGuire on his acoustic guitar and continues, strong, when the band drops in. Hundreds of hands reach to the stage, connecting occasionally with the sweating band members. The sound of the thundering encore surprises even those audience members responsible for it. At four a.m., after signing autographs, Trooper is invited to join the chief in the VIP lounge. They are also encouraged to attend a beach party that is about to begin. Risking offense, the tired musicians beg off, opting to sleep until their nine a.m. morning call.

Trooper's show in Gingolx is the last of a series of 16 shows that started 25 days earlier on June 9, in a recording studio in Calgary, Alberta, where they recorded a live-to-air performance for a room full of avid Trooper-fan contest winners. Mr. McGuire celebrated his 55th birthday twice on the tour: on the 12th, with 14,000 Thunder Bay, Ontario, fans that sang "Happy Birthday," and again the next night in Atikokan, where he was presented with a hand-carved canoe paddle with his name engraved on it. The final week of the tour carried the band from a sold-out night club in Moncton, New Brunswick, to an SRO outdoor concert at Casino Nova Scotia in Halifax, to a full day of flying that culminated in a wild night at the Bud Country Festival in Grande Prairie, Alberta, to another full day of flying and driving, deep into BC's beautiful and remote Nass Valley.

In three and a half weeks, the eight members of the band and crew had shared countless adventures, some of which were chronicled in a two-page story in the July 2 weekend edition of the *Globe and Mail*. Joined in Thunder Bay by writer Peter Cheney, the band had opened the door to the backstage of their on-the-road lives in what some would call a foolish act of trust. Mr. Cheney ate, slept, partied, and traveled with the band for five days. By the time the Trooper entourage rolled into Toronto, they had been invited to join Mr. Cheney and his family at their home, in an oasis-like Toronto neighbourhood, for a Corona-fueled barbecue celebrating Mr. Cheney's recent induction into the band. Standing in the heat of grilling steaks and vegetables, with a beer in one hand and a large fork in the other, he announced that he was proud to be the sixth member of Trooper.

Sailing down the unfinished highway that only recently connected Gingolx to the rest of the world, Mr. McGuire has mostly recovered from the initial ambivalence he experienced after reading the resulting 4000-word story. Confirming once again that we all see our shared world differently, the article had reached deep into his own perceptions of his life on the road, pinching and scraping at areas not usually considered. He was particularly sorry that Mr. Cheney and the *Globe and Mail* photographer, Mr. Lum, had witnessed what was the worst attended show of the tour, and possibly the worst attended of the year. Although the Thursday night Acton, Ontario, date was the only show of the five that was not a sell-out, the article and its accompanying photos seemed to focus disproportionate attention on the somewhat glum reality of that evening. More important, on first reading, the story seems, in Mr. McGuire's view, to fail at conveying the "vibe"—the powerful, positive undercurrent that floats Trooper through even the most challenging situations. And then there's the band and crew. "Hired guns," he thinks, is not the best way to describe the excellent men who help create that amazing vibe, every day, on the road.

A few cellphone-transmitted reviews, conveyed to Mr. McGuire at the airport, add alternative, and more positive, views of the story to the mix. His wife says it's good. She likes it better on second reading. The band's Web meister likes it a lot. It is, according to less self-conscious readers, a serious and respectful piece that presents a working band with dignity. Mr. McGuire returns his black Motorola phone to the inside pocket of his jacket. Standing alone with his luggage in a remote corner of Vancouver International Airport's South Terminal, he is guardedly relieved.

The dining area of the small Terrace, BC, airport is full to bursting with a motley crew of forty Gingolx Crab Festival performers waiting for planes to take them home. Mr. McGuire listens to the boisterous laughter that surrounds him. He lowers the screen of his silver PowerBook and clicks the lid into place.

"It's a good gig," he thinks to himself, smiling. "...a good life."

INDEX

54°40, 157

A&B Sound, 66, 76, 197
Acton, ON, 258
Adams, Ryan, 23
Adolphe, Jerry, 256
Air Canada, 47, 140, 156, 162, 210
Airdrie, AB, 178
AJ's Hangar, 46
Alberta, 18, 47, 77, 79-80, 101,
    103-104, 106, 113, 116, 120,
    143, 145, 147, 175, 177-179, 217,
    228, 240, 242, 245, 247-251,
    253, 257-258
Allen, Dave, 157
Allen, Steve, 192, 194
Altman, Robert, 165-166
Amazon.com, 18, 211
Amélie, 173
Amores perros, 173
Anger and After, 73, 113, 114, 121,
    122, 123, 197, 231
April Wine, 42, 44, 49-50, 234,
    240
Aqua, 93
Arctic Ocean, 84
Armstrong, Louis, 58, 151
Assiniboia, SK, 71
Astor Theatre, 141, 143
Atikokan, ON, 127, 252, 254, 258
Atlantic Ocean, 136
Average White Band, The, 28

"Baby Woncha Please Come
    Home", 152, 153, 154

Bachman, Randy, 147-149, 158,
    182, 207
Baffin Island, NU, 234
Baker, Frankie, 94, 99-101, 109,
    123, 129, 133, 138, 155, 159, 217,
    222, 225, 230, 240-241, 250,
    252
Baker, Ginger, 129
Banff, AB, 120, 129
Baratta, Frank, 254
Barenaked Ladies, 166
"Barrett's Privateers", 52, 138
Barrhead, AB, 178
Barrie, Robert, 134, 137
Bay Roberts, NFLD, 32, 34-37,
    52, 158-159, 161
    Klondike Festival, 158
"Bay Roberts Boy From
    Newfoundland", 159
BC Ferry, 85, 108
Beach Boys, The, 122, 207
Beatles, The, 52, 88-89, 90, 122,
    141, 149
Beijing Bicycle, 173
Bennett, Doug, 86, 245
Bernal, Gael García, 131
Bif Naked, 53, 106
Big Sugar, 53, 158
Bill Lewis Music, 207
Blog, 18, 23, 32, 38, 77, 107, 119,
    134, 136, 151, 165-166, 248-
    249
Bonham, John, 90
Bonsor Hall, 89
Bourbon Street, 223

Bow River, 250
Bradbury, Steve, 34, 159
Brand, Stewart, 139
Brandon, MB, 70, 219
Brantford, ON, 234
Brazil, 66-67
Bridgewater, NS, 160-161, 224-225
British Columbia, 48
  BC, 17, 57, 59-60, 65, 67-70, 74, 76-78, 86-88, 90-92, 94-95, 99-102, 108, 113-114, 119, 121-122, 127, 161, 165-168, 170, 176, 179-180, 182-184, 187, 189, 193, 195, 197-202, 204, 206, 210-212, 223, 229-230, 245-247, 254-255, 257-259
Bromley, Bruce, 91
Brown, James, 89
Brown, Scott, 24, 30, 35, 39, 49, 52, 65, 78, 100, 123, 130, 150, 154-155, 159, 178, 222, 228, 230, 238-240, 252
Bryant, Boudleaux, 208
Burnaby, BC, 89
Buzzi, Ruth, 58
Byrne, David 172

Calgary, AB, 90-91, 106, 219, 240, 249-251, 257
Campbell River, BC, 245
Camrose, AB, 104, 145, 247
Canada Day, 48-49, 51-52, 141, 157, 229
Canadian Armed Forces, 92
Canadian Auto Workers, 133
Canmore, AB, 219, 247-248
Cape Breton, NS, 32, 43, 134, 136-139, 227

Carlin, George, 230
Casino Nova Scotia, 258
Casino Regina, 68, 77
CBC, 93, 147, 248
CFUN, 89
Charles, Ray, 23, 89
Cheap Trick, 145-146
Cheney, Peter, 251-253, 258
Chesney, Dave 90
Chilliwack, 181, 231, 256
Church, Frank, 69
Church, Larry, 69
Cinéma Paradiso, 173
Citadel Hotel, 40
Cloutier, Paul, 59, 240-241
Club 279, 60, 156
Clyde, Buddy, 88-89
CMA Awards, 79
CN Tower, 42
CNN, 93, 107, 235
Coen brothers, 172
Cold Lake, AB, 230
"Cold Water", 94, 129
Colebrook, Bob, 181
Conception Bay, NFLD, 35-36, 159
Coquihalla Highway, 101-102
Coquitlam, BC, 59
Courtenay, BC, 60, 65, 68, 108
Cozy Bones, 23, 65
Cranbrook, BC, 76, 78
Crouching Tiger, Hidden Dragon, 173

Da Vinci's Inquest, 180
Dalhousie, NB, 38-39
"Darlin' Be Home Soon", 52
Darrington, WA, 234, 240
David, Hal, 189, 206

Davis, Miles, 28
Dean, Paul, 158
Debbie K Debbie, 254
Deep Purple, 141
Deer Lake, NFLD, 161
Demme, Jonathan, 172
Dexy's Midnight Runners, 235
Dickinson, Steve, 131
Doc Walker, 256
Doobie Brothers, The, 92, 116-117, 133
Doug and the Slugs, 86
Drake Inn, 247
Drayton Valley, AB, 179
Drifters, The, 122
Dublin, Ireland, 225
Duke Point Ferry, 65
Duvall, Robert, 173, 199
Dwarves, The, 132
Dyconia Resort, 39, 41
Dylan, Bob, 188

eBay, 18, 68, 211
Edmonton, AB, 18, 77-78, 101, 103, 113, 145, 147, 149, 175-176, 217, 219, 228, 239-240, 242
Egoyan, Atom, 46
El Crimen del padre Amaro, 131
Ellis, Warren, 136, 235
Elmes, George 43-44
Empress Hotel, 170
Erickson, Del, 88
Exotica, 46

Family Guy, 169, 180
Fargo, 171-172
Farmer's Daughter, 68, 73, 217
Feynman, Richard P., 173-174

Flamboro Downs, 58, 60
Fleet Club, 68
Flickr, 247, 249
Forster, Judy, 255
Fort Frances, ON, 127
Fort William Park, 253
Fredericton, NB, 223, 229
"From Me to You", 89
Full Monty, The, 173

Gage Park, 141
Gallipoli, 173
Garcia, Jerry, 28
Garland, Judy, 29
"General Hand Grenade", 157
Genghis Blues, 173-174
George, Lowell, 28
George Street, 51-52, 157, 170
Geraldton, ON, 155-156, 160
Ghost in the Shell, 173
Gibson Flying V, 93
Gibson, William, 241
Gilliam, Terry, 66-67
Gingolx, BC, 256-259
Glace Bay, NS, 37-38, 48, 134, 136
Gogo, 30, 39, 42, 50, 65, 76, 78, 92, 101, 117, 123, 129, 150, 152-155, 166, 217, 222, 239, 254
Gold, Kerry, 86
Goodwyn, Myles, 50, 234
Grand Hotel, 76
Grande Prairie, AB, 79, 258
Grateful Dead, 28
Great Big Sea, 53, 158
Greenway, Brian, 49-50
Grey Gardens, 39
Griffith, Melanie, 172
Grimnebulin, Isaac 21
Guess Who, The, 122

Halifax, NS, 32, 37-38, 40, 45, 47-48, 51, 53, 92, 131, 134, 140-141, 223, 258
Hamilton, ON, 58-60, 140-141, 157
Hanna, AB, 240
"Happy Together", 78, 123, 129
Harbour Grace, NFLD, 33-34, 35
Hard Rock Cafe, 58, 60, 156, 226
Harlow, Al, 86-87, 253
"Hash Pipe", 47, 52, 129
"Help Me, Rhonda", 122
Henderson, Bill, 86, 182, 231
Henry, Joe, 127, 176
Herman's Hermits, 122
Hewitt, Tim, 18, 211-212
High Level, AB, 24, 77, 79-80, 99, 175
Holiday, Billie, 28
Honeymoon Suite, 43, 50
Hope, Bob, 92
Horseshoe Tavern, 60
Hot Shots, 91, 104, 117
Howard Johnson Hotel, 46, 221
Hudson Bay, SK, 117-118

I Mother Earth, 106
Il Postino, 173
Île-à-la-Crosse, SK, 143-144
In Harmony Music Festival, The, 65
IronHorse Saloon, 223
Iroquois Falls, ON, 22-24
It's a Living, 93, 217
"It's Not Unusual", 122
"Ivan Skavinski Skavar", 153

Jackson, Peter, 183
Jesse Colin Young and the
Youngbloods, 206
Johnston, Tom, 117
Jones, Tom, 122
Jordan, Peter, 85, 93, 217
Jus Jordan Arena, 23-24

Kamloops, BC, 92, 114, 117
Kamoniwannalaya, 218
Karaoke, 23, 38, 41
Kaspuskasing, ON, 149, 151-152, 154
Kelowna, BC, 75-76
Kelly, Kevin, 139, 181
"King of The Road", 122
Kingston, ON, 45-47, 133, 221-223, 233, 239
Kirkland Lake, ON, 150, 152, 154
Klondike Days Exhibition, 145, 147
Kooler, The, 101
Kuujjuaq, PQ, 234-239

La Cage Aux Folles, 173
LA Weekly, 183
Lakeview Hotel, 75
Lambkin, Patricia, 254
Lavin, Tom, 86-87
Leach, George, 256
Led Zeppelin, 239
Lee, Brent, 150
Leighton, Ralph, 174
Lennon, John, 29
Les Paul, 85, 122-123
"Let It Ride", 149
Lethbridge, AB, 92, 116-117
"Lili Marlene", 153
Little Feat, 28
Liverpool, NS, 141-142, 234
Livingston, Jack, 227

Lloydminster, SK, 219
Lloydminster, AB, 101, 241
London, ON, 132-133
Looney Tunes, 128
Lotus Pond Vegetarian Restaurant, 66
"Love Hurts", 208
Loverboy, 158
Low, Bryon, 197, 200-201
Lower Deck Pub, 40
Ludwig, Frank, 99

MacKenzie River, 84
MacLean, Gary, 70
Maclean's, 240-241
Malo, Greg, 254
Manitoba, 70, 219
Marathon, ON, 127
Marsalis, Wynton, 153
Marsden, Gerry, 206
Marshall amp, 114
Martel, Laurel, 161
Mattawa, ON, 152, 154
Mattel, 93
Maui, HI, 117
MCA, 93, 104
McGuire, Connor, 31, 53, 57, 65-67, 73, 83, 93, 109, 121-124, 150, 163, 166, 168, 170, 180, 182, 188, 194, 196-199, 201, 204, 223-225, 231, 235, 246, 248, 250
McGuire, Debbie, 53, 57, 83, 121, 123, 142-143, 150, 168, 170, 180, 182, 188, 192, 195-199, 201, 203-204, 210, 224, 228, 230-231, 246, 248, 250, 254-255
McGuire, Mickey, 69, 75, 88, 93,

101, 123, 153, 154, 168, 187, 212, 231-233, 240, 241, 246, 248
Melhuish, Marty, 141
Merritt, BC, 149
    Mountain Music Festival, 149
Midland, ON, 39
Miller, Roger, 122
Mississauga, ON, 43, 46
Mitchell, Joni, 208
Mitchell, Kim, 217
Mojo Radio Network, 60
Moncton, NB, 43, 48, 50, 258
Money Talks, 91
Montreal, PQ, 133, 222-223, 234-235, 239
Moody Blues, The, 122
Morton, Jelly Roll, 151
Mount Forest, ON, 32-33, 131, 133
Muirfield Drive, 88, 153, 206
"Mustang Sally", 155
My Left Foot, 173

Nakusp, BC, 230
Nanaimo, BC, 65, 89, 92, 108
Nass River, 256
Nass Valley, 181, 256, 258
National Gallery, 221
National Geographic, 240
Nautical Nellie's, 157
Nazareth, 160, 208, 226-227
Neil, Graham, 219
Nelson, BC, 68
New Brunswick, 38-39, 43, 46-50, 222-223, 225, 232, 234, 258
New Liskeard, ON, 23-24
New Waterford Girl, 173
Newfoundland, 32-37, 48-51, 53,

156-161, 170, 217, 226-227, 234, 239
Nirvana, 28, 219
Nisga'a Nation, 181, 256
Norbury, Judy, 68
North Bay, ON, 24-28
Northfork, 199
Northwest Territories, 101
Nova Scotia, 32, 38, 40, 47-49, 131, 135-139, 141-143, 160-161, 178, 224-226, 232, 234, 252, 258
Nowell, Bradley, 28
Nunavut, 68, 161, 217

"O Canada", 51
Oakville, ON, 42-44
Okanagan Valley, BC, 75-76
"On Broadway", 122
Ontario, 21-25, 28-33, 38-39, 41-46, 57-59, 61, 70, 77, 91, 104, 127-128, 131-134, 140-141, 148-152, 155, 157, 166, 169, 220-221, 225-227, 231-234, 252-255, 258
Ontario Cookie Lady, 42, 44, 133
Orbison, Roy, 208
Orpheum Theatre, 231
Oshawa, ON, 133, 225, 253, 255
Ottawa, ON, 57-59, 181, 215, 220-221
Owen Sound, ON, 226
Oz, 58, 60

Pacholuk, Mike, 240, 245
Peace Arch News, 65, 255
Peace River, AB, 127
Pena, Paul, 174
Penner, Fred, 161, 215, 217, 219

Penticton, BC, 69-70, 75-76, 119
Perdido Street Station, 21
Phase One Studio, 148
Playboy Bunny, 240
Pointe Claire, PQ, 223
Port Colborne, ON, 44,45, 46, 231-232
Port Hardy, BC, 77
Port Hawkesbury, NS, 136-137
Port Moody, BC, 229-230
Poverty Plainsmen, The, 79
Powder Blues, 86
PowerBook, 23, 28, 29, 38, 46, 57, 59, 94, 101, 103, 106, 107, 115, 139, 140, 150, 158, 169, 188, 192, 198, 201, 222, 227, 228, 259
Prairie Oyster, 256
"Pretty Lady", 17, 95, 130
Prince Albert, SK, 72
Prince George, BC, 74-75
Prince Rupert, BC, 246-247
Princess and the Warrior, The, 173
Princess Mononoke, 47, 173
Prism, 86, 253-254

Quebec, 31-32, 234-235, 237-238
Quesnel, BC, 99-100, 230
Queen Street, 60-61
Quitting, 173

R&B, 89, 202, 204, 234
"Raise A Little Hell", 18, 30, 45, 85, 145, 155, 219
Rankin Family, 45
Rankin Inlet, NU, 68, 161, 217
Rankin, Jimmy, 45
RCMP, 40
Reason, 199, 202, 204, 209, 210

Red Deer, AB, 231, 245

Regina, SK, 60, 68, 77, 92, 116-117, 168-169, 219

Reno, Mike, 159

Richards, Scott, 104

Richmound, SK, 106-108

Rio Bent, 65, 67, 231

"Rise and Fall of Flingel Bunt, The", 206

Rock the Dock Festival, 160-161

Rogers, Stan, 52

Roth, Norm, 207

Run Lola Run, 46, 173

Russo, Matt 117

Rutherford, Morgan, 68

Salmon Arm, BC, 92, 99-100, 106

Salt Spring Island, BC, 182

Salty's Beach House, 76

Sam the Sham and the Pharaohs, 111, 122

Saint John, NB, 48-49, 225, 232, 234

Sarnia, ON, 228

Saskatchewan, 71-73, 104, 106-108, 116-118, 143-144, 218-219, 231-232

Saskatoon, SK, 68, 73, 104, 145, 218-219

Saunders, Ida, 236-238

Savoy Theatre, 37, 43, 48, 136

Sayer, Ron, 207

Schwartz's Hebrew Delicatessen, 223

Semiahmoo Bay, BC, 167

Shadow, 167-168

Shadows, The, 206

"Shakin' All Over", 122

Shannon, Del, 89

Shawna-Rae, 73

Shields, Kenny, 158-159

Shower, 173

"Silhouettes", 122

Simon, Paul, 42

Simmons, Patrick, 117-118

SL Feldman and Associates, 201

Slave Lake, AB, 106

Sling Blade, 38, 76, 172-173

Smith, Brian (Smitty), 17, 23-25, 30-31, 33, 38, 41, 65-66, 78, 91, 113, 116, 117, 123, 128, 130, 133, 140, 150, 178, 207-208, 212, 222-223, 241

"Smoke on the Water", 141

SOCAN Awards, 17-18, 45

Something Wild, 172

Songwriting, 169, 176, 187-188, 191-192, 194-197, 201, 208, 210, 212, 228-229

Spider-Man, 39

St. Albert, AB, 127

St. Anthony, NFLD, 227

St. George's, NFLD, 160-161, 217

St. Paul, AB, 80

St. John's, NFLD, 33-34, 37, 48-49, 51, 53, 156-158, 160, 170, 227, 234, 239

St. Stephen, NB, 46-48, 222-224

Stage 13 Festival, 145

"Stand by Me", 89

Stellarton, NS, 225

Stephenville, NFLD, 161

Stewart, Tommy, 149-150

"Stop! in the Name of Love", 122

Strathroy, ON, 43-44

Streetheart, 158

Sublime, 28

Subway Steve, 37-38, 43, 125, 161
Sudbury, ON, 29, 31-32, 166
Sunshine Village ski resort, 119
Supremes, The, 122
Surrey, BC, 90, 94, 109
Sweet Hereafter, The, 173
Sydney, NS, 48-51, 85, 131, 136-137, 160-161, 232
Sylvan Lake, AB, 249

"Takin' Care of Business", 147, 149
Temiskaming, PQ, 31-32
Temptations, The, 89, 231
Terrace, BC, 259
"These Eyes", 149
"Thin Brown Line", 133
"Thin White Line", 25, 49, 136, 147, 161, 165, 208, 257
Thornton, Billy Bob, 172
Thunder Bay, ON, 128, 155-156, 251-253, 255, 258
Timmins, ON, 22
Tom Bihn, 139, 150, 181
Toronto, ON, 18, 21-23, 33, 45-47, 58, 60-61, 131, 140, 148, 150, 155-156, 160, 162, 223, 226, 231-232, 255, 258
Trapper John's, 52
Triton, NFLD, 226
Trooper, 18, 25-26, 32, 35, 41-45, 50, 52-53, 60, 68-70, 85, 90-94, 99-100, 106-107, 109, 113, 116-117, 121-123, 130, 133-134, 136, 144, 146-147, 150-151, 157, 178, 181, 183, 201-202, 204-205, 207-212, 217, 221, 224-225, 227-228, 230-231, 234, 240-241, 252-253, 255-258

fans, 43, 68, 106, 134
first album, 104
karaoke disk, 23, 41
logo, 42
Web site, 77, 147, 211
Turner, Fred, 158
"Two for the Show", 61, 207

Uhl, Brian, 211
Uhl, Heather, 58, 92, 113, 211-212
Underwood, Mark, 178-179
Utne Magazine, 174

Va Savoir, 173
Valleyview, AB, 245
Vancouver, BC, 53, 65-66, 74, 86, 88-90, 93, 106, 108, 134, 140, 162, 197, 200, 207, 228-229, 235, 241
Vancouver Island, 65-66, 106, 108
Vancouver Sun, 86, 229
Vermilion, AB, 143
Victoria, BC, 60, 65-66, 68-69, 108, 168, 170, 182
Vidocq, 173
Voodoo Lounge, 50
Vulcan, AB, 251, 253

Wainwright, Rufus, 23
Wasaga Beach, ON, 38-39, 41
Weakerthans, The, 166
"We're Here For A Good Time", 18, 38, 44, 51, 100, 129, 130, 147, 150, 153, 154, 155, 157, 257
Weezer, 47, 129, 185, 188
West Edmonton Mall, 18, 101, 219, 245
Whistler, BC, 65

Whitby, ON, 41-42, 133

White Rock, BC, 21, 23, 31, 57,
    65, 73, 86-88, 90-91, 95, 108-
    109, 113-114, 119, 121-123, 127,
    150, 158, 161, 165-167, 170,
    176, 179-180, 182-184, 187,
    189, 193, 195, 197-202, 204,
    206, 208, 210-211, 213, 220,
    223, 229, 231, 243, 254-255

Whitehorse, YT, 90

Wilco, 188

Williams, Hank, 208

Williams Lake, BC, 70, 75

Williams, Lucinda, 31, 128

Winnipeg, MB, 70, 92, 117, 162,
    217, 219-220

Winsor, Ian 43

Wired, 139

"Wooly Bully", 122

Wright, Steven, 104

Y tu Mamá también, 173

Yarmouth, NS, 38, 139

Yellowknife, NWT, 228

Yi Yi, 173

Young, Neil, 181